Performance Affects

Performance Affects

Applied Theatre and the End of Effect

James Thompson

First published 2009 by
PALGRAVE MACMILLAN

Palgrave Macmillan in the UK is an imprint of Macmillan Publishers Limited, registered in England, company number 785998, of Houndmills, Basingstoke, Hampshire RG21 6XS.

Palgrave Macmillan in the US is a division of St Martin's Press LLC, 175 Fifth Avenue, New York, NY 10010.

Palgrave Macmillan is the global academic imprint of the above companies and has companies and representatives throughout the world.

Palgrave® and Macmillan® are registered trademarks in the United States, the United Kingdom, Europe and other countries.

ISBN-13: 978-0-230-22160-4 hardback
ISBN-10: 0-230-22160-2 hardback

This book is printed on paper suitable for recycling and made from fully managed and sustained forest sources. Logging, pulping and manufacturing processes are expected to conform to the environmental regulations of the country of origin.

A catalogue record for this book is available from the British Library.

A catalog record for this book is available from the Library of Congress.

10 9 8 7 6 5 4 3 2 1
18 17 16 15 14 13 12 11 10 09

Printed and bound in Great Britain by
CPI Antony Rowe, Chippenham and Eastbourne

To Bridget and Molly, with love

Contents

viii   *Contents*

Part II   Performance Affects

Acknowledgements

I would like to thank all colleagues who worked on the *In Place of War* project. They are Michael Balfour, Ananda Breed, Ruth Daniel, Rachel Finn, Charlotte Hennessy, Jenny Hughes and Alison Jeffers. A particular thanks to Rachel for providing invaluable support on seeking permissions in the last stages of preparing the manuscript and Jenny who made the whole project possible. Colleagues in the School of Arts Histories and Cultures and especially those in Drama have provided encouragement to all the Applied Theatre work in the University of Manchester. It is their enthusiasm that makes working in the city so enjoyable and rewarding. A particular thanks to Viv Gardner, Tony Jackson, Johannes Sjöberg and a massive thank you to Maggie Gale – her comments on many different stages of this book have helped hugely.

I am also indebted to colleagues in the broader applied theatre/drama/ performance field whose openness and warmth make them great friends and collaborators. Thanks always to Paul Heritage, who made me understand what working in a University could be, and to Bill McDonnell, whose insights on questions of ethics and politics have been vital for this area of practice. Thanks to David Grant for spirited encouragement of all applied theatre endeavours and particular appreciation to Helen Nicholson, who shares a passion for practice and research in this area and is an inspiration to all of us who continue to strive to create a place for applied drama/theatre inside universities.

I would also like to thank the artists whose work has inspired a number of the debates and ideas that exist in these pages. There are many who show incredible tenacity to make beautiful work happen in the most surprising contexts. Ruwanthie de Chickera continues to amaze in her capacity to create theatre projects in the testing world of present-day Sri Lanka, and Janine Waters continues to amaze in her capacity to create theatre projects in the testing world of present-day Manchester: two artists who in different ways – perhaps unknowingly – shaped many of the key concerns of this book.

Thank you to all MA Applied Theatre students at the University of Manchester and all PhD students past and present. Emilie Brothers, Kat Low, Ranjit Khutan and Zoe Zontou demonstrate the future health of a participatory and progressive performance practice. *Performance Affects* was completed while I was on research leave funded by the Arts and Humanities Research Council. I would like to thank the Council for their support, which has been vital for completing the book, and for the funding they gave to the *In Place of War* project between 2004 and 2008.

Finally, thanks to Debbie, Hannah, Leah and Jess. Leah, thanks for the fajitas (being cooked as I write this), Hannah, well done on finishing your drama coursework (being performed as I write this), Jess for being the best ever house-guest (you are brilliant) and Debbie, with love, always.

Shorter versions of Chapter 1 and Chapter 2 have been previously published and have been revised substantially for this book. They appeared respectively in Sheila Preston and Tim Prentki's *The Applied Theatre Reader* (Routledge, 2008) and Sue Jennings's *Dramatherapy and Social Theatre, Necessary Dialogues* (Routledge, 2009). I would like to thank the publishers for permission to revise these works for this edition.

Extracts in the text from the following are all © The Johns Hopkins University Press and reprinted with permission.

Malpede, K. (1996) 'Teaching Witnessing: A Class Wakes to the Genocide in Bosnia', *Theatre Topics*, 6, 2, 167–79.
Salverson, J. (1996) 'Performing Emergency: Witnessing, Popular Theatre, and The Lie of the Literal', *Theatre Topics*, 6, 2, 181–91.
Eng, D.L. (2002) 'The Value of Silence', *Theatre Journal*, 54, 85–94.
A'ness, F. (2004) 'Resisting Amnesia: Yuyachkani, Performance, and the Postwar Reconstruction of Peru', *Theatre Journal*, 56, 395–414.
Haedicke, S.C. (2002) 'The Politics of Participation: Un Voyage Pas Comme Les Autres Sur Les Chemins De L'Exil', *Theatre Topics*, 12, 2, 99–118.

Every effort has been made to trace all copyright holders, but if any have been inadvertently overlooked, the publisher will be pleased to make the necessary arrangements at the first opportunity.

Introduction:
Hedonism Is a Bunker

The Russian-American anarchist Emma Goldman (1869–1940) is famous for castigating a young comrade who thought that her enthusiasm for dancing was inappropriate 'for an agitator'. He had insisted that such behaviour was 'frivolous' and that her obvious enjoyment was unbefitting a figure such as her: revolution and dance, for this earnest young anarchist, did not mix. Goldman, however, was furious and responded with what has become one of her most famous statements. In her autobiography, *Living My Life*, she explained that joy was a vital part of her radicalism:

> I did not believe that a Cause which stood for a beautiful ideal, for anarchism, for release and freedom from conventions and prejudice, should demand the denial of life and joy. I insisted that our Cause could not expect me to become a nun and that the movement would not be turned into a cloister. If it meant that, I did not want it. 'I want freedom, the right to self-expression, everybody's right to beautiful, radiant things.' Anarchism meant that to me, and I would live it in spite of the whole world – prisons, persecution, everything. Yes, even in spite of the condemnation of my own closest comrades I would live my beautiful ideal. (Goldman, 2006, p. 42)

Many who try to mix art and politics today might recognise the tendency to joylessness expressed in the criticism of her young comrade, and also wish we had the confidence to announce our dedication to *beautiful radiant things* with such clarity. The response from artists to the criticism of a lack of seriousness has more usually been to dampen commitment to concepts such as the beautiful (mentioned three times in the quotation above) and retreat to a certain asceticism in our aesthetics.

1

While *Performance Affects* is not seeking to rehabilitate Goldman's philosophy in its entirety (her views on the use of violence, for example, would raise eyebrows), her enthusiastic defence of joy offers an important point of departure.

For the purpose of this introduction, there are two related perspectives on 'self-expression' suggested by Goldman that are useful to consider. First, art is understood to have a role in the present, as a protective force with an 'in spite of' quality that enables people to tolerate suffering, not so that they become immune to it, but so that they have the energy to continue to resist. This is not dance as an opiate, but as a source of nourishment. Second, participation in the joyful is part of a dream of a 'beautiful' future, in the sense that it becomes an inspirational force. Far from being a diversion, it acts to make visible a better world. This aligns *Performance Affects* with the idea of the utopian developed by Jill Dolan, where performance makes 'palpable an affective vision of how the world might be better' (Dolan, 2005, p. 6). These perspectives are foundational to this book, where the focus is on how we can ensure the protective and resistant qualities of theatre and performance without minimising or denying their capacity for inducing enjoyment and pleasure. Goldman's comrade might look aghast at the abandon she displayed in her dancing and a more modern activist might dismiss the nightclubber as 'hedonistic', but dancing 'in spite of a world of prisons and persecution' needs to be given more critical attention and, ultimately, credit.

Performance Affects concentrates on projects in sites of war, disaster or crisis where disparagement of joy is harder to support: it might just be that hedonism is a bunker in these settings – protecting people from the worst of the situation so that they may come back safely into a world that they still desire to change. When Rovit and Goldfarb, in their account of performance during the Holocaust, note that there was little research on the area due to the feeling that 'the grotesquerie of such events suggests frivolity and even sacrilege' (1999, p. 4), they are indicating a similar mistrust. While the performance events in concentration camps should rightly be considered extraordinary, their existence in no way minimises the reality of the appalling conditions in those settings. Instead they offer a remarkable testament to people's tenacity and endurance: a form of resistance that is too rarely acknowledged or taken seriously.

During applied theatre workshops that I conducted in Sri Lanka in the year 2000, the participants organised social evenings of singing and dancing. Most of my critical attention – in terms of research and practice – was focused, however, on the work during the day. Perhaps I had internalised the vision of Goldman's comrade, who considered that the evening entertainment was not the place of 'proper' political work. I also knew my Artaud, Brecht and Boal (but perhaps not my Barba or Grotowski[1]) and was uncertain about the evening's hilarity and sense of celebration, preferring the serious but aesthetically sparse work of the image theatre, improvisations and forum theatre. The *effect* of this day work was planned but, in contrast, there was no intended *effect* of the social events. This is an exaggeration, of course, but while both the daytime and the evening activities could be categorised as performance in this particular war zone, the latter did receive second billing. *Performance Affects* is my response to this mistaken hierarchy and is offered as a recalibration of the relationship between the two areas of practice. It seeks to realign what is perceived as the proper place, time and form of 'applied theatre' so that the struggle for a *beautiful ideal* rediscovers the intimate correlation between the political and the aesthetic at its heart.

Applied theatre

If the evening entertainment is given equal critical weight in an analysis of the political role of cultural expression, can the phrase 'applied theatre' continue to have any validity? Were the social gatherings applied theatre or were they a related activity that applied theatre should acknowledge? Or were they, ultimately, a cultural activity that challenges the very use of the term? Certainly a narrow understanding of applied theatre as a particular series of games, exercises and techniques seems unsatisfactory in the many places where performance has and needs a much broader set of forms. Participatory, process-orientated workshops, inspired by the work of Boal, while producing commitment and debate in many situations, hit metaphoric road blocks in Sri Lanka as this particular context refused to let some techniques past.[2] However, if we include the evening events under applied theatre's 'umbrella', so that almost any cultural act becomes applied theatre when a particular context determines that it has social impact, it can easily be argued that the term has become too expansive: so loose a definition as to become meaningless.

Performance Affects is not, however, a death knell announcing the untimely demise of the term. Its intention is more to act as a form of boundary testing and ultimately reinvigoration of a certain realm of political performance practice – whatever it is or may come to be called.

The aim, therefore, is not to go over the ground of previous writing on 'applied theatre' or 'applied drama' (see Nicholson, 2004; Taylor, 2003; Thompson, 2003) but to discover some of the problems and then opportunities for the practice that has commonly been considered within its limits. In developing a critique of the developments of the field, I do not seek to abolish the term. It exists, and, even if people might be keen to write its obituary, condoning or condemning its use is perhaps less relevant. It seems perverse to announce that it should not be used, when it will remain a category accepted by many practitioners, the title of university and college courses, and, in particular, a term that continues to galvanise an interest in theatre and performance amongst many artist facilitators, students and participant groups. It is part of the scene in the UK and is also used in a number of other countries and contexts. There are, of course, similar terms that the use of applied theatre in no way seeks to disparage (for example, social theatre or applied performance) and the practice in the UK has close links to the notions of participatory theatre and community performance used elsewhere (see, for example, Kuppers, 2007). These different designations will be used in *Performance Affects* when the emphasis that they suggest is desired. The argument here is that the term has now become independent of the semantic problems with its constituent words – applied and theatre. The purpose of this book is to argue that applied theatre might or might not survive as an organising category, but what is more important is that what commonly falls under its auspices needs to rediscover its connection to other art practices generally and a radical aspiration for performance in particular.

The end of effect

Performance Affects arrives at the end of a research project on performance in war zones (*In Place of War*) and after a number of years of practice both in sites of conflict and in other settings. Undertaking and documenting performance in war zones has demonstrated that the parameters of what is and is not 'theatre for social change' are particularly porous. Goldman's dancing was part of her political commitment, and those evening social events in Sri Lanka were intimately connected to people's relationship to the conflict in that country – to try to unravel a social from an aesthetic theatre in these contexts becomes impossible. The purpose and problems with the work undertaken might be a better starting point than a desire to categorise and divide one practice from another. Some prison theatre in the UK, for example, favours a workshop style that focuses on a discussion of criminal behaviour, while some conflict settings demand attention to anything but the war. Much applied theatre in British schools has been closely integrated with the curriculum, while theatre projects in disaster zones have at times avoided any mention of educational objectives. None of these provide a *right* way to run applied theatre programmes, but all reveal certain aesthetic and political choices that need to be considered. Rather than debating whether they are or are not applied theatre, this book aims to consider those choices and to suggest new forms of aesthetic and political orientation.

Performance Affects has two related definitions for the performance practice that falls within its interest. It is clearly concerned with projects that claim they are focused on change, on issues of social justice and on the participation of those who are economically, socially or culturally marginalised or discriminated against. Second, it is also about practice that is closely connected to particular sites – for example, prisons, camps, or schools – and attached to the interests of particular communities – for example, refugees, disabled people or the elderly. The point to emphasise, however, is that projects that fall into the second part of this definition cannot be automatically connected to the first. Working in a particular site or community does not inevitably lead to an attention to social justice. Part of the challenge of this book, therefore, is to explore what political and ethical ramifications exist in 'applied theatre' projects with a particular site or community focus and examine how these projects might more explicitly connect to some of the radical intent of the first part of this definition. Working with a group of refugees, for example, has a politics that needs to be questioned, but it is not, by some default process, one that is inevitably critical, or one that can claim an automatic contribution to social change.

The phrase 'the end of effect' has been adopted to indicate a desire to refocus on the connection between the forms applied theatre takes and its political aspirations. It was inspired by Phelan and Lane's edited collection *The Ends of Performance* (1997), where contributors offer different accounts of the challenges or 'horizons' of the field of performance studies. This is in terms of its reach beyond theatre and anthropology and how a field premised on the disappearance of its object of enquiry can research and write the 'invisible'. The horizon is, then, a point of opportunity for performance – *where it can go* – and also of limitation – *where it stops*. It suggests opportunity, purpose, limit and invisibility. While my use of the *end of effect* does not overlap entirely with the focus of Phelan and Lane's book, it borrows the sense of *end* in three related ways: it denotes the limits of applied theatre's focus on certain types of outcome; it questions the purpose or intent of existing practice; and it demands an alternative configuration of the field's political and aesthetic ambition.

Questioning the limits of a sole focus on effect is important so that the potential for problematic impact is documented and made explicit. Aspiration and idealism are not to be discouraged, but consideration of the possible dangers of the practice might ensure that what is undertaken recognises how it is contained or restrained by the many forces under which it operates. Similarly, thinking about limits aims to offer a critical perspective on how certain practices can be manipulated to help justify, at worst, forms of abuse and, at best, a maintenance of an undesirable status quo. The *end of effect* as a statement of limitation, therefore, has an ethical focus – it concentrates on how things are done – and a political focus – why things are done and what the problems with those aspirations may be.

The focus on purpose is similarly structured and draws attention to the fact that the *intentions* of applied theatre are frequently poorly articulated, or include ambitions that are far from radical. Practitioners can be unsure why the work is being done ('to what end?') or indicate that it is being done for somewhat dubious reasons. Of course this is not always the case, but an explicit discussion of purpose at least may offer clarity as to the political vision behind an applied theatre practice. Articulating why a project is being created, and why every part of the project is being developed, ensures a close attention to the effect of the work – and, once again, its social and political implications. In discussing both limits and purpose, *Performance Affects* is also making the case that applied theatre has tended to miss aspects of practice that could strengthen its claims. The argument here is that it is limited if it concentrates solely on effects – identifiable social outcomes, messages or impacts – and forgets the radical potential of the freedom to enjoy *beautiful radiant things*. The concentration on *affect*, discussed in detail in Chapter 4, seeks to broaden the scope and offer a different *end* for the field.

Finally, *the end of effect* indicates a concern for applied theatre's political and aesthetic ambition. *Performance Affects* suggests that the field should make alliances with other forms of practice, draw inspiration from different cultural forms and learn from disciplines both within and beyond the field of performance studies. At some point in this process of reorientation, applied theatre as a category might be hard to distinguish from a broader commitment to an aesthetic–political project.

This might be taken as a call to end applied theatre and develop a new unnamed form of practice, or reinvigorate those projects that will continue to use the term. It is on a consideration of this future practice that the book itself ends.

Affects

As will be explained in more detail below, Part I is called *The End of Effect* and offers three examples of practice where applied theatre's purpose, limits and ambition were challenged. Part II takes the main title of the book, to develop a proposal for a shift in focus from *effects* to *affects*. A central argument is that those evening sessions in Sri Lanka, the love of dance expressed by Goldman and more generally the themes of joy and celebration are rarely given significant attention in discussions of political performance. Perhaps the most notable exception is *Utopia In Performance* by Jill Dolan, which makes a strong case for the importance of 'exquisite moments' and offers an analysis of the times the author felt 'charged, challenged and reassured' (2005, p. 5), echoing the protective *and* inspirational force of performance mentioned above. Dolan's discussion of the 'affective and effective feelings' (Ibid., p. 2) provoked by performance is written in what I would call an *affective register*, and it is this register (both practice-based and analytic) that becomes the major focus of Part II. The final three chapters, therefore, work as a proposal for how the problems outlined in Part I might find new possibilities in the realm of aesthetic sensation. While a full definition of affect is given in Chapter 4, the substance of the proposal is that by working solely in the realm of effect, where performance communicates messages or concentrates on identifiable social or educational impact, the practice becomes restricted or weakened. By failing to recognise affect – bodily responses, sensations and aesthetic pleasure – much of the power of performance can be missed. Attention to this realm, it is suggested, might be a place from which a particular politics of practice can be developed: one that, I will argue, avoids many of the problems outlined in Part I.

Performance

The primary use of 'performance' in this book is as an inclusive term for all those artistic practices that include the participation of groups and individuals as they present themselves to others. This might be in dance, music, poetry recital or theatre and could take place in a small room or in a huge arena – and, vitally, might be done by people who are not usually permitted to call themselves artists. Performance is used to illustrate the widest possible set of artistic forms and also avoid the assumption that a staged event is one that only uses the spoken word or some linear narrative structure. Of course, many theatre productions include song and dance – but the use of the word 'performance' here is intended to help indicate that there is a range of cultural forms that might exist in any one 'staged' moment. In *Performance Affects* the main interest is in participatory artistic processes and productions but at times performance is used to refer to celebrations or public actions more broadly. Where I do use the word theatre, it will indicate that the project, process or event was orientated towards the creation or presentation of a spoken-word drama or stage play. As discussed above, I keep to the term applied theatre both out of respect for its current usage and also because it hints that much of the practice captured by it does tend to be 'theatrical' in the way explained here.

A secondary use of the term performance comes when certain social processes are said to perform. At a simple level this implies that they are constructed to make an appeal to a particular audience. However, it also suggests that they are *performative* in the linguistic sense, so that they do something beyond their mere existence. A memorial, for example, might perform because it is actively involved in creating the memories or history it proclaims only to represent. Or a camp for child soldiers is said to perform because it is organised to demonstrate something to an audience beyond the simple fact of imprisoning young men. In using performance to refer both to artistic processes and to a variety of social phenomena, *Performance Affects* inevitably draws attention to how these versions of performance overlap, interact and sometimes compete. Performances with communities are happening within wider social performances, and the limits of the former can only be understood within a close analysis of the framework of the latter. Performance affects are, therefore, the sensory responses to both social and artistic processes, but here it is more often how the deliberate attention to affect within forms of cultural expression can position people in relation to their wider social and sensory context that is important. These *performance affects*, as will be argued in Chapter 4, can be vital in providing resources for combating the negative *effects* of the worlds in which people live.

From Part I to Part II – from *effect* to *affect*

As has already been mentioned, the book is divided between Part I – *The End of Effect* – and Part II – *Performance Affects* – and each follows very different formats and writing styles. Part I is concerned with examples from practice and how they have troubled the notion of applied theatre and helped articulate its different *ends*. Chapter 1, for example, discusses an applied theatre project in a camp for child soldiers and asks whether a later massacre can in any way be attributed to the original programme. This then leads to a discussion about the problematic relationship between applied theatre's relative invisibility and demands for a public articulation of purpose. The chapter uses de Certeau's categories of 'strategies' and 'tactics' to explore the ambitions of the practice and how the political scope of small-scale projects may be structurally limited. Lack of awareness of those limits becomes one of the dangers of these types of projects. The response from Chapter 1 is to propose a politics of tenacity and survival that might be all that is possible in the tightly controlled and highly circumscribed situation in which the young men lived. Chapter 2 starts in tsunami-affected Sri Lanka, but then borrows examples from different countries and contexts, to explore cultural responses to disaster. It develops an argument for the end to an uncritical acceptance of certain models of practice that are based on theories of trauma and narrative recall. Arguing against a default 'aesthetics of injury' in applied theatre, it makes the case for considering the richness of different performance forms that exist in various communities. Rather than assuming that populations are 'traumatised' and can be relieved through narrative-based storytelling, the chapter argues for an ethnographic emphasis that accepts different models of suffering and necessarily different modes of survival. By exploring the way that communities have resisted violence or disaster with their own cultural resources, a broader picture of transformative art processes can emerge. Chapter 3 draws this part of the book to an end, with an account of performance and memorialisation in Rwanda. The discussion of this context marks the turning point in the book, so that a theatre workshop in Kigali prison acts as a fulcrum over which the shift from effects to affects takes place. In a country where the state is involved in using the arts in projects of reconciliation, a problematic version of the country's past becomes the enforced plot line for performances and everyday discussion. Creating any space for complexity or critique in this context is difficult but a tentative solution is discovered during a visit to a memorial that displays bodies of genocide victims. The *affect* of these bodies starts a process of examining how attention to sensation may provide a protective space apart from the reach of the problematic national discourse. Affect does not become a simple response here, but a term to be debated and a starting point for critical commentary or further performance. Chapter 3 also ties this directly to method, so that a tendency in memorials, and a tendency in research, to tidy up the past becomes translated into a desire to find a means to research and write about performance that maintains the difficultness of affect, rather than resorting to comfortable proclamations of certain effect.

Part II marks a strong change of tone and writing style. Each chapter takes one aspect of affect and develops an argument for why it is important for a politically committed performance practice. They are offered as both proposal and polemic – and the limited attention to practice in this section of the book is an implicit suggestion that the ideas need to be tested. Chapter 4 offers a detailed account of the notion of affect – its theoretical origins, current usage and how it delineates a powerful terrain from which an aesthetically focused politics of practice might be developed. It articulates a 'non-hermeneutic' (non-interpretative) realm for artistic practice and research, which, although it could be dismissed as a retreat from political ambition, is here given a strongly political frame. Chapter 5 explores the concept of beauty and argues that it is emblematic for the discussion of affect. It is a vital part of the case for an aesthetic dimension to radical performance and seeking beauty, rather than being 'frivolous', could be a means to enhance a project's critical power. As suggested in this introduction, beauty has certain protective features and in Chapter 4 this is extended so that working with the beautiful is said to provide a critically comparative edge between artistic work and its social context. The chapter offers a brief discussion of theories of pain to illustrate how applied theatre's frequent reliance on the experience of suffering as its inspiration might be counterproductive. Beauty, in this instance, becomes a means of resisting and critiquing the shape of the world, in a way that maintains our capacity to engage with it. The final chapter, *About Face*, concludes the arguments in Part II by exploring the ethical and political dimensions of affect in more detail. While both affect and beauty will have been presented as having political force, Chapter 6 tackles the question of politics more directly. It examines how the encounters between people in performance processes can become the site of felt individual responsibility and a moment through which universal claims to right or good can be made. Relationships created through an intense interpersonal encounter are presented as a vital place through which political commitment can be generated, and also through which politics retrieves its necessary ethical dimension. Finally, the sensate world of affects, outlined throughout Part II, is examined as a realm of political action in which intimate theatre workshops, evening cultural events and larger-scale public performances are all interrelated and mutually dependent.

Goldman's dispute with her over-earnest comrade is, in contemporary accounts, misquoted as 'if I can't dance, I don't want to be part of your revolution'. This sentiment is clearly admired here, as it suggests that she enjoyed dancing for what it gave her in her life and also that dance was part of her vision of a better world. Social change needs dancing now, and the dancing will not end once it has been achieved. *Performance Affects* wants to go one stage further. While taking something of the Goldmanesque spirit, it aims to articulate a place where the actual work of social change is bound up in how we create, who creates and when we create art. Dancing, and other forms of aesthetic expression, might be places of respite, but the argument here suggests something more radical – they are also integral and necessary parts of change itself. In a world of inequality, social injustice and endemic violence, they could be acts of resistance *and* redistribution, made in an intimate and sensory key. This is a proposal that would probably leave Goldman's comrade exasperated and more contemporary 'serious' political activists somewhat perplexed. I hope, however, that, through its elaboration in the pages that follow, it encourages readers to maintain their commitment to working with groups and communities in dynamic and joyful performance projects – and to continue to make real everyone's right to *beautiful, radiant things*.

Part I
The End of Effect

1
Incidents of Cutting and Chopping

Q: Did any incident occur while you were with these others?
A: An incident occurred of cutting and chopping.
　　(Court transcript from survivor, Jaganathan Uttamanathan)

We are concerned with the battles or games between the strong and the weak, and with the 'actions' which remain possible for the latter.
　　(de Certeau, 1984, p. 34)

On 25 October 2000, 27 Tamil boys and young men were killed at the Bindunuwewa rehabilitation centre in the hill country area of Sri Lanka while being held as surrendered child soldiers. Most died from cut or burn wounds and the President at the time, Chandrika Bandaranaike Kumaratunga, called it 'an unfortunate incident'.[1] There were 69 police officers present in the vicinity of the camp on the morning of the massacre, but the event was blamed on an attack by local villagers (see Keenan, 2005a, 2005b). This chapter analyses a theatre project that took place in the centre in July 2000, some three months before the *incident of cutting and chopping*. The project involved both a training programme for the staff, offering the instructors guidance about using participatory theatre within their rehabilitation initiatives, and a series of theatre workshops with the young men that were run over several days. The workshops included a range of theatre games and exercises that encouraged a relaxed and cooperative atmosphere amongst a group of participants aged between 13 and their early twenties. Each day improvisations and devised scenes were developed, leading to a short performance on the final day of the project to all camp residents including staff. I had overall responsibility for the workshops and ran them with one Scottish[2] and four Sri Lankan colleagues who were all part of the intercommunity *Big Circle* Applied Theatre network in the country.

The argument presented here starts from the end of my book, *Applied Theatre*, where, on briefly mentioning this massacre, I asked whether '[t]his is the place where it ends?' (Thompson, 2003, p. 197). This chapter, and the book as a whole, takes on this question in an attempt to reveal the complex web in which this and all applied theatre initiatives are caught – and to explore both the intentions and the limits of community-based or participatory theatre practice. Although friends and colleagues involved in the original project have asserted that there were no connections between it and the massacre, another Sri Lankan colleague, on being asked whether he thought there was a link, replied that *'of course there was'*. While he may have had other political or philosophical reasons for his conviction, it is vital that his assertion is fully tested. If applied theatre, or at least my practice of applied theatre, is in any way complicit in the wider set of factors that made the massacre possible, then for me it must end. This book starts from this very real personal dilemma, and it shapes the search for a form of critical performance practice that is properly resistant to the worse aspects of violence and mistreatment, which must be its minimum standard.

With the Bindunuwewa project in particular, it is important to examine in detail whether my colleague's *'of course there was'* has any real force. I do not believe there is a simple causal relation between the two events, but how the project was embedded in a wider system of practice and discourse that left a group of young men vulnerable to attack is a crucial area of analysis. The chapter investigates, therefore, how the problems revealed in this example can illustrate the broader limits of applied theatre in conflict or crisis situations. The argument to be made, in light of this project and the subsequent 'unfortunate incident', is that applied theatre's claims need to be re-examined and a politics of the practice needs to be rearticulated (or perhaps rediscovered) so that it is decoupled from any possible complicity, however tenuous, with incidents of violence. Whether this can happen is the challenge of this chapter and frames many of the arguments in the rest of the book.

Incidents of cutting and chopping uses a range of quotations taken from enquiry reports, internet sources and local Sri Lankan newspapers to examine some of the discourses surrounding the operation of the rehabilitation centre and consequently the theatre project.[3] They are used to reveal some of the threads that bound a series of workshops into relations of power that are difficult to ascertain if attention is only given to the execution of the games and exercises within the boundaries of the camp itself. They aim to indicate the variety of contextual constraints in which the massacre and the theatre project were situated and to illustrate the interconnections that exist around any practice. Importantly, this is not a realm of determining factors that petitioned at the gate of the practice and, once the camp was entered, could be forgotten. Social and cultural discourses within particular contexts do not circle theatre practice waiting for an opportune moment to strike, but condition within and through the actions of every project – sometimes willingly and deliberately and sometimes accidentally or in competition with each other. Roth and Salas's work on memory, history and crisis, for example, illustrates how narratives have a capacity to 'precipitate, facilitate, and retrospectively frame traumatic events' (2001, p. 4). This indicates a temporal line that is important here because the narratives around the Bindunuwewa camp, and the wider civil conflict in Sri Lanka, helped to inaugurate the camp and determine what took place within it and subsequently were marshalled to explain why the massacre had taken place. Similarly, Khalili's work on Palestinian commemoration in Lebanon demonstrates how the smallest, often private, act can become a 'public political event' through a range of framing practices (2005, p. 33). This contrasts with Dolan, who, borrowing from writers such as Habermas, has suggested that the public sphere's 'very informality keeps it free of the surveillance that constrains more structured, regulated systems' (Dolan, 2005, p. 90). The argument here is that the informal, in sites of conflict, is rarely 'un-surveyed': the private seldom remains strictly private, and the public struggles to elude regulation.

The interrelation between the hidden work inside a camp – including a theatre project – and the mechanisms for constructing the public politics of the treatment of child soldiers, their death and the investigation of that death, is, therefore, central to the argument of this chapter. While these mechanisms are shown to be predominantly local, drawing on legal, journalistic and government sources from within Sri Lanka, it is important to add that there is a strong suggestion of an international agenda and audience. When we stepped into the Bindunuwewa camp in July 2000, therefore, to conduct a *simple* theatre project with the young men, the question remains as to how or whether these agendas were strengthened, shaped or challenged by our presence. The claim of the chapter is that reflection on these concerns forces a more explicit articulation of the relation between applied theatre and a 'public' politics. A relationship that is further explored in Chapter 6, where the limitations of the distinction between public and private is examined in more detail.

In an introduction to a *TDR: The Journal of Performance Studies* special edition on social theatre in 2004, the following description of this interaction was given:

> The view that social theatre is simply a matter of taking theatre to sites that have no theatre or where theatre has been disrupted or destroyed needs to be challenged by the argument that the practice of social theatre is a complex process of interdisciplinary performance. From the performance studies perspective, 'non-theatre' venues are in fact sites of multiple performances. Prisons, refugee camps, hospitals, etc., are not empty of theatre nor do they only experience the theatrical when a social theatre project is staged. These locations are arenas rich in performance moments – sometimes small and subtle and at other times huge and obvious. These places and the regimes of knowledge and practice that operate within them are performed. (Thompson and Schechner, 2004, p. 13)

According to this perspective, the political realm is also a site of performance and this chapter is, therefore, examining how the performance of the camp met the theatre project within it. As will be shown, the camp was constructed for a particular audience in mind, but the authors of that performance forgot how it could be read by unintended others. What the conceptualisation of 'social theatre' quoted above misses, however, is that *performance moments* within a particular context can be multiple, in violent competition, and ready to absorb and use any theatre work that might take place within them. To develop this analysis, de Certeau's concepts of *strategies* and *tactics* will be borrowed to create a differentiation between forms of political action that 'sites of multiple performances' permit – for *the actions that remain possible* without placing people in danger. In particular, de Certeau's use of the word *perruque* (wig) will be adopted to examine a more modest claim for applied theatre where projects might merely be engaging with 'an ethics of *tenacity*' (1984, p. 26. Italics in original).

Before examining these terms in more detail, the next section of the chapter documents three areas that are important for understanding the wider context in which the theatre project took place. These are the intersections of international and local politico-cultural worlds, the way the project may have shown itself or become *part of a show* beyond the immediate moment of the work and, finally, developing the work of Khalili mentioned above, the relationship between the private spaces of applied theatre and its public ramifications. This is not a complete list of the relevant determining factors for this particular programme but, hopefully, it will illustrate areas that are relevant to other applied theatre projects – and start a process of questioning the possible limits of the practice.

An international incident

> During the evening he [Captain Abeyratne, the Officer in Charge] went over to the police outside the camp asking them to disperse the crowd that was chanting 'kill the tigers[4], skin them alive'. He then said: 'This is an international question; get rid of those people'. (Police CID HQ, Bandarawela, 2000)

> Abominable crimes are being committed against young Tamil children in Sri Lanka by the rebel group known as the Tamil Tigers. They have been, and still are, forcibly conscripting even 10 year old children, boys and girls, for battle against the Sri Lankan Army. Some of these children have been programmed into suicide bombers. (Kadirgamar, 2000)

Sri Lanka has seen a civil conflict lasting over twenty years in which one of the main protagonists, the Liberation Tigers of Tamil Eelam (LTTE), has been frequently accused by international bodies of actively recruiting child soldiers. UNICEF has been at the forefront of these accusations, although after the 2002 ceasefire[5] it established a working relationship with the LTTE to support programmes through which recruits under the age of 18 were released back to their families. In June 2004, however, the cooperation appeared to have broken down when UNICEF once again called on the LTTE to halt child recruitment from Tamil areas. A press statement from 26 June 2004 announced:

> After promising signs in April that the LTTE was taking seriously its pledge to release the children in its ranks, recruitment has been accelerated in recent weeks, including of children under the age of 18. (UNICEF, 2004)

While reports differ as to the exact number of children who currently serve with the LTTE, it is clear that international attention to the existence of these young people has been one area in which the Tigers have gained notoriety. As Harrison, the former BBC reporter to Sri Lanka, notes, 'allegations of child recruitment have dogged the Tamil Tiger rebels for years' (Harrison, 2003). What is particularly significant about this international journalist's attention to the issue comes in what she wrote next. Having commented on the pressure that the LTTE face over child soldiers, she continued that it was 'so much so that they have become a powerful propaganda tool used against them by the Sri Lankan military and other opponents' (Ibid.).

This is where one of the protagonists from the quotations above makes an appearance. The 'Tamil struggle' is waged very directly in the international arena with Tamil diasporic organisations, particularly in Europe and Canada, driving fundraising campaigns based on a sense of the injustices committed by the Sri Lankan state. On the other side, the international community has listened to the case made by Sri Lankan government officials for the LTTE to be proscribed as a terrorist organisation – partly because of its continuing use of children in active service. Although already a banned terrorist organisation in the UK and the USA, the LTTE joined a Europe-wide list on 30 May 2006. Part of the credit for the action taken by the international community was given to the former Foreign Minister, Lakshman Kadirgamar, who campaigned for action by international bodies to starve the LTTE of funds. The existence of child soldiers remained a powerful *propaganda tool* in that battle and this is evidenced in his address to the conference in Canada quoted above. The fact that Kadirgamar, himself a Sri Lankan Tamil, was assassinated on 12 August 2005 in his own home in Colombo, presumably by the LTTE,[6] is an indication of how seriously the propaganda *battle* was taken.

The first act of tying the threads, therefore, is to note that the rehabilitation centre in Bindunuwewa was necessary as a concrete example of the existence of child soldiers. It served a double-edged purpose in providing an example of the 'terrorist' nature of the LTTE and simultaneously proving the 'humanity' of the Sri Lankan government. When Kadirgamar spoke of the *abominable crimes* of the LTTE, the camp gave him a living example of those crimes and evidence of the apparent goodwill and magnanimity of the state. The camp – *and perhaps all that went on in it* – performed for him and his audience, and, considering his later assassination, for some it worked too well. The centre in Bindunuwewa must, therefore, be understood within a geopolitical enterprise undertaken principally by the foreign minister to cut off international support for the LTTE. And, although it could be assumed that its existence was enough for this political message to be communicated, it also appears that what happened within its boundaries was important. The following is found in the Presidential Commission of Enquiry report into the massacre:

> In his submission Prof, [*sic*] de Silva has referred to the keen interest shown by the Foreign Minister in rehabilitation work. (Kulatilaka, 2001, p. 46)

There is, therefore, a direct link between de Silva, the Director of the National Youth Services Council (NYSC), the government agency with responsibility for the camp, and the minister. What happened inside the centre – rehabilitation work that included theatre – was therefore an important part of that wider performance of the government's positive treatment of child soldiers to the international community.

It was particularly difficult to get into the Bindunuwewa rehabilitation centre. A UNICEF staff member and Sri Lankan colleagues had been trying for several months before the permission was finally granted from the NYSC. Once inside and running the workshops, the negotiations with the Officer in Charge, Captain Abeyratne, were predominantly straightforward. However, permission to enter in the first place took numerous phone calls, faxes, proposals and letters. The sensitivity was obvious and to be expected as the war was ongoing. What we failed to recognise, however, was that this reluctance was due not only to the lack of clarity about our intentions or the prevailing tense security situation in the country, but also to the need for our presence in the camp to operate within the performance structures established for it. These were not acknowledged in our local dealings with administrators, but were only revealed gradually in the period after the massacre. To illustrate this, the quotation from the Presidential Commission above becomes more significant when placed in the context of what comes before:

> Prof, de Silva further placed before the Commission certain meaningful steps taken to train the working staff namely, (a) An opportunity was afforded to Capt. Abeyratne and Capt. Mahanama to attend a conference in Congo in December 1999. (b) A seminar for training of officers on basics of counselling with Dr. Chris Hobbs and Dr. Helga Hanka (UK) in February 2000 was held at the Bindunuwewa centre (this was sponsored by the UK Government). (c) Counselling programme by Dr. Elizabeth Jareg (Norway) in March 2000. (d) Counselling programme – Conflict resolution through theatre by James Thompson (UK) in July 2000. In his submission Prof, de

Silva has referred to the keen interest shown by the Foreign Minister in rehabilitation work. (Ibid.)

The 'conflict resolution through theatre' therefore becomes framed as part of the good intentions of the government, and tied into the investigation of the massacre that ultimately led to all convictions being quashed on appeal and those who were responsible for the welfare of the young men being exonerated. The theatre workshop programme is incorporated into a process that seeks to 'retrospectively frame traumatic events' (Roth and Salas, 2001, p. 4). While this reveals a complicity between the theatre project and the broader performance of the camp – part of Kadirgamar's *propaganda battle* – it does not automatically mean that it played any role in the precipitation of the massacre. This is retrospective framing, which places the theatre in a deeply uncomfortable relation with Kadirgamar's project without automatically assuming that it gives it the status of cause. But this assertion needs further analysis.

The international pressure on the LTTE's child soldier recruitment was directed by the Sri Lankan government and supported by the 'non-political' UNICEF. While it is easy to condemn child soldier recruitment, the Sri Lankan government can have no monopoly on virtue in the civil war. Their involvement in supporting a breakaway former eastern LTTE commander in his regional fight with the northern Tiger leadership shows that they are not squeamish in harbouring someone who is widely known to recruit young people forcibly.[7] The Bindunuwewa centre, however, provided a site from which the goodwill of the government could be proved in international arenas, and the existence of foreign consultants in liaison with international agencies running programmes in this centre further strengthened the impression that the government was part of the international mainstream, pursuing projects governed by accepted human rights norms. Kadirgamar, therefore, took great interest in the rehabilitation programme because it was a necessary part of his broader project.

The anthropologist Argenti-Pillen, in her work on the effect of international NGOs on local discourses of violence in Sri Lanka, has examined how in a complex and conflict-riven political arena many projects seem to avoid or ignore context in the justifications of their activities. Her attention is focused principally on how what she calls the 'trauma industry' has come to dominate the programmes of agencies such as UNICEF. It can be argued that the practice emanating from this 'industry', which allows theatre, for example, to be framed as helping people heal through the telling of stories or expressing their pain, also becomes divorced from the wider political environment. Argenti-Pillen explains how 'elites in Colombo have thereby acquired a paradigm by means of which they can discuss violence without having to mention its context' (2003, p. 186). While the problems with this paradigm will be explored in detail in the following chapter, it is the link to human rights, and a similar obliviousness to context, that are important here.

In allowing the discursive frames employed by UNICEF to explain the theatre project, we were in danger of paying too little attention to the local/international political machinations that permit projects to exist and gain legitimacy in the first place. Whether the 'trauma discourse' or the 'human rights paradigm' are the most appropriate or not for applied theatre is to be debated in due course, but here my point is that in a conflict situation these discourses operate within historically and culturally particular parameters. They did not govern the practice of Kadirgamar and the policy decisions that determined the creation of the rehabilitation centre, but were borrowed and operationalised by him to help explain decisions already made. The Machiavellian qualities of this should not be overemphasised, because it is possible that there was a sincere belief in human rights held by the government of the time. However, the use of the child soldiers and the supporting discourses of UN agencies must be seen as part of a *strategic* political project. They were made to perform as part of a particular vision of the conflict, and the existence of the camp was, therefore, integral to a competition of narratives that was being played out publicly. Since applied theatre operates primarily in sites that are bound by these competitions – whether that is prison, classroom, hospital, camp or war zone – attention to a public and political terrain becomes vital. It is not good enough to understand the discourses that operate within a particular location, but we must also understand who is using them, for what ends and in what circumstances. When someone urges the support of human rights in a crisis situation, we need to ask what claims they are making for their own actions and who is excluded within their conception of rights. If someone proposes a project for victims of a conflict, who has decided who the victims will be and which of them will receive what type of support?

The application for clearance for the project in Bindunuwewa, combining the *rights* of the young people to cultural expression with a claim for the powerful ability of the arts to rebuild lives, might have been easy to construct but it overlooked how the rights discourse operated within a highly contested political field where many different voices borrowed the authority of international human rights standards at different times to justify their actions. Human rights claims have now become so entrenched into antagonistic discourses in war or conflict situations more generally that it is hard to extract any report of human rights abuses from a competition of truths (that might encourage as much as prevent further conflict). While there have been terrible abuses in the war in Sri Lanka, work within a human rights paradigm is always going to be easily instrumentalised by one party to the conflict. Conceptualising the theatre project in Bindunuwewa as a human rights initiative, therefore, failed to recognise the systematic use of rights discourses by the government and opposition political groups. This, therefore, enabled the theatre programme to be understood quite easily as part of Kadirgamar's project of proving the abominable character of the LTTE and further demonstrating the exercise of positive, human rights standards by the government.

Applied theatre, of course, always operates within and through the competing discourses of the situations in which it is practised. Participatory, workshop-based theatre might aim to help individuals or groups generate a critique of structures of power in which they live, but institutions, the practices that exist within them, and the comings and goings of applied theatre will always be embedded in wider discursive, political and cultural processes. These processes are involved in a historical development of the institutions and the multiple meanings that emerge from them – part of what Rancière called the 'distribution of the sensible', which will be discussed in detail in Chapter 6. It is perhaps naïve to believe that individual participants within the confines of transitory projects can develop any 'spontaneous' resistant power (Dolan, 2005, p. 90). A question to ask is whether the activity of the project is more likely to fit with the dominating discourses (even those that are mutually antagonistic) or be rendered invisible. De Certeau refers to the power of these discourses as a 'grid of discipline' and offers a more positive response by suggesting where and how they may be 'evaded':

> If it is true that the grid of 'discipline' is everywhere becoming clearer and more extensive, it is all the more urgent to discover how an entire society resists being reduced to it, what popular procedures (also 'miniscule' and quotidian) manipulate the mechanisms of discipline and conform to them only in order to evade them. (1984, p. xiv)

So applied theatre, in the case I am discussing, was easily subsumed or reduced to operating within the tight parameters of the grid that surrounded the camp in Bindunuwewa. Rather than having power to overcome what de Certeau views as 'extensive', it was in fact more likely to *conform*. However, if we accept these limits, there is also a clue here to a more modest mission for this form of performance practice. We might hope, as is mentioned above, that theatre can generate a critique of a structure of power, but in fact perhaps we can only presume, with our 'miniscule and quotidian' art form, to 'conform in order to evade'. And, before we decry the pessimism of this vision, it is important to remember that, in a war zone, evasion can be life-saving. Whether the theatre project in July 2000 provided or could have provided a means for this evasion is, of course, still to be questioned, but if the conformity of the work is not inflected with the gentle politics of *safely evading the worst abuses of power* it can make no claims to be a critical or radical practice.

While conformity for de Certeau can be a precursor to resistance, this needs to be questioned in the example here. Conformity, in Bindunuwewa, could have meant that the project was either a helpful aside in the international political campaign to prove the terrorist status of the LTTE or, as I will go on to argue in the next section, evidence of the 'favourable treatment of Tamil people over the Sinhalese'. It may have hoped for evasive power, but untangling it from the 'competing grids' is a complex task.

A showpiece

> The rehabilitation program went well. The government even used it as a showpiece. (*Sri Lankan Observer*, 2000a)

> It is possible that the massacre which occurred on the eve of the Deepavali festival was stage-managed to trigger ethnic tensions in the country and besmirch the Government's image. (*Daily News*,[8] 2000)

When Captain Abeyratne, the Officer in Charge of Bindunuwewa, came down to the camp edge to help disperse a crowd that had gathered outside on the evening of 24 October, he called what was happening 'an international question': he urged the police to 'get rid of those people'. Although it is impossible to understand the exact reason for him combining the mention of an international context with a demand for the police to move on a mob, the coupling of the two does suggest that the camp leader was aware of the wider significance of his work. The local disquiet interrupted the international appearance that, perhaps, it was his job to maintain. In the end the disturbance was not quietened and the following day many more people were clamouring at the camp's boundary. By early morning they had stormed into the grounds and within less than one hour the whole incident was over.

What will be discussed in more detail here is the *show* of the camp. All contexts in which applied theatre projects take place show themselves in some way and the organisation and reception of that display is important for understanding the problems faced by particular projects. In the quotations above the word 'showpiece' is used to describe the camp and, coupled with the comments made by the Captain, it is easy to draw the conclusion that the camp was a performance with an international audience in mind. The quotation from *The Daily News* suggests that the government, having organised its own *show*, could only conceive of the attack as the construction of some other power. The conviction that the killing was stage-managed says more about the hopes of the camp's founders than offering a sufficiently nuanced version of why the massacre happened. These quotations emphasise once again that the camp was emblematic and its existence was used to generate political capital in the moves to have the LTTE marginalised by the international community. The *show*, therefore, both affected the activities in the camp and was particularly concerned with sustaining an impression beyond the local context. The theatre project, as one of those activities, could only hope to 'conform' to the image of rehabilitating surrendered child soldiers or remain a trouble-free *private* activity – one that did not interfere with the wider performance.

However, understanding the theatre project as conforming to one set of performance imperatives can forget that this was a war zone. De Certeau's view that the 'grid of discipline is everywhere becoming clearer and more extensive' emerges from a society broadly at peace and does not provide a model that can be straightforwardly applied to a conflict situation. The 'grid' in Sri Lanka is 'extensive' but violently contested – and perhaps more usefully conceived of as a series of interlocking, competing grids that change over time. The potential of creating a politics of evasion, therefore – the *tactics* that will be discussed below – is subject to a series of opposing 'stage-management' teams. So, for example, Kadirgamar's use of the camp was within an international terrain in which there were multiple interpretations of the rationale for the incarceration of these Tamil youths. Although the construction of the significance of the camp might have been carefully controlled within a speech to an international body, in many other situations the camp could not be bound to a single purpose. Other readings, based on a range of historical and cultural positions, offered radically different visions of the camp's rationale. These were both international (for example, Tamil diaspora versus Sri Lankan government) and also, crucially, local. It is these local interpretations that, I believe, were forgotten by the policymakers in their attempts to create a metapolitical strategy, and it is this omission that could be partly responsible for the massacre. The Captain's pleading for the crowd to be dispersed illustrates a literal moment when different versions of the camp's purpose collided. The Captain wanted the emerging angry response from the local community to disappear – not to compete with, and thus complicate, the international version that he was entrusted to maintain.

In a return visit to Bindunuwewa village in 2006, a number of local people were interviewed about the massacre six years previously.[9] There were many different memories but a dominant theme was the fear that the LTTE were now in the hills above them plotting their revenge on the community below. There was a clear sense of a deep fear at the power and reach of the Tigers. It is not the job of this chapter to deal in detail with the differing versions of the causes of the massacre, but it is frequently noted that a disturbance within the camp on the previous night led a number of local people to fear that the 'Tigers' in the camp were about to come flooding out of the centre and kill them. On the evening of 24 October, the young men in the camp had held a meeting with the officers in charge and levelled a number of complaints about their treatment and containment in the centre. This apparently escalated to a point where the second in charge was assaulted by one of the young men. He left the centre and arrived in the village with blood on his shirt from the blow. Whether he did this to escape real fear or to encourage revenge by the people in the village is not clear, but the sight of the officer was understood to indicate that the 'Tiger cubs' were revolting and was widely seen as instrumental in stimulating the first crowds to gather. The fear of the Tigers, a product of years of civil conflict during which the LTTE have been accused of a number of massacres and have been demonised in the majority Sinhala community press, meant that for many the subsequent attack on the centre was viewed as defensive. Clearly there was manipulation of that sense of vulnerability and there was massive negligence (if not cooperation) from the police, but hundreds of previously non-homicidal individuals did congregate at the camp that morning and participate in the massacre. To take up work tools and engage in *chopping and cutting* means that deeply held structures of belief were somehow threatened by the existence of the

camp and news of the disturbance. Kapferer has analysed 'the interface between nationalist mythologizations drawn from textual sources
and popular action' (1988, p. xi) in relation to Sri Lankan violence,
and, although the exact mechanisms for this connection are complex,
clearly a set of meanings and processes were generated by the camp, and
particular incidents within it, that provoked a certain terrible response.
These readings of the camp created an 'interface' with the local community that was outside the control of the supranational picture and
'showpiece' that others were trying to sustain. Haugbolle illustrates
this tension in her work on memorialisation in Lebanon, where she
notes that 'state-sanctioned narratives are received and transformed in
uneven (and unexplored) ways by the specific localities' (2005, p. 191).
Here, in a small village in Sri Lanka, a state-sanctioned narrative performed in conferences in the international arena met the villagers'
deep suspicion of the LTTE (even young surrendered members) who
were housed on the hill above them. And in this case that local feeling
adopted its own set of justifications that transformed the state's vision
and developed its own appalling logic.

The rehabilitation centre in Bindunuwewa was originally used to
hold young men caught by the army during the insurrection of *Janatha
Vimukthi Peramuna* (JVP or People's Liberation Front) in the 1980s. This
armed movement of Sinhala youth was brutally put down in the late
1980s (see Gunaratna, 1990). The camp was then used for a short while
as a place for the treatment of drug users before being transferred to
its function as a centre for the training of surrendered child soldiers
in the late 1990s. The local, predominantly Sinhala, village had varied
responses to the arrival of the Tamil youth in their area. In most reports
the good relations between camp and village are mentioned, with tales
of young Tamil internees working in shops or helping out locals with
a variety of tasks. For example, the local region (Uya) Housewives'
Association were reported to have had the following reaction to the
massacre:

> We cannot believe this has happened. We knew many of the boys last
> year when our organisations helped them to stage a musical show to
> collect money for a trip to Kataragama. (*Sri Lankan Observer*, 2000b)

This suggests an easy, problem-free interaction. Elements of this music
show were certainly performed during the theatre project in July 2000
and the young men were positive about their experience. However,
within a number of the reports there is also an undercurrent of disquiet

with indications of a fear of possible relations between the young men and local young women and also the availability of services (particularly water) to the camp that were not made available to the village. The showpiece thus appears to have *shown* the local community a number of competing visions of the relations between Tamil and Sinhalese people. Linked to the international display was a positive discourse that insisted that the Sinhalese and Tamils had no problem with each other and many people in the area would urge this interpretation. However, competing, and especially resonant in light of the election campaign that had happened in the weeks before the massacre, was the view that the government was more preoccupied with helping Tamil 'terrorists' than supporting the impoverished Sinhalese villagers. This discourse also directed its criticism to the national government, which was seen to be more concerned with maintaining its international image than fighting the Tigers vigorously. In a sense the political position that argued that the national politicians were too soft on the Tigers and were too concerned about international opinion found an easy symbol in the existence of the camp. A fairly insecure institution located above a village became a short cut for the discrimination *against the Sinhalese* that was at odds with the international message hoped for in the showpiece. As Foreign Minister Kadirgamar held up the camp as proof of the Tigers' recruitment of children and his government's commitment to human rights through the humane treatment of those that had surrendered, nationalist politicians were claiming that the camp indicated that the government was too concerned with the human rights of the Tamils and not enough with the Sinhalese.

Once again the theatre project is caught up in these different positions (and could be used to prove the veracity of both). UNICEF's role in the project, and mine as a non-Sri Lankan, could easily be worked into the international vision of the showpiece but they could simultaneously further sustain the opinions and rumours that circulated locally. While the staff at the camp were at pains to emphasise the degree to which the young men were welcomed into the village and that there was no hostility, the post-massacre analyses indicate that this was the product of a hoped-for local *show* of the camp and perhaps less an accurate vision of how it played out in different communities of interest in the region. The belief that the Tamils were treated favourably (the access to water) and that there was more care for their human rights than for the local Sinhalese (the fact they received rehabilitation when returning Sri Lankan army recruits got little support) was a mobilising rhetoric which the sight of myself and the Sri Lankan team going to the centre every day could have sustained. A theatre project behind closed doors, therefore, cannot claim that it was only an event within the parameters of the camp. As Khalili noted when discussing how a private, small-scale initiative was 'evacuated of its private aspects [...] and became a public political event' (2005, p. 33), there is no easy division between private acts and a more public process. The question to ask is whether our project – private in Khalili's words or 'miniscule' in de Certeau's – was 'evacuated' to become something that made the massacre more likely or less likely. The larger question, of course, is how applied theatre practitioners might intervene in the process of the 'evacuation' of their work.

Although asking 'which show are we part of?' is a vital aspect of the critical examination of applied theatre practice, it is, therefore, not sufficient. When considering projects in complex situations we might be able to discern the different competing or complementing positions that condition the context, but we cannot subtract ourselves from one in a hope that we can be singularly attached to another. We need, instead, to explore how we can develop a more sophisticated art of evasion that can protect the most vulnerable – an art of evasion that in the chapters that follow is linked to a shift of focus from effect to *affects*. In the context of Bindunuwewa, we were problematically quiet about what we were doing because there were few opportunities for speaking about the work. We left the 'evacuating' of our private practice to others. There is no guarantee, however, that articulating a clear position would have necessarily prevented the co-option of this practice into some dubious and ultimately murderous position. If, for the sake of argument, we had asserted that this project was done specifically to draw attention to the human rights abuses of the Tamil Tigers, the work could still have been incorporated into competing discourses within the region. In the village of Bindunuwewa, and the surrounding area, this might have proved a Sinhalese nationalist position that their rights were marginalised, whereas in the international arena this could have confirmed that the government was dutifully obeying human rights norms. A simple statement of purpose, an articulation of meaning or *effect*, would not have prevented its manipulation. Much of the rationale for our practice in the centre – particularly the rhetoric of human rights – could, therefore, be implicated in, or perhaps was manipulated to support, the decisions that left a large group of young people vulnerable on this hillside in the first place.

Competing narratives and the public meets the private

> The Tamil Students Forum of Colombo District vehemently criticize the blatant Murders [*sic*] of innocent Tamil Youths, who were arrested by the Security Forces for suspicion, under the emergency regulation and rehabilitated at the Bindunuwewa refugee camp. (Tamil Students Forum, 2000)

> By the time the police arrived with the Army the show was over. The 'stories' circulating in the village could not be verified from the police. (*The Island*, 2000b)

> Almost as soon as the attack was over, a number of competing narratives and explanations began to vie for supremacy in the public sphere, feeding off the lack of clear information available from trustworthy sources. Among the most popular initial stories were two diametrically opposed accounts. (Keenan, 2005a, p. 21)

> Inmates of the B [*sic*] Rehabilitation Centre, all young Tamils, were attacked on the morning of 25th October 2000 by a mob of an estimated 2000 comprising villagers and outside elements ferried in, while the Police stood by, abetted and participated in the outrage [...] Almost immediately, persons at the top began making statements that were inexcusably misleading and calculated to shift the blame onto the victims. B. M. Premaratne, SSP of the region told the media that the Tamil youths had broken into the store of the Centre, armed themselves with implements for attack and provoked villagers by displaying their genitals and throwing stones. (UTHR (J), 2005)

All these quotations in relation to the massacre testify to the way different versions of the events were circulated or disseminated by different groups. There were 'stories circulating', 'narratives and explanations vying for supremacy' and 'misleading statements' made. The quotation from the Tamil students' leaflet insisted that the inmates of the camp were innocent Tamil youths and certainly not the surrendered child soldiers in the picture painted by the government. The fact that many of the young men that we worked with in the camp were over the age of 20 indicates that the public face of the centre as a place for children did not match with a more complex history of each resident. The age limits on the category 'child soldier' were certainly stretched for the show. The argument here is that applied theatre projects frequently take place in sites that produce and are produced by narratives competing in the public sphere and yet they are often hidden or lack visibility. Perhaps in deliberately seeking to work with refugees, prisoners, troubled teens, the disabled or the elderly, there is a strong political desire to engage with those social issues in which that competition is most acute and highly contested – from within communities that are made invisible. If we accept this *applied theatre tendency*, the question remains how the relationship between the *vying in the public sphere* and the actual theatre work is explicated. In the whirlwind of documentation that emerged after the massacre – of which the quotations above are the tiniest example – where are the accounts from the theatre workers?

In writing about the massacre in the past (Thompson, 2003), I positioned the problem for practitioners as an ethical negotiation between contingent and absolute statements of purpose or values. While these concerns should not be dismissed, the emphasis here will be shifted to examine the problematic relationship between the public and the private in applied theatre. It will also be argued that this axis is usefully illuminated by considering the difference between *strategic* and *tactical* performance practices. First, however, I will consider the public and the private – two interacting spheres that combine in awkward and demanding ways in both applied theatre projects and practitioners' discussions of their work: spheres that, in Chapter 6, will be shown to be very hard to distinguish.

One view would insist that the workshops in the camp in Bindunuwewa were a largely private affair. We ran games, improvisation exercises, movement and acting sessions leading to a series of short scenes performed within the boundaries of the camp. The immediate reception of the work was with the audience of young people and staff. There was, of course, the wider audience of those people that saw us entering and exiting the premises each day but they did not see the theatre work itself. While many applied theatre projects have a strong public face, I would argue that a large proportion of the work takes place within the confines of institutions, communities and closed settings. This means that they have a limited or strongly mediated interface with a broadly conceived public sphere. Clearly some applied theatre projects – in the widest possible sense of the practice – have a far more direct interaction through large-scale events, festivals, carnivals and major forms of public expression, but much of the repertoire is necessarily relatively invisible. Many projects can, therefore, be considered as a form of private practice and much of the writing on applied theatre discusses moments, problems and dilemmas that occur within these hidden moments. While the applied theatre practitioner will often be working in a setting where she or he rejects the public discourses that condition it (for example, in a prison where she or he disputes retributive discourses on punishment), that rejection is rarely constructed or announced as a specific competition with those discourses. However, as argued above when noting how discourses do not wait at the gate or circle above the world of practice, it is false to conceive of the private and the public having a firm boundary marking one off from the other. Public politics is performed within private moments and private actions seep into public discourse. Although sociologist Tambornino might argue that 'a delicate balance must be maintained between the private and the public, between that remaining in the shadows and that exposed to bright light' (2002, p. 22), the concern here is how shadow practices become illuminated by others, and how that illumination can be a process of imagining and inventing what is assumed to be happening in those hidden places.

With the Bindunuwewa camp, there was a dynamic interplay of a range of competing public discourses, as is indicated by the quotations from the 'circulating stories' and the discussion of the international show above. However, while the internal operation of the camp became drawn into the public investigations after the massacre, there was only a limited attempt by the team of theatre practitioners, at the time of the project, to make explicit connections between the private moments of the workshops and the public debates concerning the camp. The concern for human rights and so forth was outlined in applications to do the work, and in conversations between colleagues and staff from UNICEF, but the degree to which all frameworks for explaining the camp were being co-opted within different strategic political projects only became clear when a number had coalesced in that moment of *cutting and chopping*. Applied theatre (in this version of it) struggled to articulate the significance of the private moments in a way that could disturb (or perhaps *evade*) those forces that had their own power to imagine and then publicly disseminate the rationale for the work. Tying *effects* into a broader schema – for example arguing 'the theatre was another example of the government's genuine concern for the rehabilitation needs of these children' – would have too easily folded the private into the public. Captain Abeyratne might explain to his superiors what we were doing, those superiors might use what we were doing for their ends and simultaneously local villagers would generate their own interpretations that were spun from their existing perspectives on the camp. There is no simple, automatic power to affect these processes, but practitioners where possible should be cognisant of their implications.

The *end of effect* is, therefore, partly located in the interface between the private and the public – and at that site/moment, in Tambornino's balance between the shadows and the bright light, the articulation of the purpose of applied theatre needs to be carefully considered. Practice will struggle to contain readings that it spawns, particularly in those contexts dominated by highly and violently oppositional visions of the world (a particularly acute version of this is the subject of Chapter 3). In effect, because the private never remains completely private, we must be fully engaged with how the work is refigured, co-opted or put in the service of diverse public discourses. We must perhaps patrol the public/private interfaces of each moment of applied theatre practice (which do not exist simply at the door between the workshop room and the outside) to discover means of continuing to permit space for the intimacy of the practice while engaging safely and critically with the contexts and discourse in which the work is located. This requires an advocacy of the private (a politics of the intimate) and a critical encounter with the public (the shape of which is the subject of Part II). This meeting does not mean cooperation with powerful voices operating in different contexts but a wry 'conformity' that still allows space for evasion. This is an engagement with a strategic and tactical realm that will be analysed below. These concerns are echoed in the chapters that follow in Part I, with Chapter 2 proposing an ethnographic perspective that locates performance practice outside the narrow politics of trauma relief, and Chapter 3 that holds onto *affect* so that we do not compete on a discursive terrain that may be complicit with genocide. Here we need to discover a tactical politics – that is between public and private: one that is content to work both in the shadows and in the bright light.

Applied theatre as strategy or tactic?

The necessity for a more carefully planned and deliberate development of the interrelation between the public and private aspects of applied theatre – what Chapter 6 calls an intervention in the 'distribution of the sensible' – is not only a call for the private practice to have a correlating act of 'public' explanation or advocacy. While this would be a good idea, the argument here is that, in order to manage the interaction of private and public in contested situations, applied theatre needs to consider the difference between *tactical* and *strategic* performance practices. According to de Certeau, the difference between these indicates alternative forms of political action and the varying positions from which those acts can happen. He explains *strategy* in the following terms:

> I call a *strategy* the calculation (or manipulation) of power relation-
> ships that become possible as soon as a subject with will and power
> (a business, an army, a city, a scientific institution) can be isolated.
> It postulates a *place* that can be delimited as its *own* and serve as the
> base from which relations with an *exteriority* composed of targets
> or threats [...] can be managed. As in management, every 'strategic'
> rationalization seeks first of all to distinguish its 'own' place, that is,
> the places of its own power and will, from an 'environment' [...] It
> is also the typical attitude of modern science, politics, and military
> strategy. (de Certeau, 1984, pp. 35–6)

Political strategy allows a person, group or organisation with 'will or
power' to manage the threats that are exterior to it. In a war zone,
clearly this is at both a military and a government level but also between
competing strategists who are vying to have power over a particular
environment. For those who cannot find a place from which to act strategically, de Certeau offers *tactics* – 'ways of operating' including everyday practices such as 'clever tricks' and 'knowing how to get away with
things' (de Certeau, 1984, p. xix). He expands in the following:

> a *tactic* is a calculated action determined by the absence of a proper
> locus. No delimitation of an exteriority, then, provides it with the
> condition necessary for autonomy. The space of a tactic is the space
> of the other. Thus it must play on and with a terrain imposed on it
> and organized by the law of a foreign power. (Ibid., pp. 36–7)

In de Certeau's configuration, therefore, where some have the power to
act strategically – to make interventions to change an environment –
others can only resist within the boundaries in which they exist. As
he explains, 'a tactic is determined by the *absence of power* just as a
strategy is organized by the postulation of power' (Ibid., p. 38. Italics in
original). While this distinction is perhaps best understood as degrees
of potential rather than in absolute terms, I would argue that it is useful generally for the applied theatre community and vital for the case
discussed here. For example, many participatory theatre projects, when
working with marginalised, isolated or oppressed groups, hope they can
generate strategic action with that community when in fact they can
only operate at the level of tactics. Applied theatre projects might instil
in participants rich and complex means of coping and subtly resisting

the worst of a context, but rarely are they able to equip people to transcend it. In fact, in not noticing how many communities are held in cultural, physical and historical settings from which a strategic vision of change is very difficult to adopt, applied theatre may be raising dangerous expectations. In not actively differentiating between tactical and strategic political action in an 'empowerment' agenda, for example, we may be encouraging attempts at strategic action which, particularly in conflict zones, are fatal. So the celebratory theatre workshop, the problem-solving role play or the forum theatre session in most applied theatre circumstances are *tactical* performance practices that might provide immediate means of living through and dealing with the present, but cannot claim that they structurally alter it. As de Certeau claims, what a tactic wins 'it cannot keep' (Ibid., p. 37). Forum theatre is, perhaps, the form that forgets this most, as communities come up with solutions to scenes of oppression (such as insisting that you need to be more assertive or deal with the boss in a different way) as a source for transforming oppression. These are, however, tactics. If a forum theatre session with a community proposed interventions based on reformulating the economic relations on which a workplace operates, or developing a system-wide approach to reporting and prosecuting human rights failures, it would be making strategic demands. While these are impressive political goals that need complex alliances of different groups to be made possible, oppressed groups within the realm of the often 'private' theatre project are largely in positions from which it is difficult to have the power to make them real. To urge otherwise, in a situation of a radical imbalance of power, makes those groups vulnerable to the strategies of the more dominant.

This is exactly the situation in which the young men and boys at Bindunuwewa found themselves. While I am comfortable that the workshops in Bindunuwewa did not create a context that encouraged the group to make strategic demands, it could be argued that their protest the night before the attack, which in some ways precipitated the massacre, could be presented as a failure to recognise the limits on action for those young men. This is, of course, not to blame the young men for the brutal attack upon them, but to suggest, to rephrase the chapter's epigraph, that, in the battle between the strong and the weak, the actions which remain possible for the weak are sadly limited.

My argument here is that, because applied theatre operates in situations that are governed by both the tactical and the strategic, we must carefully consider the actions that might be inspired by the theatre process and the decisions taken by the facilitators. These terms are, of course, neither absolute nor fixed, but they are categories that support an analysis of particular, context-specific moments. While the process of the workshops and explanations of those running them might appear to be different realms, they can each become part of a strategic political programme. Kadirgamar used the Bindunuwewa camp in a *strategic* campaign that could easily co-opt both the 'rehabilitation' work of the theatre workshops and the discourse of human rights that we might have used to frame them. This is why this book discusses the problems of the activity of applied theatre itself and dilemmas pertinent to practitioners. Acts of reflection and interpretation are as much part of the politics of applied theatre as the content of the work. One of the problems of this analysis is that, in questioning whether theatre within oppressed, vulnerable or marginalised communities can have any strategic political outcome, the argument could be read as a proposal for a retreat from political action. However, de Certeau's analysis insists that the tactical is political and is in fact part of a broader concept of political intervention to be discussed in Chapter 6. In discussing the scope of the possible in situations of crisis or conflict, I am seeking to avoid an easy programmatic politics that forgets the very real dangers in which people live. In highly circumscribed and violent environments, the tactical can be a powerful political terrain that enables survival and resistance, whereas pretending to have the capacity for engaging strategically can put people's lives in danger. The modesty of this claim is, therefore, politically necessary and ethically responsible. The tactical realm is the one in which performance programmes might find a space that ensures that they may counter but not (in this particular context) confront the wider strategic political world.

To develop this argument, I want to use another term from de Certeau – that of the 'wig' or in French *perruque*. This concept is useful for this context because it reinserts a political intent into the 'private' applied theatre practice – but one that is focused on the playful, critical and tactical. De Certeau described the *perruque* in the following:

> *La perruque* is the worker's own work disguised as work for his employer. It differs from pilfering as nothing material is stolen. It differs from absenteeism in that the worker is officially on the job [...] Accused of stealing or turning material to his own ends and using machines for his own profit, the worker who indulges in *la perruque* actually diverts time (not goods, since he only uses scraps) from the factory for work that is free, creative, and precisely not directed toward profit. (Ibid., p. 25)

So while the institution of work cannot be overturned by this individual at this moment – as with the institution of the Bindunuwewa camp and similar locations of community-based performance – you can indulge in the *perruque*. While there is a debate to be had about whether this 'esthetics of "tricks" [...] and an ethics of tenacity' (Ibid., p. 26) is the only possible form of radical political action in contemporary contexts, I would suggest that in war zones, places of extreme crisis, or highly restricted or controlled environments this provides an optimistic polit-ics of survival. In seeking to 'make a *perruque* in the economic system' (Ibid., p. 27) whereby people become surreptitiously 'poets of their own affairs' (Ibid., p. 34), we have a form of resistance within a coercive system that has an element of freedom and creativity. When talking of coping or living through violence, as this book will do, the term *per-ruque* ensures that this is framed as an active form of resistance rather than a passive resignation. It certainly aims to restrict the inflated aspir-ation for cultural practice that may be brought into a context without realising the dangers of the strategies that are played through it. By way of example, de Certeau explains the resourcefulness of a 'North African living in Paris' who is forced to live in a 'low-income housing develop-ment' as a case of the *perruque* enacted in people's daily lives:

> [He] creates for himself a space in which he can find *ways of using* the constraining order of the place [...] Without leaving the place where he has no choice but to live [...] he establishes within it a degree of *plurality* and creativity. By an art of being in between, he draws unex-pected results from his situation. (Ibid., p. 30. Italics in original)

The young men and boys in Bindunuwewa certainly had no choice about where they were currently living, but perhaps the express intent of the theatre project should have been to support them in finding ways of using its constraining order. Rather than conceptualising the project as one that supported their 'human rights' or enabled them to articulate strategic demands, it could have provided a space that devel-oped a degree of plurality or creativity, where 'order is *tricked* by an art' (Ibid., p. 26. Italics in original). Applied theatre might, within these constraints, become a tactical art form that encourages the *perruque*, allowing people to 'draw the unexpected from their situations'. This is not a retreat but a form of resistance that does not forget a primary responsibility to people's safety.

To return to the major questions of this chapter, it is important to know whether our project did in fact develop the 'art of being in between' or rather give the young men a false confidence in their ability to make strategic demands. And, even if they were stimulated by the *perruque* and an 'ethics of tenacity', maybe in this highly fragile setting these provided little protection from the myriad of events that led to the eventual massacre. I cannot be sure of the answer to these questions – as I mentioned above, it was only one colleague who insisted there was any connection between the theatre project and the massacre. The very fact that our programme was part of the post-massacre investigations, however, has made it important to ask whether it was part of the pre-massacre calculations. While the final answer cannot be authoritative, an overarching response is that my colleagues and I insufficiently recognised the strategic political performance in which Bindunuwewa was situated. The question to ask, therefore, is: how might similar projects provide a set of experiences that enable a group to manage, exist and survive in overwhelming situations with a sense of playfulness and safety? How might performance practice operate on a tactical level between private actions and their inevitable public ramifications? Of course, whether a closer attention to the *perruque* would have ensured that this particular group had the resources to prevent the massacre is impossible to know, and perhaps unfair to ask. Ultimately, whether it was a competition at the strategic level, between local, regional, national and international players, that conspired to make these young people vulnerable or the villagers' desperate, appalling tactic born of fear, the *perruque* might have been, in the end, a mediocre protection against the *cutting and chopping*.

Making a *perruque*

As a group working through a major UN body, however, my colleagues and I had some access to a strategic world in which we only inadvertently engaged. In leaving the centre every day we straddled the private world of the small barrack in which the workshop took place and the broader public world of child soldier rehabilitation policy. As argued above, this is not to say that the public and the private are synonymous with outside and inside the institutional base, but, with the benefit of hindsight, we could have had a greater presence in the public realm of 'bright lights'. This perhaps should be an additional responsibility for applied theatre practitioners. It is where our acts of interpretation, presentation and discussion of the work become a crucial part of its political whole – a whole that is taken up in the discussion of applied theatre's politics in Part II. We should not only think of the project as the play of the *perruque*, but should aim 'to make a kind of *perruque* of writing itself' (Ibid., p. 28). I am not claiming we should make speeches to conferences in Canada, but as theatre practitioners and academics (in my case) we need to experiment with our own 'tricks' to challenge the smooth facades of the institutions in which we are forced to live (those UNICEFs and universities) and in whose strategies we are implicated. These actions could perhaps be seen as a necessary complement to the other tactical, 'private' or intimate applied theatre moments.

So what might a public *perruque* performance form look like? This is, of course, a question for the whole of *Performance Affects*, where it is argued that attention to the politics of *affect* is necessary in both execution and explanation of applied theatre projects. The politics of affect is linked directly to the play of the *perruque*. If my criticism of the project in Bindunuwewa is that it failed to recognise the realm of the strategic while simultaneously not articulating its tactical purpose, there is perhaps a double performance practice proposed: one that insists that within the often hidden projects of applied theatre we are not working for, supporting or helping the running of institutions but seeking to perform a *perruque* within them and another that, in a place beyond the confines of those sites, aims to comment on the abusive strategies involved in maintaining them. This is making a *perruque* in the other situations in which practitioners might find themselves, whether that be in the university class room, on public stages, in seminar rooms, in articles, at conferences or at other forms of public event. While this is not a demand for a return to the clumsy didacticism found in many forms of 'political theatre' (and, for clumsy, read deadly in war zones), it is a recognition that applied theatre needs to find a means of acknowledging the politics of its practice. This demands an interplay with the public and the private of that practice – so that the private world recognises its public-ness, and in public we somehow find a means of presenting the private in a way that does not position the practice within over-convenient disciplinary or discursive boundaries. I am arguing for new practice-based alliances: for some way of linking the care and resilience hoped for in those private projects with the subtly subversive possibilities of public performance.

Bindunuwewa was caught in a web of strategic performances that 'vied for supremacy' after the massacre and sought to use the 'show-piece' prior to it. These manipulations, provocations and half-truths should not be beyond the scope of applied theatre practice. They needed to be acknowledged, revealed and questioned because they were the frameworks that permitted the practice in the first place. Some form of additional work is needed to take up this challenge. This is not to reject the act of creating the participatory, tactical project with the young men, but perhaps, in the absence of careful research into those wider performances and an explicit engagement with them, our project could be criticised as one that *in no way mitigated* their vulnerability.

Throughout this chapter I have used the word 'performance' to describe in particular Kadirgamar's use of his showpiece camp and also referred to the camp itself performing for certain constituent groups. My argument is that because this institution, and the policies that permitted its construction, performed in different ways for certain audiences, there could be a place for public acts that reveal how those discursive and institutional performances operated. This echoes Klaic, who urged that 'artists focus not on the unfolding tragedy itself but on the ways it is being presented, reported, perceived and metaphorized by other dominant discourses' (Klaic, 2002, p. 160). While it might be a tall order to claim that this is the job of those applied theatre practitioners whose art lies in working creatively, and intimately, with groups and communities, without that wider focus, applied theatre will continue to be an easy target for the strategic manipulations of others.

Perhaps the alliance to make – or the barrier to break – is between the applied theatre practitioners and those performance artists who specialise in public spectaculars, site-specific interventions and transgressive *perruque*-like critical acts. And a conversation between what need to be allied fields of practice will help applied theatre people remember the potential of intervening 'publicly' and perhaps allow the performance activist to experience the *affect* of engaging 'privately'.

Postscript

Since 2005, five years after the massacre and around the time of Kadirgamar's assassination, the *In Place of War* project along with playwright Ruwanthie de Chickera and the Stages Theatre Company in Sri Lanka have been working on a public performance in response to the massacre at Bindunuwewa. While this event was planned for 2007, and then postponed to early 2008, at the time of writing it still has not taken place. A preview in late 2007 met with positive response from an invited audience; however, the deterioration of the situation in the country has meant that the team involved in the project has had to consider the risks of any further act of public performance. 2007 and 2008 saw not only widespread military action, but also a spate of disappearances, attacks on journalists and threats against public critics of the current government. A relative of one of the artists involved in this project warned that there is 'a time for showing and a time for documentation' – and in 2008 showing was heavily circumscribed. At the end of all the commissions of enquiry and court cases, there were no convictions for the murder of the 27 young men and boys, and two of the policemen on duty on the day are still in very senior positions. In addition, there has been a slow forgetting of the story as more recent atrocities have entered public consciousness. New massacres have become stories to be used by different strategists, while local communities are left with the tactics of evasion: of doing everything they can to stay safe. A tactical, documentation-only arts practice may be the best approach for performance in this time of further brutal *cutting and chopping*. While the demand not to show has been questioned here by the claim that work is shown whether we choose it to be or not, the restrictions on the *perruque* in the context of extreme violence must be taken seriously.

This is not the end of performance projects, though. There are still artists making public interventions at what is a time of appalling civil violence. However, it is a context in which the space of the quiet and tactical might become one of the few situations in which work can safely continue. The public performance that was proposed on the massacre necessarily became a low-key, intimate private performance event: it has only existed as *preview* rather than *view*. Its existence was, however, a testament to the 'ethics of tenacity' in artists and activists in Sri Lanka and perhaps, in its own small way, it shone a necessary light on the injustices of that *incident of cutting and chopping*. This project in no way minimises the acknowledged problems with the original, but starts the process of suggesting, to paraphrase the title of Phelan and Lane's book, an *ends of applied theatre*: a proposal that is now taken up in Chapter 2, where *Performance Affects* meets the disaster of the 2004 Asian tsunami.

2
The End of the Story?

> I will not speak too long because there are still things unsaid, too terrible for you to hear, and too terrible for me to say, and my heart is heavy with them. Nkosi. [Begins song.].
>
> (Woman witness at South Africa's Truth and Reconciliation Commission. Cited in Segall, 2005, p. 149)

One of the central arguments of the previous chapter was that participatory theatre work is explained by discursive systems, some of which we may (perhaps inadvertently) encourage and some of which feed from our work in ways that we might not choose. This chapter focuses on one such 'system' and seeks to question its hold on theatre and performance studies. It aims to move beyond what I will argue are its limits, to construct a vision for applied theatre that is strongly historically situated and culturally specific: one that both rejects this particular theoretical framework and questions the practice that emerges from it. The chapter focuses on theories of *trauma*, approaches to *trauma relief* and related practices of storytelling and narration. It would be wrong to argue that all applied theatre projects have been dominated by or are situated within these fields but, as will be demonstrated below, many practices are either directly or indirectly affected by their terms of reference. The claim here is that a dependency on theories of *trauma* narrows the potential of the work and aligns applied theatre with some deeply problematic assumptions and practices. In order to develop this argument, the origins of *trauma* as 'one of the signal concepts of our time' (Leys, 2000, p. 10) will be explored and then I will outline how it has been adopted by or translated into performance practice. The chapter will, therefore, move backwards into the field of trauma studies, and then move forwards into the ramifications of this alignment for theatre and performance. Murphy has referred, when discussing trauma, to 'the effects of a seepage from the clinic into broader public discourse' (Murphy, 2007, p. 69) and it is exactly this *seepage* from a psychological/psychoanalytic category into the realm of performance that is the concern here. One of the conclusions of the chapter is that cultural practices in sites of disaster, war or crisis must escape the clutches of what Schaffer and Smith have called 'the dominant paradigm for understanding the processes of victimization, remembering, witnessing, and recovery' (Schaffer and Smith, 2004, p. 9) if a claim for resistant or radical impact can be maintained. In addition, by rejecting a framing of the practice within *trauma studies*, there are inevitable consequences for the form, style and feel of community-based performance that also need to be discussed.

Trauma relief is a dominant mode of practice and discourse (a 'master term'[1]) that has become an explanatory tool for many programmes with individuals and communities in crisis. It is used both theoretically (particularly linked to literary studies; see Caruth (1995)), technically (see, for example, manuals on psychosocial care by Ehrenreich (2001) or the *Disaster Mental Health Response Handbook* (2000)) and less formally in everyday speech and lay diagnoses of suffering. With its connections to the field of Holocaust Studies and origins in a body of knowledge emerging from the First World War through to Vietnam era research on Post-Traumatic Stress Disorder (PTSD) (Argenti-Pillen, 2003; Caruth, 1995; Felman and Laub, 1992; Leys, 2000), *trauma studies* has become an important paradigm from which a range of micro-practices, including some theatre and performance projects, find their theoretical rationale. This chapter argues that these theories (and practices) emerged from a certain historical moment and geographical site and cannot be transferred fully to new times and new places.[2] The case here, however, is not only that this has led to treatment demands that have at times been uncritically adopted by theatre practitioners, but also that the very foundations, on which 'trauma relief' is based, are also contested. The idea that trauma leads, for example, to an uncontrolled return of the past in the present – discussed below – while providing a rich canvas to sketch the debates on representation or 'speakability', in fact has only limited support in empirical research. If *trauma* does not lead inevitably to a replication of the negative event in dreams, nightmares and flashbacks in the present, what does this mean for the links between terrifying experiences and different communities' means of coping? What does this do to an assumption about the importance of storytelling? In challenging the *trauma diagnosis* as a basic framework for understanding memory, witnessing and working through the appalling, the chapter hopes to open up a more complex picture of cultural forms of living with and resisting violence: a picture that aims to present a broader and more inclusive vision for radical or resistant performance practice.

Within performance studies in general and in applied theatre in particular, the assumptions emanating from the popularity of the *trauma diagnosis* have led to the prescription of 'telling one's story' as the preferred method and necessary precondition for 'relief', 'liberation' or 'healing'. According to this approach, constructing a narrative from the pain of the past allows it to be contained or healed. The prescription for cure has then transformed itself into a proscription as the binary opposite of speaking your experience, that is, silence or 'not-telling' is somehow denigrated as a dangerous retreat, a failure or the site of continued harm. The argument here is that theatre makers and performance scholars have recognised an apparent congruence between their storytelling forms and the speaking out urged in projects with 'trauma survivors' and have subsequently sought to make an alliance between two fields of practice. Taylor, for example, has noted that 'the individual focus of trauma studies clearly overlaps with the public and collective focus of performance studies' (Taylor, D., 2002, p. 152) but she does not critically analyse the dubious claims contained within much of the trauma literature and therefore she fails to recognise the overlap as a place of limitation. These encounters, both in the pages of journals and, I would argue in a more damaging way, in the sites of practice, have led to a set of connections at the heart of applied theatre practice that, put simply, link *theatre work to story work to trauma relief* in a deeply problematic chain.

The argument presented here, therefore, seeks to decouple theatre practices with communities that have suffered crisis or violence from the field of trauma studies. In focusing instead on the range of cultural practices that these communities undertake, it seeks to validate diverse and culturally specific responses to crisis. It does this rather than define all practice within the trauma paradigm (as some of the examples below try to do) or ignore those that fail to be legitimised by the theory. It suggests that the insistence that survivors 'tell their stories' is a culturally particular approach that can become dangerous if applied universally. *Tell your story* can become an imperative rather than a self-directed action and this results in a set of practices and assumptions that inculcate themselves into human rights and relief operations in many locations, ignoring and potentially interrupting culturally particular modes of mourning, coping or crisis management. And, in being a popular framework for theatre in community settings, storytelling can be in danger of having a similarly debilitating impact on existing, local performance practices.

If a sole reliance on storytelling is compromised, what claims can applied theatre make? What is the purpose of applied theatre if theatre-based trauma relief programmes are often part of the globalisation of a particular form of knowledge that damages the adaptations and strategies that many communities already have in place? Can we claim that performance has any place with people who have suffered from war, crisis or personal disaster, if it is no longer about the relief of personal, 'shattering' trauma? Rather than dismissing performance practice entirely, the chapter proposes an approach that respects the strength of the culturally particular. This is a position that, for example, validates silence as a form of resistance, that accepts numerous artistic forms as appropriate responses to horror and that respects multiple, context-specific modes of dealing and living with the appalling. This might, of course, include storytelling but the argument here is that this should no longer be the default position for participatory performance makers. As in other chapters in Part I, this is a call for broader model of applied theatre – and an end to simple or singular effect.

The chapter will draw on the literature on trauma studies, writing in theatre and performance and practice-based examples. To frame the debate I will outline two incidents that prompted the subsequent analysis and these will be called 'stones' in the 'life story' of this chapter. This is a nod towards (and a gentle mocking of) a 'tell your story' device used within Narrative Exposure Therapy (NET) (see Schauer, Neuner and Elbert, 2005). In an exercise from the NET manual, a person's life story is told and then visualised using a rope, flowers and stones. On the front cover of Schauer, Neuner and Elbert's book on NET, there is a photo of a rope laid on a beach that has flowers and stones placed along its length at strategic intervals. It was taken 'during a therapy session with a traumatized Sri Lankan child' by therapist Dr Claudia Catani, who goes onto explain that it was 'a very moving moment to finally see one's own life with its personal pattern built of flowers and stones disentangled in front of the survivor' (Ibid., no page number).

Each flower is said to represent a good incident in someone's life and a stone a problematic one – a potentially traumatic moment. It is an image that will be used here to provide the metaphor for the two vignettes that frame 'problems' with the direction of this form of therapeutic intervention. Although NET is one practice of many, it is indicative of many trauma-based therapies that arrive in disaster zones soon after terrible events. It is also particularly appropriate because NET is directly connected to one example and the setting of the rope picture (a beach in Sri Lanka) is the context of both. My *stones* will be analysed in light of the origins of the trauma diagnosis, the prescriptive 'imperative to tell' that emerges in the literature and how this constructs a heightened importance and reliance on storytelling. Finally, the two examples will inform what has been condemned as the 'failure of silence' and I will end with a defence of the multiple performance forms that cannot be contained in the limited binary of 'telling' or 'not-telling'. That multiplicity, I will argue, should be central to the applied theatre repertoire.

Stone 1

After the Asian tsunami in December 2004, a huge relief effort channelled resources through a range of international agencies into the disaster-affected countries. As the second-worst hit country,[3] Sri Lanka received financial aid but also a plethora of specialist teams dealing with all aspects of disaster relief. Prevalent in these groups were a large number proposing a bewildering range of therapeutic or psychosocial interventions. Some of these were invited, but the majority simply arrived with their elaborate plans for offering relief to the 'tsunami-traumatised population'.[4] Narrative Exposure Therapy was one of these and, with others, NET teams rapidly set about finding 'survivors' who would benefit from their services. The *stone* here is not a direct account of what was done in the refugee camps and emergency shelters but the sense of disbelief expressed by Sri Lankan colleagues who were working in development and psychological services prior to the tsunami.[5] The quote from the NET manual about the picture immediately indicates some of the concerns expressed by many of the professionals in Sri Lanka. First, the child is given a mental health category of 'traumatized' with little clarity about how a therapy session on a beach would have been able to adequately assess this. Then, the exercise appears 'moving' for the therapist, and, if it was moving for the child, it is not clear whether that 'movement' was desired or solicited – and finally the grammatical slippage in the quote (whose 'own life'?) implies that the life story was disentangled in front of a survivor, not by them. Conversations with two colleagues,[6] who rapidly became gatekeepers to the psychosocial teams that came into the country, indicated that these 'slippages' were endemic. They identified three major concerns with the groups they encountered. First, many teams considered all Sri Lankans to be in need of psychosocial support or trauma relief by the very fact that they were living in areas touched by the tsunami. The child was a 'survivor' whether they considered themselves to be or not, and Sri Lankans who questioned whether there was a need for 'trauma' therapy were themselves 'in denial'. Second, the *telling of stories* was a dominant approach and used indiscriminately in chaotic settings. Communities were frequently asked to *tell their stories* with next to no follow up or clarity as to what was to be done with the stories told. Third, terminology used to explain the interventions had no direct translation in the two major languages (Sinhala and Tamil) and the diagnostic tools for detecting trauma asked questions and used terms that were both inappropriate and meaningless within the context. Galappatti notes that, although for the reasons hinted here 'attempts to "counsel" survivors were actively discouraged as an initial intervention', there was:

> A widely held assumption that speaking about their experiences and feelings with 'counsellors' would be emotionally beneficial for people who had faced the loss of their families, houses, livelihoods and who were living in temporary camps. (Galappatti, 2005, p. 2)

The emerging anger[7] at these assumptions, and the practices they led to, represent the first *stone* in this account. In post-tsunami Sri Lanka, trauma discourse and trauma relief therapies did not arrive as a slow-moving seepage from the clinic – they were somewhat desperately referred to as the 'second wave'.

Stone 2

While the first stone is general and somewhat impressionistic, the second refers to a specific moment from a theatre-based intervention. In February 2005, a British arts organisation was running a series of projects in a tsunami-displaced people's camp in the south of Sri Lanka. While they ran sessions involving a range of art forms, they also brought two registered dramatherapists to conduct theatre workshops with children. There is no claim that the motivation for this is fully known, but I would suggest that it must have been based on certain assumptions about the needs of the young people and the intercultural transference of dramatherapy methods. Again, it is the basis and then effect of those assumptions that are the target here. This is not an attack on dramatherapists specifically, as the argument is that they share a disciplinary predisposition that is held by many theatre practitioners working in similar settings. The dramatherapists in this *stone* worked in the camp for several weeks with a somewhat transient group of school-age children. In one incident early in the project one of the dramatherapists, having played some theatre games, asked the children to tell their stories of the day that the tsunami hit. One child started to cry and left the group and later the dramatherapist complained, somewhat at a loss, that they were 'not prepared to tell their stories' and 'all they want to do is play'.[8] This *stone*, then, touches on the notion of intercultural application of forms of theatre work in disaster zones, the appropriateness of the timing of cultural work in relation to other needs and the precise demand for participants to tell a story of a terrible event.

Trauma – 'a cut into the soul'

A *trauma* was originally a medical term for a wound in the flesh that through the course of the twentieth century was adopted by psychiatric and mental health professions as a psychological injury. Although in much of the literature it is uncertain whether the term is being used in a metaphoric or a literal sense, it is still understood as a wound where the brain is in some way marked directly by an experience. Caruth explains this process in the following terms:

> Modern neurobiologists have in fact suggested that the unerring 'engraving' on the mind, the 'etching into the brain' of an event in trauma may be associated with its elision of its normal encoding in memory. (Caruth, 1995, p. 153)

Although, as Leys has pointed out, this is in fact contested in the neurobiological literature (Leys, 2000, p. 265) and the 'modern neurobiologists' here are not named, the claim made is that trauma results in a different form of embodied memory when compared with non-traumatic events. The subtle confusion in the literature between 'wound as literal' (in a physical sense) and 'wound as metaphoric' (where an event is *wound-like*) is a common feature of trauma studies, where technical definition can drift into a literary or everyday explanation. When, for example, Kellerman and Hudgins in their book on psychodrama with trauma survivors note that in war 'people are wounded, abused and neglected and respond with characteristic pain, rage and despair' (2000, p. 11), it is unclear whether they are talking about wound-like quality of suffering or actual physical injury. This lack of precision has problematic results when it comes to designing interventions, as will be explained later. In another example, Hamera discusses the aftermath of genocide in Cambodia as a place where:

> Memory does not always equal information retrieval or expressive force, much less solace. It is, rather, a wound. (Hamera, 2002, p. 69)

Again the memory of suffering is described as a wound – an affective force that will be discussed more fully later within the notion of *performance affects* – but its literal quality, which is a defining feature enabling many of the claims of the trauma literature, is uncertain.

Schauer, Neuner and Elbert's definition of trauma as a 'cut into the soul' (2005, p. 5) is a further example of the osmosis between the neurological and the literary. Although a cursory glance at their explanation indicates a somewhat dubious religious framework (soul?) that might struggle to translate into non-Christian/Judaic/Islamic traditions, it is the relation between specific psychological definitions and subsequent treatment procedures that is important here. Taking into account the argument that traumatic events imprint the brain in ways that others do not, Caruth explains trauma as:

> [a response] sometimes delayed, to an overwhelming event or events, which takes the form of repeated, intrusive hallucinations, dreams, thoughts or behaviors stemming from the event, along with numbing that may have begun during or after the experience, and possibly also increased arousal to (and avoidance of) stimuli recalling the event. (Caruth, 1995, p. 4)

Traumatic incidents, then, overwhelm the memory-making facilities of the person to create a numbness close to the event and an uncontrolled revisiting at periods sometimes long after. The *etched* brain replays the event as an actual return to the moment rather than a version that is a representation of the event mediated through recall. Traumatic events are, therefore, the most extreme moments of horror, loss or violence that disturb usual patterns of memory to create traces or fragments that appear unpredictably in the future. These definitions, which are based on disputed empirical evidence, are in turn commonly linked to diagnoses of Post-Traumatic Stress Disorder, where past incidents continue to disturb an individual in the present in the form of nightmares or terrifying flashbacks.

This chapter accepts that symptoms mentioned in PTSD inventories are real for those that suffer them but makes a number of related observations. First, PTSD cannot be understood outside the political and social developments that facilitated the acceptance of the definition. Again, Leys's work on the genealogy of trauma is instructive here:

> It was largely as the result of an essentially political struggle by psychiatrists, social workers, activists and others to acknowledge the postwar sufferings of the Vietnam War veterans that the third edition of the American Psychiatric Association's *Diagnostic and Statistical Manual of Mental Disorders* (1980) accorded the traumatic syndrome, or PTSD, official recognition for the first time. (Leys, 2000, p. 5)

This is echoed in Saunders and Aghaie's work on mourning, where they take in the whole field of trauma as a product of specific historical time:

> Trauma, as both a concept and a diagnostic category, is a Western artifact, the product of a specific sociopolitical and clinical genealogy that emerges with late modernity and is assembled out of Euro-American experiences of industrialization and war fare, its gender relations, and its conceptions of normalcy and deviance. (2005, p. 18)

PTSD, therefore, belongs to a particular historical moment that was part of a project to gain acknowledgement of the suffering of Vietnam veterans. In order for these people to be accepted (and receive some recompense), it was important to show that the event of the war itself caused their present-day suffering. This in turn led to an emphasis on the idea of trauma being a literal reliving of the past, rather than a representation of it that was dependent on the interaction between the person, their existing circumstances and the event. If the 'trauma' was seared into memory and then replayed, the event itself (and not the person) could be blamed for the current symptoms. While the political expediency of ensuring that Vietnam veterans were made the *innocent* victims of their circumstances is understandable, as Leys again has noted, 'the theory of the literal nature of traumatic memory continues to gain widespread adherence, even as it remains inadequately formulated and weakly supported by the scientific evidence' (2000, p. 265). In fact, research on the dreams of veterans has indicated that they had complex relationships with the life and other concerns of the person, rather than replaying exactly the moment of the traumatic event (Ibid., p. 235). The effect of the combined political and scientific project was that people displaying symptoms related to past terrible events became victims (a category for American GIs that many people in Vietnam might be reluctant to accept) and that the symptoms were given an inevitable or universal quality that was not reliant on the person or their situation.

If the symptoms listed within PTSD diagnoses are understood not solely as the literal regurgitation of the actual event, but a complex interaction between sufferer, the event and their contemporary situation, it becomes important to emphasise that the meanings attached to these symptoms must be vastly different across cultures. Dreams or hallucinations, for example, cannot be detached from cultural systems of interpretation. As will be demonstrated later in the chapter, if the meanings attached to memories of an event are different, any treatment must engage with those differences and not ignore, minimise or deny them. The final point to make about PTSD is that it is a particular diagnosis that cannot be mapped onto all individuals who experience uncomfortable or terrible events. For many, as is fully acknowledged in the literature, involvement in an appalling incident does not lead to *any* PTSD symptoms. For example, the *Disaster and Mental Health Response Handbook*, issued by the Centre for Mental Health in New South Wales, Australia, states that:

> [i]t is important to note that PTSD is **not the normal response** to a threatening experience. Most people recover from such an event without formal intervention. (2000, p. 39. Emphasis in the original)

Also, psychodramatist Marcia Karp shows that 25 per cent of people experiencing extraordinary incidents will develop PTSD symptoms and 'half of those people will improve over time, even without treatment' (Karp, 2000, p. 67). If it is acknowledged that most do not develop these PTSD symptoms, it becomes important to ask why the teams who entered Sri Lanka soon after the tsunami took it as a default diagnosis. If, based on Karp's calculations, 75 per cent do not develop PTSD symptoms and 87.5 per cent improve with no intervention, why is 'an imposed fetish such as trauma' smuggled in (Feldman, 2004, p. 183)?

A-historical and a-cultural trauma

The tendency of the definition of trauma to confuse what it claims to be universal psychological traits with the culturally particular can be seen in a range of practices. In the following quotation from Schauer,

Neuner and Elbert this is fairly stark. For these writers, the 'core' of psychological trauma is:

> the alienation from life of a wounded soul. In the moment in which pain and harm is purposefully inflicted by one human being onto another, breach of humanity has occurred. Trauma destroys the human kernel that resides in moments or acts that occur within a social context: communication, speech, autobiographical remembrance, dignity, peace, and freedom. Trauma isolates the survivor, alienates life, freezes the flow of one's personal biography. (Schauer, Neuner and Elbert, 2005, p. 1)

While in no way wanting to minimise the 'pain and harm' caused by many appalling events, concepts such as 'soul', 'humanity' and 'human kernel' coupled with 'dignity, peace and freedom' mix the quasi-religious with a human rights discourse, all under the umbrella of a clinical diagnosis. Although this throws doubts onto the universal claims of what 'trauma destroys', the same edition assertively claims that 'there is no evidence for the hypothesis that the prevalence and validity of PTSD depends on cultural factors' (Ibid., p. 12). If the very definition they use for trauma already relies on concepts that are self-evidently not automatically translatable to different communities (ask a Sri Lankan Buddhist about human kernels for example), the universality is suspect. Even though a treatment specialist such as Ehrenreich might claim that 'reports from countries as diverse as China, Japan, Sri Lanka, Mexico, Colombia, Armenia, Rwanda, South Africa, the Philippines, Fiji, Bosnia, England, Australia, and the United States, among others, show that the emotional responses to disaster are broadly similar everywhere in the world' (2001, p. 11), the argument here is that this a-cultural position denies radically different experiences and responses.[9] By way of example, Ranck has discussed how 'trauma is locally constructed' (2000, p. 198) in Rwanda, Tankint working in Uganda has referred to suffering's 'different meanings in different cultures' (2004, p. 13) and Langford has analysed Laotian belief systems, where abiding by Western practices of speaking out about illness with terminally ill patients would have weakened a sufferer's *khwan* or spirit (2005, p. 168). In a review of arts practices in African war zones by Isar, a form of therapeutic storytelling connected to trauma relief was roundly condemned:

> Given foreigners' scant understanding of African social and psychological dynamics, particularly with respect to coping strategies, the

position of the individual within society, and group structures of inclusion and exclusion, the evaluators believe the adaptability of such approaches is uncertain and potentially dangerous. (Isar, 2003, p. 29)

'Trauma' therefore does not translate easily as a concept to different settings or cultures. Means of coping with disasters in different parts of the world often 'already exist in the cultural repertoire of the society' (Perera, 2001, p. 196) and any interventions drawn straightforwardly from the trauma literature or borrowed from the treatment protocols that have emerged from those sites in which the discipline developed are likely to interact in a complex and perhaps problematic way with existing practices.

Unfortunately because the word 'trauma' has become so attached to difficult events – all disasters becoming 'traumatic' – it is assumed that what is popularly considered a trauma leads to what is specifically diagnosed as PTSD. This link is far from obvious, but the treatment specificities from PTSD slip easily into treatment proposals for all who experience events that are too quickly labelled traumatic. While Caruth maintains a sense of the universality of the experience of trauma, collectivising the traumatised as a people who 'carry an impossible history within them' (Caruth, 1995, p. 5), others seek to re-historicise their fate by insisting the 'closed interiority of trauma' is in fact 'inadequate to address the diverse experiential histories, languages of suffering, structures of feeling, and storytelling modes evidenced in diverse cultural traditions around the world' (Schaffer and Smith, 2004, p. 10). In both *stones* there is an assumption that all people living in tsunami-affected areas of Sri Lanka, or war regions more generally, were affected by trauma and would therefore have symptoms and treatment needs linked to what in a different context is categorised as PTSD. Although 'trauma professionals' may deny that this slippage is made, this happens both in theory (so according to Feldman 'the trauma-aesthetic smuggles in a medical narrative as a philosophy of history', 2004, p. 185) and in practice, where in the often chaotic and highly complex moments of crisis the language of a trauma diagnosis dominates: populations are 'traumatised' and people are 'numbed' by the event.

The process of universalising the particular in trauma studies is recognised by Caruth when she notes that:

This singular *possession of the past* [...] extends beyond the bounds of a marginal pathology and has become a central characteristic of the survivor experience of our time. (Caruth, 1995, p. 151)

It is, however, difficult to uncover the status of this assertion. Is it constitutive, in that it explains that the survivor experience *is* characterised by this difficulty in transforming the past into self-controlled memory experiences? Traumatic memory in this version is the central experience of all survivors. Or is it performative in that Caruth hopes, by naming it as such, that all survivors will claim this *possession of the past* as the central characteristic of their experience? I have already argued above that a possession of the past is a political and historical construct that denies the agency of the victim in shaping how they live with their memories. Whether Caruth is deliberately or unintentionally creating that *experience of our time*, the effect of naming, writing, documenting and developing a discipline around a 'marginal pathology' has meant that it has come to be projected onto all circumstances as the 'central characteristic of the survivor experience' (whether those survivors claim it themselves or not). Again the peculiar 'marginal' pathology becomes generalised and theory and practice are organised around an assumption that all people who experience 'trauma' require the same set of treatment procedures. The specific problems of flashbacks, numbing, dreams and so forth become an a-historical given with inevitable consequences (and 'correct' treatments). In this process a discipline has emerged with its own advocates, professional and commonsense practices that are ready to transfer themselves to any context at extremely short notice: the second wave.

For the purpose of the argument here, there is a simplistic set of connections made that lead to the dramatherapist in the *stone* example asking a group of children to *tell their story*. It is based on Caruth's theoretical formulation of the relation between history and trauma in the following:

> Not having been fully integrated as it occurred, the event cannot become [...] a 'narrative memory' that is integrated into a completed story of the past. The history that a flashback tells [...] is, therefore, a history that literally *has no place*, neither in the past in which it was not fully experienced, nor in the present, in which its precise images and enactments are not fully understood. In its repeated imposition as both image and amnesia, the trauma thus seems to evoke the difficult truth of a history that is constituted by the very incomprehensibility of its occurrence. (Caruth, 1995, p. 153)

The history is incomprehensible because it exists in a different form of memory from 'narrative memory'. If traumatic stress is the inability of the actual moment to be incorporated into memory (due to the shock engraving it in a particular way) then the sufferer gets flashbacks or uncontrolled revisions of the incident. It follows that the sufferer needs to be able to speak through the moment so that it gets properly formed – so that it becomes fully understood. It needs to become a completed story of the past for the person to escape the repeat (which is para-doxically both an image of the event and an inability to remember it). The argument then continues to claim that anyone who has suffered trauma needs to speak about it (undertake what Moss calls 'memory work', 2001, p. 174) and, because any event that is bad is understood to be traumatic, everyone going through a bad experience must speak about it in order to be cured, relieved or given 'closure'.

These leaps happen almost subtextually in much of the writing, as the repeated assertion of the importance of relief from trauma, and of telling your story to be given that relief, become the performative acts that move the particular discourse from the pathological margin to the centre; a centre that has become institutionalised in training courses, organisations and knowledge-generative processes from which the teams of 'trauma' consultants then travel as they take their expertise to crisis zones across the world. As discussed in Chapter 1, the trauma model becomes 'enlisted in human rights frameworks for telling and listening to stories [as] this psychoanalytic model spreads through glo-bal circuits into dispersed local sites' and it also 'serves to locate nar-ratives produced in dispersed global locations in the field of trauma and to reinterpret them as a part of the contemporary literature about trauma' (Schaffer and Smith, 2004, p. 5). The result is that a minority response to awful and terrible incidents, based on particular, culturally located events, is transformed into a near-universal set of theories and practices.

The imperative to tell

One of the many symptoms of traumatic stress is said to be that indi-viduals will struggle to describe past incidents in detail. They may get flashbacks or have frightening dreams but they find it difficult to give a narrative account of the original event. The awfulness of the experi-ence is somehow beyond cognitive recall and therefore beyond the bounds of a 'narrative' or structured memory. Much of the treatment proposed for conditions such as PTSD therefore seeks to bridge these different memory forms so that a troubling, easily triggered, reliving can become shaped into less injurious forms of memory (ideally one that permits the events to be contained within a narrative form that the person is more able to control). The irony here is that a condition whose central property is said to be the inability for the event to be remembered – it is merely relived – results in a demand that it must be remembered in order that a person may be freed from endless repetition. This chapter does not deny the difficulty that people who experience terrible events have in telling others about them, but aims to emphasise and respect that struggle and its specificities. It seeks to position that struggle within culturally particular sets of meanings rather than devolve all power to the original event. Moving too rapidly from a respect for the difficulty to an emphasis on a solution once again jumps dangerously from the case-specific analysis to an over-simple universalised response. This can be seen in the trauma literature, where the accounts of the strength of those people who are able to speak of their histories is transformed into an imperative that the telling must be undertaken. For example, in an account of a theatre project with child refugees, Kurahashi sweepingly asserts that 'studies on children with PTSD confirm that it is imperative for them to articulate their feelings' (Kurahashi, 2004, p. 32)[10] and, more subtly, psychiatrist Laub creates an instruction in the following:

> [T]he survivors did not only need to survive so that they could tell their stories: they also needed to tell their stories in order to survive. There is [...] an imperative need to *tell* and thus to come to *know* one's story, unimpeded by the ghosts from the past against which one has to protect oneself. One has to know one's buried truth in order to be able to live one's life. (Laub, 1995, p. 63. Italics in original)

Although the imperative here seems to start as a desire among the survivors of past horrors, it is possible to see how the desires of some become projected to be the needs of all. The theatre practitioner in the example from the camp in Sri Lanka made this leap and therefore anticipated needs on the basis of the discipline of trauma studies rather than a fully culturally sensitive appreciation of the needs of the young people. The 'imperative need to tell' becomes validated so strongly in the literature that it is easy to see how this shift from the *imperative within* the survivor to an *imperative without* – from the therapist to the client – emerges. Felman, for example, argues that 'a therapeutic process – a process of constructing a narrative, of reconstructing a history and essentially, of *re-externalising the event* – has to be set in motion' (Felman and Laub, 1992, p. 69. Italics in original).

She creates a compulsion that publications such as the *Disaster Mental Health Handbook* from Australia argue strongly against. This practice-orientated manual offers much less directive, and ultimately less doctrinaire, advice:

> Such natural talking through of what has happened is often the beginning of a process of making meaning of the experience, a giving of testimony, and ventilation of feelings. If it occurs in such natural groups or settings, eg. a shelter, it should be supported. *However, it should not be expected or forced.* (2000, p. 66. Italics in the original)

A further example of the emergence of the authoritarian compulsion can be seen in another quotation from Laub:

> This imperative to tell and to be heard can become itself an all-consuming life task. Yet no amount of telling seems ever to do justice to this inner compulsion. There is never enough words or the right words, there is never enough time or the right time, and never enough listening or the right listening to articulate the story that cannot be fully captured in *thought, memory* or *speech*. The pressure thus continues unremittingly, and if words are not trustworthy or adequate, the life that is chosen can become the vehicle by which the struggle to tell continues. (Laub, 1995, p. 63. Italics in original)

The *struggle to tell* is certainly shown to be difficult in this account, but it remains the exemplary relationship a person can have to her or his past. Although the implication in the quotation from Laub is that it is an internal process, it is, however, a journey that appears inevitable. It is 'all-consuming' and generated through an 'inner compulsion'. This contradicts Langford's more subtle analysis, where 'telling the truth' to the terminally ill Laotian elder causes anxiety and perhaps harm. Rather than a natural 'life task', 'truth telling institutionalizes a Judeo-Christian ideal of an expressivist, introspective, and autonomous self, confronting itself in its final moments' (Langford, 2005, p. 169). By the time this discourse of inner compulsion or internal imperative reaches other academic communities or the world of practice, however, the ambivalence is no longer there and that 'struggle to tell' can become compulsory: Kurahashi's participants suffer from PTSD and must express themselves. Another example from a theatre perspective comes from Moss, in her analysis of Lebanese-Québécois theatre, where the link between PTSD and storytelling is explained as follows:

> [T]he symptoms of post-traumatic stress disorder [...] are involuntary returns to the horrific events in which the person experiences the anxiety not present before and confronts the enigma of survival [...] To work through the trauma, the person must speak of it, bearing endless testimony to the impossibility of survival. (Moss, 2001, p. 174)

Similarly, psychodramatist Kellerman insists 'as most clinicians and researchers believe these days, for full healing to occur the core trauma must often be revisited to release dissociated emotions and change trauma-based cognitions' (2000, p. 14). For Moss, and these unnamed 'clinicians and researchers', survivors do not struggle or maybe only have a desire to speak – now *they must* speak. So, while telling is clearly represented as difficult, it is also proposed as necessary. Laub writes that 'one *has* to know one's buried truth' (my emphasis) suggesting this requirement. Although telling for some people can be 'all-consuming', what is important to acknowledge is that an internal condition can too easily be refigured as an external compulsion. What is a specific response is in danger of turning into a Golden Rule: an imperative.

When Laub speaks about the ghosts of the past 'against which one has to protect oneself', he does, however, hint at the direct opposite argument. Why, we might ask, should we not, in order to protect ourselves, keep our ghosts hidden? Does this not indicate that perhaps sometimes one has to bury one's truth in order to live as well? The possibility that this burial might be appropriate, however, gets swept aside in the dominance of the *tell your story* demand. There is a suspicion that many examples of coping are in fact forms of self-deceit. This was seen in the *stone* examples, where psychologists visiting Sri Lanka accused local practitioners of being in denial when they resisted their trauma-based diagnoses, and the dramatherapist who was exasperated about the inability or refusal of the children to tell their tsunami stories. The discourses governing their practices did not create a space for understanding or permitting these responses. They were perhaps guided by the ethics of suspicion, evidenced in Ehrenreich's *Guidebook To Psychosocial Intervention*, when he explains that when victims of a disaster may appear to be doing well 'this may be illusory' (2001, p. 12). An assumption that people coping with situations of disaster are deluding themselves, particularly when held by people from outside the site, can only result in a sense of practitioner superiority that can too easily transform into a dangerous imposition of 'compulsory' treatments.

As already argued, symptoms of traumatic stress, while affecting the minority, are assumed to be latent in all. Miller and Tougaw in writing on testimony and trauma recognise this in relation to Holocaust studies when they explain:

> [T]he Holocaust has produced a discourse – a set of terms and debates about the nature of trauma, testimony, witness, and community – that has affected other domains of mediation on the forms the representation of extreme human suffering seems to engender and require. (Miller and Tougaw, 2002, p. 4)

The Holocaust studies discourse and the PTSD studies framework have therefore created a 'set of terms and debates' around specific cultural and historical moments that have come to dictate which 'forms of representation of extreme suffering' are engendered or required. Specific cultural responses to appalling events thus become the general and reactions to 'traumatic events' in different locations and different moments of history become affected by their 'requirements'. And it is giving narrative shape to one's story that is 'engendered and required' due to the strength of the convergence of Holocaust and trauma studies. The Holocaust itself is not made comparable in these shifts, but the debates it has produced become the parameters for discussions of radically different historical incidents.[11] As Tougaw and Miller explain, 'if every century has been marked by extreme experience, it has become almost compulsory in ours to document disaster' (Ibid., p. 11) and when it comes to the survivors of 'traumatic incidents' this compulsory documentation is translated into a requirement to tell their stories: a requirement that may 'enfold the narrative within the individualist, humanist, and secular frameworks of Western rights, overwriting the customs and beliefs of the victims' (Schaffer and Smith, 2004, p. 5).

Trauma, the 'importance of storytelling' and the connections to theatre

In a discussion about the importance of the Fortunoff Video Archive of Holocaust survivor testimony, Laub makes the following comment:

> Yet it is essential for this narrative that *could not be articulated* to be *told*, to be *transmitted*, to be *heard* [...] Such endeavors make up for the survivors' need for witnesses, as well as for the historical lack of witnessing, by setting the stage for a reliving, a reoccurrence of

the event, in the presence of a witness. (Laub, 1995, p. 69. Italics in original)

While the importance of this archive is not in doubt, this quotation once again seems to place the need to tell one's story as essential: as a-historical and not something constructed by the world we live in today. That said, the relevance of these comments for the argument here is the connection they make to the practice of theatre. This was touched upon in noting how Moss uses trauma studies in her critique and it can be traced again in the project that Laub is insisting on. In announcing that the archive is 'setting the stage for a reliving, a reoccurrence of the event, in the presence of a witness' he establishes a set of terms that can easily – and problematically – link this process to the construction of a performance. This dynamically illustrates why the practice of creating theatre with certain groups of people can very easily find an explanatory framework within the discourse of trauma and specifically research on testimony: a form of justification that Feldman refers to as 'the facile fusion of trauma-aesthetics and testimonial display' (2004, p. 186). Theatre makers have borrowed from these disciplines to justify and explain their practice because they already use quasi-theatrical terminology that emphasises the repeat and the staging of that repeat: because they emphasise the importance of telling a story in front of witnesses (whether that be the therapist, archivist or audience) (see Taylor, D., 2002, p. 152). The danger of this interdisciplinary borrowing is that 'making theatre' as a response to traumatic experiences uses a theory that is, as has been argued above, particular to a specific form of stress experienced in a minority of people and in a particular historical and cultural moment. It is also a problem because it is a theory that insists that the display of trauma is non-representational and therefore, rather than being 'twice-behaved' (Schechner, 2006, p. 29), it is in fact once-behaved and liable to spread trauma to the witnesses/audience. Although, as will be argued later in the book, performance can be a force – an *affect* – this need not be conceived of as a 'contamination' (Leys, 2000, p. 268) in the way trauma studies proposes. The impact of the original event is strongly mediated by the person affected and the context in which they find themselves. Performance processes affect people in specific, nuanced ways that cannot be reduced to the transference of traumatic memory between a sufferer and a witness and, therefore, an understanding of the relation between a performance by a person or community in crisis and the subsequent effect on an audience needs to be reconfigured beyond this medical contagion model.

If theatre is only conceived in this way, it is in danger of universalising and prescribing how people should respond to appalling incidents. Their options become restricted to a testifier and witness model that reduces the multitude of forms of encounter that may be generated.

It has already been noted how Taylor sees a 'clear overlap' between trauma studies and performance studies, and this apparently natural alliance is articulated in the community-based performance and applied theatre literature where either the language of trauma studies is used or the imperative to tell is repeated. So, for example, the rich history of the famous *Madres de Plaza de Mayo* who protest for justice for their disappeared children every Thursday in Buenos Aires becomes a 'trauma-driven performance protest' (Taylor, D., 2002, p. 155) and, in relation to a war on the other side of the world, Malpede argues that in order to explore the topic of Bosnia and genocide in the theatre classroom:

> The students also needed a conceptual orientation to help process the material. In other words, they needed to understand the basics of psychological witnessing, of testimony psychotherapy, and of current ideas about trauma and recovery. (1996, p. 168)

Trauma, therefore, drives women in Argentina and provides a 'conceptual orientation' for understanding the experience of the people of Bosnia. The struggle for the disappeared in a dirty war in South America apparently can be understood within the same theoretical boundaries as the sexual violence against Muslim women in contemporary central Europe. As a counter to Taylor and Malpede, Edmondson has expertly documented the danger of a trauma framework in the analysis of performance in northern Uganda (Edmondson, 2005) and Isar, as quoted earlier, has raised similar questions about theatre within development settings. The following extract from Isar explicitly challenges the relationship between uses of theatre in a conflict zone and its basis in western forms of psychosocial practice:

> Much more questionable in the evaluators' minds, however, is CCG's [Centre for Common Ground Angola] experimentation with playback theatre (PBT).[12] The basis of PBT is a technique developed in countries such as Australia, Canada and New Zealand, as a form of psychotherapy for the traumatized. Someone from an assembled group tells his or her real life story to the theatre troupe that acts it out to the group, who then discuss the scene afterwards. The evaluators have serious misgivings about CCG attempting this practice for

a number of reasons. The technique originates in a western concept of psychosocial healing that encourages the victim (or 'survivor') of trauma to release distress by expressing and externalising the experience. It is not rooted in an understanding of African society and how African group culture deals with terrible personal experience. (Isar, 2003, p. 28)

This is an excellent statement of the problem of the globalisation of the trauma studies approach and is a strong suggestion that its transference is inappropriate because the methods for dealing with the terrible are far from universal. 'African group culture' clearly has understandings and practices – but these are rarely documented or validated.

In another example, Segall, while giving an impressive account of Kurdish and South African performance, shows the danger of relying on trauma studies as the 'conceptual orientation' for thinking through performance and arts responses to crisis. It is worth quoting her at length to see the move from particular account to general framework of analysis in action:

In another scene, a young boy in the video described the way everyone in his village was brought to a large bulldozed pit and shot. He was wounded and buried in the bodies and crept away at night to a neighboring village. These stories, related through oral and media forms, also circulated in songs, were reworked with ancient legends, emerged in poetic laments at funerals, and were redesigned as songs of Kurdish courage to be played during festive dances. Similarly, in South Africa, stories of the apartheid police raiding and burning homes, arresting and torturing the Xhosa, emerged in performances and songs [...] instances in both groups where performances move individuals from debilitating isolation (personal trauma) to communally embraced mourning. (Segall, 2005, p. 138)

The parenthesis in the final sentence is vital. A rich and complex account is reduced to a particular mode of understanding and, although there is no way of knowing whether in these highly diverse communities there was evidence of the symptoms of 'traumatic stress', their experiences become labelled as such. She relies on the trope of 'stories' because this is a familiar way of understanding fluid and multiple cultural performances and she seems to shoehorn radically different practices into that over-convenient category. Stories 'circulate' or are 'redesigned' as songs and 'emerge' as laments without it being clear how exactly they *remain* as stories. Because trauma studies, as does the subset of theatre practice that borrows from it, requires storytelling as its treatment and dominant practice-based strategy, cultural acts of a community in crisis are reduced to various forms of narration rather than the multiple acts of cultural expression that they in fact appear to be. Salverson in her work on popular theatre in Canada[13] warns against the limitations imposed by relying too heavily on a certain form when she suggests that 'a "container," whether popular theatre process or story, can become a straitjacket, a set of norms imposed by a leader' (1996, p. 186). However, she fails to develop the logic of her warning to the straightjacket effect of storytelling itself when she ends by insisting that this 'does not mean we must stop doing our work or telling our stories' (Ibid.). In the following extract Segall appears to acknowledge a broader set of cultural performances as potentially powerful and diverse means of dealing with appalling events, but as before they are rapidly conceptualised – 'contained' – within a framework of trauma and PTSD.

> [T]he cultural practices of rituals, songs, public storytelling, and funeral laments that perform the past in a new context emphasize the distinction between the traumatic past and the present moment. The embodied memory of well-known verses shifts out of the cognitive mode–since cognition is often disrupted by PTSD–to a physical, rhythmic release of tension, and the improvisation and spontaneity accompanying storytelling and singing–in juxtaposition to the helpless state of torture and terror–offers a measure of artistic choice and control. (2005, p. 139)

People are all given the diagnosis of PTSD and the performances are still understood as either variants or 'accompaniments' to the dominant mode, which is storytelling. What is, in fact, most remarkable about the practices outlined in the Segall article is that there are multiple art forms mentioned and many of them have no formal 'telling' or linear narrative structure (songs, laments, rituals and dances) that would be the usual 'requirement' or 'imperative' in trauma relief work. The apparently universal need to tell is met here with a whole range of arts practices, many of which, it could be argued, are as much about forgetting as remembrance. They are poorly contained within a 'telling' or a 'not-telling' framework, and instead exist as multiple means of actively displaying, ignoring, remembering or forgetting experience. Interestingly, it was Segall's own theatre work in these contexts that was about explicit storytelling processes, where the communities themselves seemed to prioritise actions such as dance. The reason for this, the language that can perhaps develop an explanation of it, and how applied theatre practitioners and other artists might support or relate to it, are of course the major concerns of *Performance Affects*.

In their work on forms of remembrance Simon, Rosenberg and Eppert discuss what they call the strategy of the *difficult return*. While this notion will be explored in more detail in the next chapter in relation to memorialisation in Rwanda, it is important here because it emphasises that remembering does not need to resolve the past in the present. A performance should not seek to heal the 'cuts into the soul' with over neat forms of resolution; instead:

> remembrance as a difficult return then becomes a series of propositions of how to live with what cannot be redeemed, what must remain a psychic and social wound that bleeds. (Simon, Rosenberg, and Eppert, 2000, p. 5)

Although the imagery here is quite brutal, the suggestion is that the past can find a place to live problematically in the present rather than be cured: that the struggle of that past's difficultness can be validated rather than always becoming a problem to be overcome. Recognising that struggle and seeking to work with it in culturally meaningful ways aims to break the link that welds the 'people are traumatised' cause to the 'they must tell their story' solution. In the account from Segall above, what is described is a community using multiple artistic methods that have complex relations to the problems of the past. This, I would argue, is perhaps an artistic version of that *difficult return* and could just as easily not be connected to discourses of PTSD and trauma. What the writer does is create a categorisation that in fact fails to contain this plethora of practices. In Segall's analysis the performances move people neatly from 'debilitating isolation (personal trauma) to communally embraced mourning' and 'storytelling and singing' is 'in juxtaposition to the helpless state of torture and terror'. This appears to oversimplify the process and predetermine the solution. While it might be claimed that 'acting out is necessary in the wake of extreme trauma' (Moss, 2001, p. 174), it seems, from reports from these diverse sites, that it has no predetermined form. In fact, people have multiple reactions in the face of terror that cannot be reduced to a radically passive 'helpless state' or a 'debilitating isolation'. The suggestion here is that arts programmes should step out from the over-convenient umbrella of trauma studies for their complex possibilities to be realised, and the more fluid concept of the *difficult return* might be a place from which to start.

The 'failure of silence'

The suggestion that in certain circumstances people do want to tell their stories or that by telling they receive some relief from the debilitating memories of the past becomes, through iteration, a rule. By the creation of a rule, a certain sense of righteousness and disdain for those who disobey becomes evident. This disdain was seen in the teams of 'trauma specialists' who descended on Sri Lanka and looked with pity on the resistance to their work as evidence that people did not know what was best for them, and in the incredulity of the dramatherapist who did not know what to do with her disobedient charges. The operation of the 'rule' is dynamically shown in the way that the binary opposite, that is, not-telling or 'silence', is discussed. It is important to examine this briefly because, by recognising the strength of the disregard for 'not telling', the potentially authoritarian nature of the trauma industry can be demonstrated. I would argue that it is from this dismissal of an ill-defined *silence* that the refusal to acknowledge the possible alternatives embedded in local practices stems.

The argument can be illustrated with two quotations from Laub:

> The listener to trauma, therefore, needs to know [...] [t]hat the speakers about trauma on some level prefer silence so as to protect themselves from the fear of being listened to – and of listening to themselves. That while silence is defeat, it serves them both as sanctuary and as a place of bondage. (Laub in Felman and Laub, 1992, p. 58)

> None find peace in silence, even when it is their choice to remain silent [...] Survivors who do not tell their story become victims of a distorted memory, that is, of a forcibly imposed 'external evil' which causes an endless struggle with and over a delusion. The 'not telling' of the story serves as a perpetuation of its tyranny [...] The events become more and more distorted in their silent retention and pervasively invade and contaminate the survivor's daily life. The longer the story remains untold, the more distorted it becomes in the survivor's conception of it, so much so that the survivor doubts the reality of the actual events. (Ibid., p. 64)

In these quotations we discover that 'silence' is a place in which 'none find peace': it is a 'defeat'; a 'place of bondage'; and by 'not telling' there is a 'perpetuation of tyranny'. Although Laub does permit silence to be a 'sanctuary', and there is certainly evidence that some might 'prefer' it, the overall emphasis here is easily read as punitive. Silence is unhealthy and not a place in which those who have suffered should remain. It is ultimately damaging, a contamination, and by extension those that either support 'not telling', or communities that seem not to realise its danger, are by implication guilty of sustaining the original story's tyrannical hold. Again, to emphasise, the argument here is not a dismissal of the importance of telling stories *per se*. Rather, it is a reaction to how this discipline has embedded within it a set of assumptions that when put into operation can lead to a denial and, at worst, a disregard for alternative and possibly multiple responses to crises. When telling becomes essentialised as an act against the tyrannical in a discipline that has a problematic global reach, how can a specific community, which has variant local methods of survival and resistance, develop explanatory regimes that can compete? How can we validate, for example, what Munk, in her work on oppositional Yugoslavian theatre, called 'eloquent silence' (2001, p. 15)?

There are two points against this marginalisation of silence that will be made here before the fuller *defence of silence* in the next section. First, there is a tendency to create a binary between speaking and silence that forgets that both are part of processes that many engage with at different times in their histories. As Lawrence has noted in her anthropological research in eastern Sri Lanka, 'in this region of protracted war, people live with many kinds of silences: protective silences, some silences that may be understood as empowering' (Lawrence, 2000, p. 178). Similarly Eng reminds us that 'silence, then, is not the opposite of speech but, indeed, its very condition of possibility, the precondition of knowing and of meaning' (Eng, 2002, p. 86). Positioning silence against speaking reduces it to a passive failure rather than giving it any possibility for agency. Silence, in fact, could be an *active* means of coping at certain points in the history of a person's relation to an appalling experience. It is not only the dwelling place of the feeble and deluded but also potentially the tactic of the strong. While Butler tends to conceive of silence only within the terms of narration and speech, she does echo this by endowing a refusal to speak with positive qualities. Silence is permitted a sense of resistance when she argues that it 'either calls into question the legitimacy of the authority invoked by the question and the questioner or attempts to circumscribe a domain of autonomy that cannot or should not be intruded upon by the questioner' (Butler, 2005, p. 12). This is a domain that, I would argue, is a valuable space for anybody who, or any community which, has been encroached upon by disaster, violence or even the practices of international trauma relief teams.

Second, it is important to emphasise that Laub here is discussing Holocaust survivors and it is difficult to tell whether the account is peculiar to certain individuals or an accurate description of them all. While the particular is to be respected deeply, it does appear that from the experience of some a generalisation is made. The argument of this chapter is that it is problematic to make a case that these experiences are translatable to all survivors of horror, at all points in history and across all cultures. Laub is not necessarily doing this, but one of the dangers of the dominance of western visions of survival and healing is that the specificity of one set of survival processes becomes the recipe for others.

Speaking and the different contexts of speaking are, of course, culturally specific. To insist that there is a definable opposite that is a defeat, when 'not-speaking' might also be the most rewarding place for a person or community to occupy at a particular time, is a potentially dangerous imposition. The trauma specialists, by creating an implicit rule against silence, through the iteration of its damaging qualities, minimise the importance of the different time frames that permit speaking and deny the possibility that silence could be a form of expression, coping, resistance and celebration of living. Silence can be active – silence about horror might not be a life without noise (see Chapter 5's discussion of beauty). The alternative to 'speaking', as seen in the epigraph and other quotations from Segall, might not be quiet, but singing, dancing or lamentation. These could all be classified as 'not-telling' approaches and fundamentally appropriate for certain communities at certain moments. It is an affirmation of these multiple forms of expression, which cannot be contained within the straightjackets of 'telling and not telling' or 'silence and speaking', which are defended in the section that follows and are central to the case for the reorientation of applied theatre towards affect.

In defence of silence (and many other forms of expression)

Writing on psychodrama with trauma survivors, Kellerman notes the following:

> Frequently, there is a contradictory (and largely paradoxical) effort to both remember and to forget, both to approach and to avoid the traumatic event in a compulsive, repeated fashion. Like a broken record that is spinning around and around, intrusive experienced images and painful memories keep coming back while there is a conscious effort to avoid them and not to think about them. Desperate

and often futile efforts are attempted to regain some kind of inner balance and emotional equilibrium in order to 'get on' with life. (Kellerman and Hudgins, 2000, p. 24)

This chapter has argued for a respect for this paradox and an acceptance of the past's place in the present as a complex and not easily solvable *difficult return*. Kellerman, however, cannot resist a desire to resolve the paradox when he elaborates later:

> Getting the traumatic experiences out into the open is in itself a liberation from the earlier tendency to repress the emotional impact of the event. (Ibid., p. 28)

Similarly, in Schauer, Neuner and Elbert the paradox is recognised but then resolved with a compulsion:

> From an outsider's perspective, it might seem that 'Narration' and 'Trauma' are radically opposed, and mutually exclusive, as people suffering these crimes are in too much pain, incapacitated by their enigmatic memory code, to share their stories. However, these two concepts are intimately connected. The atrocities cannot remain buried forever and eventually the victim will be compelled to speak. It is this dichotomy that creates the foothold for this approach. (Schauer, Neuner and Elbert, 2005, p. 2)

It is not clear whether they are 'compelled to speak' by their own motivation, but in placing this statement in a manual proposing 'exposure' to narrative I would contend the compulsion has external drivers. Similarly, Kellerman's liberation might work for some, but in insisting on it, writing it and creating professions from this basis, the complex reality of different communities' suffering, and the local meanings associated with the paradox, become overridden with a diktat: a diktat that seems to ignore the simple assertion from Salverson that 'telling stories is not always an empowering experience' (1996, p. 181). I would argue that we should accept the reality of the complex patterns of remembering and forgetting and try to understand how they are locally interpreted and acted upon. It is not only 'storytelling conventions that are distinctly local' (Hoffman, 2005, p. 339) but the full range of cultural responses to terrible events. We should approach a crisis from a position of respecting the paradoxical responses within communities rather than importing simple and singular means for their resolution. This is not to argue that silence is better than speaking, or that theatre practitioners should only be interested in the performance of non-stories rather than stories, but that all cultural activities are potentially appropriate responses if they are understood from within the contexts in which they emerge. This is the starting point for an argument for attention to performance affects, rather than a series of testimonial or narrative forms that are particular to a narrow range of contexts.

A respect for the paradox of speaking/not-speaking is well illustrated in an article by Tankint titled *Not talking about traumatic experiences: harmful or healing?* In this piece, she discusses how a community in Uganda remained silent in response to appalling suffering and she argues that this is a phenomenon to be discussed rather than a problem to be condemned:

> The silence that was a necessity during the war has not been broken since the return of peace, but seems rather to have taken root in society. Personal war experiences are kept private. In Banyankore society there are hardly any cultural forms and public opportunities of commemoration. (Tankint, 2004, pp. 5–6)

And similarly later she elaborates:

> It is considered too dangerous to talk about traumatic war experiences. Remaining silent makes people less vulnerable, it safeguards them from repercussions by the neighbours [...] talking would damage the already fragile social structure even more. (Ibid., p. 7)

In this context, therefore, talking was dangerous and silence was an appropriate defence. This might not be a situation that is recommended or celebrated, but it is difficult to criticise. The crucial point is that the specifics of this situation determine how and what is possible. As Schaffer and Smith have argued:

> Many cultures have adopted other ways of understanding and figuring cataclysmic events, including genocide [...] In the immediate face of radical suffering and distress, telling and healing can take more pragmatic forms, even in Western settings. (2004, p. 10)

If communities have a 'wealth of traditional strengths and resources' (Ehrenreich, 2001, p. 55) or Schaffer and Smith's 'other ways', the argument here is that the focus for performance and cultural activists should be to enhance and support them. We should accept their pragmatics rather than arrive armed with manuals of our own.

An ethnography of performance in crisis

This chapter has questioned both the interpretive frame of trauma studies and also the prescriptive treatments that emerge from it. It suggests that there are multiple ways of analysing the performance acts described, for example by Segall, that might not be contained within the theories of trauma, and also that these activities might not be considered examples of storytelling at all. They could just as easily be seen as performances of forgetting or 'not telling', and better still they should be understood outside these binaries altogether. The argument is, then, for an ethnographic perspective that starts with the knowledge and practices within a community before diagnoses, treatments or performance techniques are assumed to be appropriate. This was the approach of the Peruvian company Yuyachkani, who, in asking 'what social and political function' they should serve, researched 'nonnaturalistic performance modes' and translated the contemporary through 'allegory and myth' and 'song and dance' (A'ness, 2004, p. 400). They discovered forms and ideas within the traditions in which they worked, and did not need to rely on disciplinary or cultural practices from North America or Europe. Similarly, the work of Hamera validates the dance of a Cambodian woman in a refugee camp, who explained that:

> I dance. I'm not like my husband, good student like him, but I dance in camp. Music is beautiful, steps are hard and they are beautiful. I dance to keep music in my [ears] and keep talk out. (Hamera, 2002, p. 71)

This approach, then, respects her right to *keep talk out* and is prepared to accept a community's right to silence (and her assertion of the importance of beautiful dance is an echo of Goldman that is taken up again in Chapter 5).

To return to the *stones*, an ethnographic approach would mean that a detailed understanding of how talking, storytelling and grief are exhibited and given meaning within Sri Lankan society is vital before decisions are made as to what the different communities' needs might be, and certainly before programmes are implemented with communities affected by the war or the tsunami. It would, therefore, be important to ask what telling stories means to Sinhalese youth in southern

Sri Lanka and to discover how the tsunami is explained, narrated and commemorated (if at all). How are bad events remembered or forgotten within these communities? What processes already exist to deal with, live through or manage crises? In terms of the arts, what forms of cultural expression are already in place, and what are the purposes and effects designated to communal performance by the community itself? As will be touched upon later, this is not to argue that all these approaches are inevitably positive for a community, but that a commitment to performance work in these settings must start from an awareness of what already exists.

While there are numerous anthropological studies of Sri Lanka that are relevant to this argument (see, for example, Brow, 1996; Daniel, 1996; Kapferer, 1991, 1988; Obeyesekere, 1990; and Spencer, 1999), the works of Argenti-Pillen, Perera and Lawrence are perhaps the most revealing as a starting point to answer some of these questions. Argenti-Pillen in particular offers both a critique of trauma studies and 'a detailed critique of the ways in which the notion "war trauma" has been exported to non-Western societies through the implementation of humanitarian counselling services in wartorn societies worldwide' (Argenti-Pillen, 2003, p. xii). Her analysis gives both a methodological response to the problems raised by the *stone* examples here and also an insight into how the specificities of Sri Lanka might challenge the assumptions they contain.

Her overall study seeks to explore how '[h]umanitarian aid that has been designed within the framework of the trauma paradigm has reached rural communities in southern Sri Lanka' and by doing so she aims to reveal 'the effect of trauma counselling programs in operation in the village' (Ibid., p. 8). The suggestion in her work is that practices based on the trauma model are not benign in their interaction with the communities in Sri Lanka but in fact have an adverse effect. The refusal experienced by the dramatherapist is not therefore a 'treatment resistance' issue but a fundamental clash with what this form of storytelling may mean in this community. Argenti-Pillen explores the notion of the 'fear of the wild' to demonstrate that speaking straightforwardly of violent or damaging events is understood to cause harm to the speaker. Her detailed analysis of discursive practices within a particular Sri Lankan village, affected by the conflict in the late 1980s, indicates a delicate interrelation of violence 'containment' processes around speaking that would be disturbed by any uniform demand for people to 'tell their story'. This was not a static situation, as some women became 'fearless' and changed the relationship they had to violence (Ibid., p. 161), but the thrust of her argument is that 'the discourse on trauma poses a threat to the culture-specific strategies of containment of violence' (Ibid., p. xii). 'Speaking', therefore, is not a panacea but a peculiar demand that in this case interrupts strategies where 'not talking' about disappearances or discussing them through a variety of oblique methods allows violence to be contained. A specific approach from southern Sri Lanka to violence 'containment', in both the sense of keeping it in and the sense of reducing its impact, is an example of local practice that undermines the claims to universal application for 'narrative exposure' insisted upon by writers such as Schauer, Neuner and Elbert. The dramatherapist in the opening vignette, therefore, asked people to tell their story of a crisis in a place where explicit telling of that story was understood to do you harm.

Perera's research on spirit possessions and ghosts, and their relationship to mechanisms of coping with or remembering terror, is similarly instructive. In an account of a father and daughter, who after the killing of several family members became possessed by different ghosts, he argues that speaking out *as themselves* would not have been possible or acceptable. He elaborates by showing that:

> The possessions and ghost stories gave them an opportunity to express their hatred as well as their expectations of justice and revenge and the preservation of their memories in a socially and ritually accepted fashion. (2001, p. 194)

There was then a 'community recognition, acceptance and legitimization' (Ibid., p. 183) of approaches to dealing with their loss that had to be in place. Rather than resorting to speaking about the deaths or seeking support from mental health services that posed 'a serious problem in terms of availability and accessibility' (Ibid., p. 195), it was 'local methods of intervention and coping associated with popular religion' that had 'no negative cultural perceptions' (Ibid., p. 196) and were, therefore, widely practised. The two *stone* examples indicate an ignorance of these approaches and a failure even to appreciate that they might be in place.

Another example comes from Lawrence's field research in the war-affected east of Sri Lanka.[14] She reports in detail how women used local temples and rituals to express themselves in 'historical moments when dissent is impossible' (2000, p. 179). The temple location was, of course, vital for the 'acceptance and legitimisation' of the practice. Similarly, women who had missing husbands or children would go to oracles in order to learn their fate. Rather than speaking out about their loss themselves, the oracles (usually women as well) became a vehicle to express not a linear narrative of their grief but a 'bricolage of ritual practices':

> theatrical gestures, lyrics of popular film songs, motherly chastise-ments, words of empathy, traditional and invented rituals. Herein lie the gestures or words which may give to others a sense of future and create new dispositions to an altered world. (Ibid., p. 199)

Both these writers, therefore, in attending to the practices as they exist in sites of violence and crisis, generate an awareness of the sophis-ticated, complex and delicate patterns of coping, which I would argue are both ignored and more seriously damaged by a rapid adoption of a 'speaking cure'.

Methodologically Argenti-Pillen offers an ethnographic approach that should perhaps be shared by applied theatre practitioners. Rather than adopting the trauma paradigm as the explanatory framework and then constructing projects from within its logic of practice, we should start from the systems of knowledge already in place. Argenti-Pillen explains:

> The narratives of the women from Udahenagama [...] engage us to think about how survivors of wartime atrocities reconstruct their communicative worlds and interrupt the cycle of violence in ways that may be difficult for Euro-American professionals to imagine [...] I base my critical analysis on the extensive presentation of empirical material I gathered in southern Sri Lanka, and I show how the dis-course on trauma poses a threat to the culture-specific strategies of containment of violence that Udahenagama women use on a daily basis. (2003, p. xii)

As mentioned above, theatre practitioners perhaps need to withdraw from the comfort of the trauma studies 'umbrella' and discover how 'survivors of wartime atrocities reconstruct their communicative world and interrupt the cycle of violence' themselves. From this culturally spe-cific location, we then might build performance and artistic approaches with artists from the communities that extend, develop and maximise the potential for violence to be interrupted and, to repeat the words of Lawrence, create 'dispositions for an altered world'. And the 'bricolage' of art forms that are most appropriate will emerge in this negotiation.

They may be silent dance, expressive song, wild lament, shared cookery, craft-making, and, of course, they may be storytelling.

Conclusion

This chapter has sought to emphasise that the paradoxical relationship between telling and not telling is manifested in culturally specific ways and the place of artists in situations of crisis depends on the narrative, healing and performance cultures in which those crises happen. This was recognised after the tsunami in Sri Lanka when activists and local mental health workers tried to protect their communities from external therapists who descended urging people to talk about their experience, with little acknowledgement of what speaking of the past and the dead might mean in these communities. It was not recognised by the dramatherapist whose reified belief in the 'importance of the story' took no account for how storytelling was understood or might already be practised.

The dominance of the trauma relief discourse has meant that a discipline emerging in Europe and the US, from testimony models post-Holocaust and the narrative memory concepts of PTSD, has come to frame much performance analysis and applied theatre practice. This is countered here with an insistence that there is a case for an ethnographic approach to community-based or participatory performance. This would start from the community in crisis and develop artistic interventions that expand upon existing means of managing violence and disruption. Ranck discusses this emphasis in relation to programmes developed after the genocide in Rwanda. He argues that to 'counter to the dominance of the PTSD framework, many anthropologists have emphasized the role of "traditional" healers in mediating trauma through ritual, which may restore communal bonds through the exorcism of violent or malingering spirits from the body' (Ranck, 2000, p. 199). Although he still uses the term trauma, he does permit a radically different interpretation of the 'symptoms' of stress – 'malingering spirits' – to frame the nature of the intervention. My emphasis is that applied theatre, and different forms of activist performance, should not attempt to glorify all local practices and assume that they automatically have positive effects. Instead, we should engage with locally structured knowledge and negotiate with existing practices in order to extend those that the particular community understand to be positive. In the case of Sri Lanka, it is Sri Lankan mental health professionals, artists and the communities directly affected by the war and the tsunami that should be central to the design and implementation of any arts-based programmes that seek to address the worse effects of these events.

Perhaps the *difficult return* is a search for a relation with the memory of crisis that does not insist that telling a story will mean that pain will be healed and the problems put to rest – that the nation, community or individual can live on without something called 'closure'. Applied theatre is not a set of practices in itself in this configuration but should be searching for examples of practice that are alternatives to the rhetoric of the trauma relief programmes – programmes that forget that telling is not always the best solution to people's suffering. Applied theatre's repertoire might include projects that respect silence and speaking out as different actions made necessary by different circumstances. This is a mission that – returning to those opening stones – rejects the arrogance of the therapists who assume they have the best approach to 'helping people' or the theatre practitioner who cannot cope with the fact that the children will not speak about their tsunami experiences.

The approach I am advocating seeks to move beyond the binary of speech or silence – to respect instead practices that could simultaneously contain silences, speech, movements and stillness: that could express a desire to forget through dance as much as grieve through song. This situates the *struggle* to deal with the appalling as an important occurrence rather than a moment to be elided. It is a desire to start from *affect* – and then move toward its different cultural manifestations. It is not necessarily what Lawrence calls the 'middle path between speaking out and suppression of feelings' (2003, p. 69) or Patraka's struggle between 'the unmanageable and the manageable' (1999, p. 8) but rather a concentration on an affectual realm and what practices this generates in different communities. It is something embodied before it is articulated as being situated between two cognitively understandable points. Perhaps it is the actual 'poise' mentioned in the following account of the work of the artist and forensic anthropologist, Claudia Bernardi:

> Her art, then, serves as a means to negotiate speech and silence, and to address the truths of what she has seen in a way that goes beyond the merely factual. Poised between fragility and resilience, beauty and horror, the known and unknown, the submerged and the revealed, the human and inhuman, her art captures the illusive qualities of memory. (Franklin and Lyons, 2004, p. vii)

The 'poise' is taken up in discussion of tactics of memorialisation and a prison theatre workshop in Rwanda in the chapter that follows, and the delicate relationship between 'beauty and horror' becomes a theme for Chapter 5. Here, it is perhaps the marker of a respect for a community as it determines its passage through difficulty and searches for forms of expression that make that movement more possible.

I want to close here with an account from a student in the US. It comes from a paper written in response to poetry on the Holocaust where the writer seems to hold onto the idea that there is a paradox in people's response to crisis. It is presented as a paradox – and I would argue a moment of *poised affect* – that should not necessarily be resolved by those who are fortunate enough to be outside the immediate reach of appalling acts. And the word 'literature' here could be replaced by theatre or performance:

> Literature has become for me the site of my own stammering. Literature, as that which can sensitively bear witness to the Holocaust, gives me a voice, a right, and a necessity to survive. Yet, I cannot discount the literature which in the dark awakens the screams, which opens the wounds, and which makes me want to fall silent. Caught by two contradictory wishes at once, to speak or not to speak, I can only stammer. (cited in Felman and Laub, 1992, p. 56)

So the contradictory wish – to speak and not to speak – led this person to stammer. Perhaps these stammering, poised responses are the complex reactions to crises that applied theatre practitioners should engage with as we search for performance forms that contribute to the plethora of ways that people overcome, contain, resist, reveal, avoid, relieve and hide from suffering in its varied guises: an engagement that hopefully ensures that children do not have their lives carelessly exposed in rope, flowers and stone and are not moved to flee from frightening drama workshops.

3
Academic Scriptwriters and Bodily Affects

> Each time forgiveness is at the service of finality, be it noble and spiritual (atonement or redemption, reconciliation, salvation), each time that it aims to re-establish a normality (social, national, political, psychological) by a work of mourning, by some therapy or ecology of memory, then the 'forgiveness' is not pure – nor is its concept. Forgiveness is not, it *should not be*, normal, normative, normalising. It *should* remain exceptional and extraordinary, in the face of the impossible: as if it interrupted the ordinary course of historical temporality.
>
> (Derrida, 2001, pp. 31–2)

Chapter 3 locates the enquiry into the *end of effect* to the central African Republic of Rwanda. This beautiful country of 'a thousand hills' is, of course, known for the terrible genocide in 1994 and the struggles with its consequences in the years since. These events offer a challenge to practices of performance brought to the service of peace building and reconciliation and also provide a turning point in the debate here about the future of applied theatre. The specifics of Rwanda – embedded as they are with complex notions of violence, memory and forgiveness – force a detailed examination of how performance engages with national projects of memorialisation and mediations on a country's violent history. Participatory theatre is often endowed with the capacity for bringing about intercommunity dialogue or community understanding (see for example, Salverson, 1999; Schininà, 2004; or Wehle, 2005). The problems with this endowment are shown to be particularly acute within post-genocide Rwanda, where a major government agency (the National Unity and Reconciliation Commission) 'employed art and theatre as important tools to foster unity and reconciliation among

Rwandans' (NURC, 2007), and there is, therefore, a validation of the use of the arts within community-based projects at the highest level. In addition, the country as a whole has engaged in a process of recreating or 're-imagining' itself (Pottier, 2002) in the years since the events of 1994. Theatre projects targeted at reconciliation are, therefore, being fostered in an environment dominated by powerful forms of national performance.

The chapter will offer a brief outline of the history of Rwanda, including how that history has been used within community-based arts projects and a reflection on a prison theatre workshop conducted in 2005. Following a similar pattern to the previous chapter, the writing here examines the way that performance practice operates within wider discourses and how in the case of Rwanda the themes of memory, history and reconciliation manifest themselves in even the smallest workshop. The degree to which performance can create space outside dominant conceptions of the present and the past – and, in the context of genocide, whether it wants to – is a backdrop sketched to question the potential of a critical arts practice in Rwanda. The chapter turns from performance projects to an analysis of two memorial sites to develop a discussion about the relationship between 'official' and 'unofficial' memorial processes (perhaps respectively *normative* and *exceptional* in Derrida's terms). This is done in order to question the role of the international practitioner/researcher in this context and to think again about the assumptions of applied theatre as a communicative art form. If communicating the truths of the past in projects of national reconciliation is a problematic mission for community-based performance in Rwanda, where might cultural spaces that permit a more complex understanding of a Great Lakes[1] history be found? In seeking to answer this question, the debates and dilemmas inspired by three different moments will be investigated. These are the display of decaying bodies in one memorial site, an examination of the vision of prisoners dressed in pink across Rwanda and finally a return to a particular aspect of the prison theatre workshop.

Chapter 3 anticipates discussions in Part II of the book, by drawing conclusions related to the *affect* of those bodies, and the possible, radical potential of a rejection of an interpretative register for the prison workshop. Echoing the notion of strategies from de Certeau discussed in Chapter 1, here the argument hopes to find ways to disentangle performance practices from the strategies of the powerful (whether that be in memorialisation, trauma or human rights discourses) to petition for a theatre space that maintains the difficultness of the past in the present (the *difficult return* touched upon in the previous chapter). *Difficultness*, as will be explained below, implies incompleteness: an avoidance of neat resolutions or linear accounts of history that end in a happy present that has resolved the dangers of the past.

Rwanda performed

> So Rwandan history is dangerous. Like all of history, it is a record of successive struggles for power, and to a very large extent power consists in the ability to make others inhabit your story of their reality.
>
> (Gourevitch, 1998, p. 48)

> Sometimes it seemed that instead of fine arts, Rwandans had politics: the arts of statecraft, writ large and small, at the highest echelons of government and in the most basic negotiations of daily life.
>
> (Ibid., p. 258)

Rwanda is a landlocked nation of just over eight million people in the centre of Africa that became independent from Belgium in 1962. While Rwandans speak one language, Kinyarwanda, the country is divided between three 'ethnic' groups – the majority Hutu, minority Tutsi and tiny minority, Twa. Between April and July 1994, a mass killing of Tutsis and moderate Hutus was carried out by military, militia and community members leading to the deaths of over 800,000 people. Although there was ongoing civil conflict at the time, there is substantial evidence that the process had been both rehearsed and planned. While it is now indisputably designated a 'genocide' by the international community, Rwandan foreign policy continues to be shaped by inaction of the UN and controversial action by the French at the time.

The horror of the genocide is vividly accounted for in a number of publications and its speed, brutality and participatory nature are beyond doubt (see Gourevitch, 1998; Hatzfeld, 2000; Keane, 1996). However, the origins and causes of the events are, of course, more controversial. While reporting in Europe in the early days of the genocide trivialised it as further evidence of the 'inter-ethnic' hostility that bedevils the African continent, the history of relations between the Hutu and the Tutsi communities is, obviously, both complex and contested. For the purpose of this chapter, it is the contestation that is important because what is illustrated within historical accounts is that the very notions of Tutsi and Hutu are tied to and reliant upon disputed patterns of myth making and identity construction. History writing has been part of a competition of narratives that continues to this day. The ability of neighbour to take machete to neighbour, in what was referred to as the 'work' of killing, required an intense sense of difference, culpability and fear. This became, over many years, an embodied belief (on the part of some but not all Rwandans) in the 'historical' and 'natural' enmity between the two groups. While this did not appear overnight, and there are many examples of smaller-scale massacres of Tutsis in the years and decades prior to the genocide, April to July 1994 was particular and extraordinary in its extent, relative thoroughness and viciousness. While a high degree of blame can be and has been laid at the door of extremist Hutu politicians (part of a movement called Hutu Power) and their militia henchmen in the *Interahamwe*, the spread of the genocide required mass participation on the part of ordinary, predominantly rural, Hutu communities. The relationships, therefore, between narratives of history, their inculcation into the wider population, and that mass participation in a genocide show important interconnections in the discussion that follows.

The book *Les Médias du Génocide* (Chrétien, 1995) offers a thorough account of the role of print and broadcast media, including the involvement of dance and music, in inspiring a hatred of the Tutsi *inyenzi* (cockroaches) and a commitment to the work of killing them.[2] This book also provides a salutary reminder of dangers of assuming the benign or essentially positive role of the arts. The very fact that musician and song writer Simon Bikindi was a defendant at the International Criminal Tribunal for Rwanda, accused of crimes against humanity, is evidence enough that in a chapter about the 'arts' and 'genocide' the former cannot assume to be set up in automatic, non-complicit opposition to the latter.[3] However, for the purpose of this chapter, it is how *les médias* have used historical narratives, in particular since the genocide, that is the focus. In the years leading up to 1994, a particular version of the history of Tutsi/Hutu relations was articulated to justify violence. As genocide is viewed as an ultimate denouement of this particular narrative, the post-genocide country needed to rewrite history to construct a radically alternative (but not necessarily new) vision of the nation. Whether in this process history becomes any less 'dangerous', to use Gourevitch's term, is a concern to be discussed here. While the situation in July 1994 was staggering and exceptional (with few doctors, judges, teachers or other professionals left alive in the country), the process of nation building undertaken by the new government, coupled with a deliberate involvement of the arts, provides an important example of the instrumentalist use of history and memory. And, as this was part of a desire to make post-genocide Rwandan citizens 'inhabit a new story of their reality', it took a particularly performance-like turn: there are now *les médias du post-génocide* which are in need of analysis.

The historical and anthropological work of Gérard Prunier and Johan Pottier attest to the mythic qualities of the past and its detrimental effect on the present in their writing about Rwanda. Prunier sets the tone of this analysis in the following:

> Rwanda, as very small, compact and historically well-defined nation, was built in the late nineteenth and early twentieth century into a complex, unique and quasi-mythological land. With time this cultural mythology *became* reality, i.e. the social and political actors moved by degrees from their real world into the mythological script which had been written for them (in a way, with their complicity). (1995, p. xiii)

It was not that there was a simple division between the facts and fictions of history but that a complex habit of myth making was now inseparable from the making of the present and had therefore become 'real'. The question that follows this quotation is 'can man unwrite what others have written?' (Ibid., p. xiii). This succinctly expresses the challenge to the post-genocide regime and is the demand that constructs much policy in the country in this period. If, as Prunier notes, 'Tutsi and Hutu have killed each other more to upbraid a certain vision they have of themselves, of the others and of their place in the world than because of material interests' (Ibid., p. 40), how can that vision be transformed in such a way to ensure that the killing does not return?

Where Prunier has analysed the myths that were integral to pre-genocide history, Pottier develops an argument in relation to the 'new' histories constructed by the current regime. Where in the past history became marshalled to support killing with a conclusion in an almost completed genocide, the 'new' history sought to construct a nation in which the possibility of that logic was removed. This was not, however, a corrective approach – replacing obvious myth with simple fact:

> Post-genocide leaders regard Rwanda's pre-colonial past as something of a golden era, a state of social harmony later corrupted by Europeans. Vital to the justification of minority rule, their message is delivered in a well-rehearsed manner and style, marked sometimes

by omission [...] and sometimes by disregard of context. Complexity and context are continuously screened out of contemporary representations of 'the Old Rwanda'. (Pottier, 2002, p. 9)

The Rwandese Patriotic Front (RPF), which took control of the country from July 1994, was dominated by Tutsi exiles from Uganda (who had fled there after previous massacres). While it would appear justifiable that a vision of history was needed that did not pit Hutu against Tutsi, they started their narrative from a pre-colonial era (of Tutsi aristocratic rule) that they argued was then corrupted by external factors (German and then Belgian colonisation). While colonial rule has been appropriately criticised for exacerbating divisions, it is less clear that pre-colonial kings were as benign as this view insists. An evocation of this era does, however, conveniently legitimise the current regime:

Constructed sometimes with the help of sympathetic outsiders, the interlocking narratives share the common message that rule by the pre- and early colonial court was benevolent until destroyed by the European colonial powers. The world today, it follows, has every reason to be confident that the return to power of the Rwandan Tutsi diaspora will herald a new era of righteousness and social justice [...] that the country's numerically dominant ethnic Hutu, whose ethnicity was invented by outsiders, have nothing to fear unless guilty of genocide. (Ibid., p. 47)

What is significant for this chapter is how the common message was communicated, how that confidence was fostered and, of course, how theatre and the arts became part of that mission. The case here is that, while the desire to eradicate 'genocide ideology' was understandable, a 'seductively simple' (Ibid., p. 4) narrative was used to prevent investigation of many of the atrocities of the RPF (during the civil war and the subsequent war in the Democratic Republic of the Congo). This provided a founding mythology that could be too easily repudiated not only by democratic opposition to the regime but also, more importantly, by those political groups linked to the *génocidaires* who still hope to return to power.

Pottier outlines how the 'rewriting' project was developed 'towards a systematic re-imagining of Rwanda' and how it incorporated both national and international 'actors in the drama' (Ibid., p. 7):

Rewriting history [...] must be done on many levels and in different contexts: rewriting history is left not just to historians and other academics [...] but requires the further participation of journalists [...] humanitarians [...] and policy makers concerned with rural development and reconstruction. (Ibid., p. 47)

And, of course, it also required artists and playwrights. The post-genocide government instigated a rewriting project that 'benefited from the empathy and services not only of journalists unfamiliar with the region, but also of newcomer academics, diplomats and aid workers' (Ibid., p. 7) and each in their own way helped to 'popularise and spread an RPF-friendly but empirically questionable narrative' (Ibid., p. 53). While part of this process was explicitly about an actual rewriting of the country's history books, the project was broader in that it sought an adoption and propagation of the new history in all possible environments. Any academic (or theatre practitioner) either working in or visiting Rwanda is subject to these pressures and therefore must start any analysis by asking whether they are part of the programme of hiring 'scriptwriters for the task of re-imagining Rwanda' (Ibid., p. 128). This chapter is, therefore, a response to this challenge – from this particular *academic scriptwriter*.

Re-imagining projects

When the *Ballet National de Rwanda* with *Mutubaruka* appeared in front of a conference of African agriculture ministers in November 2005, they explicitly announced their role as supporting the process of national 'rebirth, resurrection, rehabilitation, reconstruction': one that hoped that 'the genocidal ideology may be banned from African soil'.[4] Of course, it should not be surprising that, in front of government officers, performance troupes stage visions of the nation that chime well with an official policy. It could be argued that in this example, in Kigali's Intercontinental Hotel, dances seemed to evoke both a rural idyllic past and a peaceful present in a way that could easily be read as a suggestion of a unified history, interrupted by colonialism and now urged as a model for the future (of course, an over-'easy' and deeply problematic vision). While this interpretation cannot be taken for granted, subsequent visits to cultural and performance groups indicated a surprising homogeneity of intent across vastly different styles of organisation.[5] The dance and theatre group from the village of Bicumbi called *Ongera Urere* (See It Again), for example, who performed to audiences across their area with little formal training or support, explained that the 'government needs some people to tell the truth of what was happening'.

Similarly, the dynamic young people of the *Association de Jeunes pour la promotion de development et de lutte contre la ségrégation/discrimination* (AJDS) created a reconciliation play that hoped to 'change the mind of the people' by showing them the 'history that people were one before the missionary period'. The idea of 'building one country' expressed by this small community-based arts organisation exactly replicated the 'new' history of the country that pre-colonial times were unified and the divisions between Hutu and Tutsi were fabricated by the colonialists. This is not to doubt the enthusiasm or sincerity of either of these organisations, but to indicate how a particular version of Rwandan history had reached the smallest groups and was now propagated by them. As explained by the director of a village-based cultural organisation from Gahini called *Abiyunze*, there were no Hutu or Tutsi dances because 'we are one'. The group had both absorbed a narrative, and now performed it – in this case to a *scriptwriter* who was ready with notebook in hand.

The first slips – from *Abiyunze* to prison

Part of the mission of these groups was for them to take an active part in the national project of reconciliation. They all repeated consistent versions of the reasons for the genocide and how the country should now move forward. This included a frequent iteration of a statement that Rwanda was one nation and extended to a prohibition on the terms Hutu and Tutsi. This narrative was evident in the discussions of the performance groups discussed above, in the rules for expressing guilt in the community-based *gacaca*[6] courts and the curriculum of the *Ingando* solidarity camps[7] for students and ex-prisoners. It was apparent in my government papers permitting me to conduct research in the country as long as I was not 'uttering words likely to instigate divisionism' and in the frequent reminders by translators that Rwanda was divided by colonial interference but now must forgive, reconcile and build a new united country. This appeared as a willed, performed process – as an informant of Gourevitch explained, 'even here in this tiny country with one language, we aren't one people, but we must pretend until we become one' (1998, p. 349). Performance projects in participating in education, reconciliation and peace-building initiatives operated within these terms. AJDS, for example, had created a Romeo and Juliet-style narrative play on reconciling communities, which, while containing a seemingly positive anti-racist message, was in fact evidence of the startling reach of the rewriting project.

While the version of history that the government prefers was repeated by a diverse range of groups and individuals, this process is, of course, not completely monolithic. The relation between the apparent homogeneity of the rhetoric and points of inconsistency provides an important area for investigation and a further illustration of why this context raises questions for applied theatre and its ability to create space outside the reach of problematic discourses. One example of this comes in the negotiations between the nationally acclaimed *Mashirika* Creative and Performing Arts Group and a government department. In an interview with the Director, Hope Azeda, she outlined the difficulty of writing an educational piece of theatre on the *gacaca* courts because it conflicted with a particular view of forgiveness held by her commissioner. Later, in developing a piece on reconciliation, she had a woman character saying to a perpetrator:

> I'm not forgiving you, forgiving you and not forgiving you does nothing for me. It doesn't bring back my husband and my children that you killed. (Azeda, 2005)

However, this line was rejected and because of this 'the whole project [was] delayed because someone, somewhere [had] not signed the go ahead papers' (Ibid.). Azeda's reputation and position within Rwanda made this negotiation possible, but it is clear that a particular narrative was preferred. There was a version of forgiveness or a reconciliation culture that, echoing Derrida's words, aimed to 're-establish a normality' that Azeda could not bring herself to write. While this does demonstrate space for negotiation that is important to recognise, a question to ask is: if one of the most highly respected performance groups in the country struggled to create alternative narratives within the 're-imagining' project, is there any potential for the arts to open up history as a problem to be explored rather than a story to be accepted? Can the woman character who refuses to forgive, who seems to insist that forgiveness 'is not, it *should not be*, normal, normative, normalising' (Derrida, 2001, p. 32), be given the stage?

While the degree of uniformity in the performances (both spoken by individuals and enacted on stage) within visits to Rwanda was notable, the negotiation discussed by Azeda above does illustrate chinks in the 're-imagining project'. Another very small example appeared when the director of *Abiyunze* explained, during a dance presentation mentioned above, that there were no differences between Hutu and Tutsi moves (because these categories were fabrications). As the director spoke, a translator was busily indicating a 'Twa dance' and a 'Tutsi dance'. 'One nation' was proclaimed and challenged in the same moment – and in reference to the same piece of performance. This sense of different cultural practices was further emphasised in a performance in Kigali prison in 2005, where it was pointed out that certain dances were associated with the Hutu, as well as particular geographic areas of the country. Divisions in Rwanda are clearly complex and likely to be clan-based, familial, geographic and economic as much as along the strict lines of Tutsi and Hutu – but there are differences, and this was replicated in different cultural forms. The official line might therefore elide and prevent a discussion of difference – and theatre in creating plays about reconciliation could be part of the programme of elision. However, these chinks did indicate the fragility of the overall story and also a sense of possible spaces for alternative visions of Rwanda that seemed to exist within cultural performances but were not permitted in the broader social and cultural context.

The relationship between the broader context and the actual event of theatre or performance practice can be further illustrated through the example of a theatre workshop in Kigali prison in November 2005.[8] Rwandan prisons have housed tens of thousands of people accused of participating in the genocide since 1994 and, even after many *gacaca* court cases and release programmes, that number was still around 60,000 in 2007 (Amnesty International, 2007). Out of the 20 prisoners involved in this workshop only two or three were not accused of crimes of genocide. During the course of the workshops, this group of prisoners tended to create stories from 1994 that presented themselves as innocent bystanders, noble saviours of Tutsis or accidental accomplices. They also created mythic stories of Tutsi royal barbarity,[9] mirroring the media narratives outlined in the book by Chrétien (1995) from the period leading up to the genocide. In addition, in general discussions they complained about the injustice of the *gacaca* courts and at least one participant wanted to emphasise that the extent of the genocide had been overstated. Of course, being accused of crimes of genocide is going to lead to prisoners minimising, denying or shifting responsibility. Hatzfeld's book of interviews with perpetrators, *A Time for Machetes* (2003), illustrates a devastating mix of frank admission of guilt and simultaneous denial of the seriousness or degree of involvement that afflicts many prisoners. The point here is to question how this 'private' workshop, to use a term from Chapter 1, related to the wider environment. In a country that was using all manner of 'scriptwriters' in a particularly effective performance of a new nation, where 'easy-to-grasp narratives' (Pottier, 2002, p. 4) were heard in many different formats, any form of cultural activity could easily be drawn into either competing with, drawing comparison to or simply repeating the available 'scripts'. The work of AJDS, *Abiyunze, Ongera Urere* and *Mutubaruka* illustrate cases of relatively faithful repetition. In a prison theatre workshop in a Rwanda where myths have always 'been synthesised into a new reality' (Prunier, 1995, p. 39), creating scenes and sharing stories was always going to be part of that troubled process. In this context, a theatre practice that drew on 'real' stories forgot that they were inseparable from a 'mythological script' (Ibid., p. xiii), and, working on mythic stories, forgot that what people had already been told 'was quite fantastic' (Ibid., p. 142). A project operating in a situation where the recent past had shown that 'myths can kill' (Ibid., p. 40) struggled when working within a paradigm that sought to communicate through myth, narrative, history or story. Similarly, explaining or offering interpretations of the project (in particular to prison officials) could only adopt the models of reconciliation or peace building that were heavily circumscribed by the broader context. A form of performance practice that was initiated with a concern to exchange stories meant that those articulated were shaped by a competition between different narratives – and in this prison in Kigali this tended to be either the narratives outlined by Chrétien in *Les Médias du Génocide* (that is, genocidal) or the problematic vision of unity expressed by the current regime. A mission to validate or provide a space for 'counter-narratives' in this context was, therefore, undermined by the limitations (and dangers) of those that were available.

The end of the prison theatre workshop marks a crucial point in the analysis here and in terms of the structure of this book. The dominant story of Rwanda's history and how it appeared to be repeated in high-level performance to government ministers and in community-based cultural associations indicated how theatre and performance seemed to be involved in maintaining history's *dangerousness*. This was further evidence of how performance is imbricated with powerful and problematic discourses, echoing the questions raised around the child soldier massacre in Chapter 1 and the uses of trauma theory in Chapter 2. The 'end of effect' seemed to be reached again if projects in this context could not escape the propagation of a dubious historical narrative that helped maintain what a 2007 Human Rights Watch report called a particularly 'tightly controlled [...] political space' (HRW, 2007b). While there were 'chinks' seen in cursory comments, in Azeda's negotiations and in the worrying denials by the prison inmates, there was not an alternative story to be neatly articulated through some form of cultural action. In line with the previous chapters, what emerges is a deep suspicion of the available narratives and the processes that sought to engage in forms of truth claiming. The slips in the dominant post-genocide narrative were not automatically of chinks of light, but often counter-narratives that could be aligned, particularly in the case of the prisoners, with appalling action.

A change of key – memorials

> What is to remain of the past? That which is the least disturbing? Or the most?
>
> (Roth and Salas, 2001, p. 1)

> Dead bodies have a posthumous political life in the service of creating a newly meaningful universe.
>
> (Verdery, 1999, p. 127)

In conducting research in Rwanda my focus was on theatre and performance – what the National Unity and Reconciliation Commission called the 'Theatre and Art of Reconciliation' (NURC, 2007) – and this enquiry was originally interested in memorial practices only to the degree that performances restaged them. However, in Rwanda the presence of genocide memorials is hard to ignore and eventually these material exhibits came to dominate my analysis and reflect back on questions raised about performance. Of course 'genocide museums' do not exist outside the discursive boundaries that have been discussed here. As Hughes has illustrated in her analysis of the *Tuol Sleng* museum in Cambodia, it is 'necessary to examine the local and international discourses that have conspired to produce the symbolic spaces and memorial declarations of post-genocide nationalism' (Hughes, 2006, p. 175). The two memorials that are the focus of the following discussion are not presented, therefore, as means to escape the production of the new Rwandan nation, but are used to explore and problematise that production some more. In particular the 'posthumous political life' of the dead bodies in the first example starts the tentative promotion of a performance of affect.

Before describing the first memorial, it must be emphasised why my research would not usually focus on displays of 'disturbing remains' (Roth and Salas, 2001); why – to put it bluntly – I did not want to see dead bodies in Rwanda. First, performance research, and applied theatre practice, is traditionally interested in moving, live bodies and how performance theorists, to paraphrase Peggy Phelan, aim to 'enact the affective force of those performances' in our writing (Phelan, 1997, p. 12). If 'our trade' is premised on the 'disappearance of the manifest visual object' (Ibid., pp. 1–2), we should be averse to a memorial practice that preserves dead bodies. Analysing performance is about re-imagining bodies no longer with us. What is interesting, according to Phelan, is the echo of the body in action and not projects that hope to refigure the figure. The bodies that we study usually start out alive and the demand to cling to the 'remains of the past' and to re-conjure the physical from the space left behind is seen to be to be a somewhat hopeless project. While my discussion of the ephemeral in Chapter 5 aims to throw some doubt onto this position, in the first instance, we are not the forensic anthropologist whose job is to make the 'bones talk' (Koff, 2005, p. 181).

The second reason for this aversion is prompted by an article by Wainaina that mocks and ultimately condemns a particular approach to 'writing Africa' in the west. This is a critique that perhaps undermines any decision to research Rwanda in the first place and needs to be acknowledged when considering the words used in the analysis that follows. He suggests, lampooning the post-colonial project to *write about Africa,* that we should:

> Describe in detail [...] dead bodies. Or, better, naked dead bodies. And especially rotting naked dead bodies. Remember, any work you submit in which people look filthy and miserable will be referred to as the 'real Africa', and you want that on your dust jacket [...] Always end your book with Nelson Mandela saying something about rainbows or renaissances. Because you care. (Wainaina, 2006, pp. 94–5)

While the decision not to put dead Rwandans on the 'dust jacket' for this book, and my avoidance of a quotation from Mandela, were fairly easy omissions, the questions about 'representing' the African dead remain. The bodies at the first memorial in Murambi, were practically 'rotting naked dead bodies' but the claims that are made for them are far from clear, as I hope the next section will illustrate.[10]

Suspended memory[11] – Murambi

The Murambi Memorial Centre is situated more than 100 kilometres south of the capital Kigali near the town of Gikongoro. The main exhibits of the centre are organised in the small classrooms of a disused school. The large building in front of these low-rise blocks, managed by the British genocide education charity, the Aegis Trust, stood empty in November 2005.[12] The classrooms display rack upon rack of lime-preserved, still fleshed bodies of the victims of the massacre that took place on the site of the school in 1994. A first reference might compare Patraka's discussion of a Holocaust museum's display of shoes which 'involved our bodies in the making of memory' (Patraka, 1999, p. 128) or Haedicke's discussion of Patraka's work where she notes how 'organic remains' compel 'the visitor's body to respond to what is seen (and smelled)' (Haedicke, 2002, p. 108). Or again, in reference to footwear, it reminds the viewer of Kristeva's writing on children's shoes at Auschwitz.[13] The smell in Murambi was not from shoes standing in for the dead, however – but the dead. There was a compulsion here, but it was not framed in seeking to imagine the missing bodies, but in a close examination of them. Gourevitch's writing on a different site in Rwanda, which also included unburied dead, is reproduced in Roth and Salas's edition, appropriately called *Disturbing Remains*:

> I couldn't settle on any meaningful response: revulsion, alarm, sorrow, grief, shame, incomprehension, sure, but nothing truly meaningful. I just looked, and I took photographs, because I wondered whether I could really see what I was seeing while I saw it, and I wanted also an excuse to look a bit more closely. (Gourevitch, 2001, p. 66)

The combination of a desire to look closely coupled with an unsettling inability to fix on a meaningful response is central to the comments offered here. What follows is a series of fragmented reactions in the form of notes that will then be examined more closely. It is important to demonstrate a shattering affect of these bodies, the 'affective force of the performative event' spoken about by Phelan (1997, p. 11), rather than engage in a process that seeks *in the first instance* to 'preserve and represent' (Ibid., p. 3). This attention to affect is not primarily linked to a trope of the failure of representation, but an argument that when 'unworded is sentenced to meaning' (Ibid., p. 17) a political relationship is fashioned that makes one part of a competition of interpretations: a competition that in this context, as already argued, has had murderous consequences.

Lime-bodies

An autopsy, investigation, dig, withered fractured image of murder. Machete cuts in shoulders, broken skulls, hair, babies, children with skull slices.

Warn-cloth-covered, stretched muscle – orange, pink, lime smelt. 'Classroom' does not fit with chalk-lime bodies on racks. The guide opens 'the children's room'. Line upon line – sleeping, tiny. Archaeology waiting for archaeologists – the bodies were waiting for something. You could almost touch. The stench held in my nose, clothes – held in the air. They had been buried but now were re-dug and on display: in school. A show that had no words on walls, no pinned-explanatory phrases. Just Emmanuel,[14] one of the four survivors – the guide. The response was just above my sternum – nauseous and furious. My nose was numbed by the residue, the smell, for the rest of the day. The bodies remained in the plume of lime stench that got up the face. April 1994 – 40,000, 50,000 or 60,000 people died on this site.[15] Into another room, the clothes of the dead hang chaotically on lines: a hall-like, assembly space. Caked garments again waiting – to be washed, perhaps reclaimed if this was a tribunal site: discarded, decaying. A Sri Lankan friend said, surveying his village a month after the tsunami, 'it's good because the bodies have gone'. One famous T-Shirt in Rwanda said 'bury the bodies, remember the dead'. My colleague in the UK on hearing about this place said, 'what are they going to do with them?' The guide Emmanuel was watching over his family. He was shot, clothes stripped and he crawled from under bodies to escape into the close-by hill – where he watched the French army arrive and clean up. And create a volleyball pitch over the bodies of the dead. This memorial site can't be permanent, can it? They must be about to do something with them? Do class room after class room of shattered, still fleshed bodies offer the best form of memorial – one half done, about to be investigated but not yet investigated? One that seems to be a research moment without the ongoing process of enquiry. Bodies that are suspended between being disinterred and re-interred.

The Aegis Trust is responsible for this site and explains its work as follows:

> Aegis observed that if Rwanda is to make a sustainable recovery, *memory* and *education* are critical factors. *Memory*, because survivors need time and space. They need to be heard within their own society and further afield. So too, Rwandan society needs to reckon with its collective conscience, to be clear about what it is remembering and why. *Education*, because new and emerging generations, on all sides of the genocidal divide, need to feel comfortable confronting the country's past and absorbing its demanding lessons. (Aegis Trust, 2006a)

Did the bodies make anyone feel comfortable and did the signless room lead us to absorb certain lessons? Did Murambi make it clear what was remembered and why? The emphasis on communicating the memory of the genocide – and perhaps I am suggesting the whole paradigm of cultural events as premised on a communicative impulse – seemed disturbed here. The first impression of Murambi was that something was certainly absorbed but not *learnt*. Murambi was breathed then exhaled – it was not read. The only clarity was the guide, who said he kept coming back because his family were there and that the bodies should stay to remind people. Remembering the dead, for this man, meant they should not be buried. A clue to Aegis's perspective on the bodies comes in the memorial in Kigali, but before moving there, how to talk about Murambi and the notes written above? Two pieces of writing offer a way in: one a return to Phelan and her work on Derrida and the other from a more traditional source – a small quotation from Theodor Adorno.

An 'aspiration to witness': Derrida and Celan

These bodies, to this western viewer, seemed to suspend traditional investigatory modes of memory and reconciliation. They were presented as a provisional, half-finished exhibition: a mid-dig display. They appeared to be a frozen epistemological project, stuck in a limelight, ready for a case to be made, but with no evidence that a case was being made. Bodies had been placed on their slatted beds as though ready for some commandeering – evidence for a tribunal, autopsy or forensic enquiry – but with no evidence that the commandeering or interpreting had taken place. Clearly they existed within the wider context of memorialisation in post-genocide Rwanda, and cannot be considered outside the projects of 're-imagination' already discussed, but here the bodies did not appear to be coerced into a narrative or easily co-opted into a memory programme.

The problem this presents is that, in existing in apparent suspension, the Murambi bodies appeared to resist attempts to discuss them. By opening them to enquiry, they would be tipped over a fulcrum on which they seemed to be balanced. If a simple story is constructed *from* them – if they are dug, probed, dissected – there would be a denial of an experience that held me in nauseous awe. Replacing exhalation with explanation could involve damaging the memorial, or forgetting its affect. The point of this memorial site seemed to be that the project of enquiry was not happening. To start one, therefore, would shift the balance: that which was suspended would be activated and we would fail to witness what was in fact a pause. Acknowledging that pause is where this chapter connects to the respect for the intimacy of the hidden applied theatre projects in Chapter 1, and the 'stammering, poised' responses with which Chapter 2 urged applied theatre practitioners to engage. Murambi was poised and, using the terms of Chapter 2, could not be located simplistically in a movement between telling and not telling.

A useful place to examine the dilemma of this moment comes from Phelan in her account of a lecture by Derrida on the poetry of Paul Celan. In this talk Phelan felt that Derrida enacted a failure. In his usually playful articulacy Derrida would manage to tap 'on the silent black-on-white words until the colors [bled] across the page and the words [revealed] the blood beneath their skin' (Phelan, 1997, p. 9). However, that day 'the poem spurns him' (Ibid., p. 10) and 'he cannot find the blood in Celan's ash' (Ibid., p. 9). Although Derrida tried to find the blood in what is presented as a struggle with interpretation, here in relation to Murambi this is replaced with a disavowal of searching for meaning. In seeking a politics of affect, as will be discussed in the chapters that follow, interpretation's failure can be transformed into a resistance to simple narration. The memorial was untapped and I did not want to start that tapping. The fact that the work of revealing the blood in those bodies did happen by other means in the visit to Murambi will be outlined later. For now, the poem that spurned Derrida mirrors those bodies that as artefacts could not simply stand in for a particular story of suffering. Derrida's response to his difficulty is to find a 'different entry point' to the poem – and it is this alternative that helps with an analysis of Murambi. He no longer taps the poem but instead 'his own aspiration to witness'. He becomes 'humble before Celan's poem' and performs 'an ethics of death and resignation that is not defeat but nonetheless yields to the harsh unanswerability of Celan's ash' (Ibid., p. 10). This helps here because it gives permission to yield before a site that I do not want to make bleed, yet does not stop the activity of the witness. We do not stand mute and still in front of the bodies, but question our ethical relation to this death – and thus a refusal here to narrate is not synonymous with a refusal to use language (or other forms of expression). This is not a Wittgenstein moment[16] or a repeat of Adorno's famous proscription of poetry after the Holocaust (see Blau, 2003, p. 7; Spivey, 2001, pp. 18–19[17]): it is a call to a different kind of action. In the case of Rwanda and the bodies at Murambi, it stops the act of interpretation because that act is implicated. In Rwanda interpreting those bodies, tapping on them, would struggle to reveal discourses outside those that either support the government's vision of the past or those that problematically minimise the genocide. Doing what appeared undone would slip from that poised moment into the rhetoric of cause and solution. By yielding before the display, something of the power of performance outside a communicative paradigm is hinted at. By making no incision into those bodies, you accept the imprint 'on the visitor's body' (Haedicke, 2002, p. 108) and exhale your response rather than explain your way around it. Phelan continues:

> Cast as witness to what is not there, the reader cannot rest anywhere within the space of the poem's unbearable stillness. The formal relation of address that usually adheres between reader and poem collapses. The formlessness of the poem's ash, the remains that stand *as* remains rather than body, cannot be assimilated into a mute object of the reader's contemplation. (Phelan, 1997, p. 10)

While this gives encouragement to the experience of the collapse that the Murambi site performs, there is of course a difference in that the remains stand as remains *and* as bodies and, therefore, one knows that contemplation will neither make them breathe nor bleed. Words of witnessing, therefore, do not seek to reanimate this suspended moment, but reperform the apparent stillness, and the affective up-in-the-nose catastrophic whirlwind of reminders, narratives, memories and retches that fleshed, limed bones stirred. Suspension in its silence is, then, not a settled or fixed memory project but a cloud ready to be disturbed and breathed by those who experience it. Reactions to breathing memory cannot be authoritative, but can only be performed in multiple, variant exhalations and this is not the contagion of trauma, but an affect of those bodies transformed in the response that my particular body has to them.

Suspended memory at Murambi, therefore, demands a disavowal of projects that seek to interpret or capture meanings that these bodies make – to read the bones. Instead the choice when confronted by suffering is a 'catastrophic language' that 'touches a kind of madness' (Ibid., p. 11). This determination to find an alternative register is not a retreat from politics, but a demand for a fundamentally different relationship between participatory art making and that suffering.

Cleaning up with Adorno

The second place for analytical support is connected to another famous quotation from Adorno. While the fact that his statements on poetry after Auschwitz hold the status of 'critical clichés' (Felman and Laub,

1992, p. 33) or an 'oft-quoted diktat' (Spivey, 2001, p. 18), the following is useful primarily for the final sentence:

> The aesthetic principle of stylization [...] make[s] an unthinkable fate appear to have had some meaning; it is transfigured, something of its horror is removed. This alone does an injustice to the victims [...] [Some] works [...] are even willingly absorbed as contributions to clearing up the past. (Felman and Laub, 1992, p. 34, cited from *Commitment*)

Although he was discussing works of art, for the purpose of this chapter, I am deliberately overlapping this with projects of memorialisation. What is particularly interesting here is his use of the concept of 'clearing up'. Being 'willingly absorbed' in 'clearing up the past' – as a historical-aesthetic project – is enmeshed with the basic practice of cleaning up. A demand to clear up is an affective desire (a flight from the abject perhaps), a philosophical position and an aesthetic urge. While the totalising reach of Adorno's dismissal of art-making or memory projects *per se* can be questioned, this quotation is useful because it is a criticism of *method*. The problem with works that 'clear up' is therefore brought into focus when considering Murambi and other memorial sites in Rwanda because a form of interpretation or research becomes ethically suspect – there is a dubious historiography of 'clearing up the past' that needs questioning.

Clearing up after atrocity is focused on bodies. Young people in Sri Lanka were awarded certificates for their work clearing bodies after the tsunami and, as mentioned earlier, a colleague there reported that 'all was now fine' because 'the bodies had gone'. The sight of a body to a western audience summons a desire to see something done. We want to bury the bodies – not only for culturally constructed reasons such as 'respect' and 'dignity', but because of apparently scientific ones such as 'hygiene' and 'public health'. Although the work of Taylor has expertly illustrated different conceptualisations of the body within Rwandan culture and there are suggestions of funeral practices where bodies are left on hillsides to decompose naturally, there is nothing to indicate that the display of remains was not seen as problematic amongst Rwandans themselves (Taylor, C., 2002).[18] So while 'clearing up the past' falls into Adorno's withering condemnation of projects that do injustice to victims of horror, 'cleaning up' is often a demand located between horror and memorialisation. It determines a relation between the past and the future. This is a liminal, transformative process that is culturally specific yet often intimately connected to bodies. Making clear – clarity – and cleanliness – are connected to their absence. Bodies are dirty, stinking and covered in insects: they spread disease and without bodies we are apparently cleaner and *clearer*. But Adorno warns us about 'clearing up' and his warning is perhaps heeded in Murambi and in the guide Emmanuel's desire not to see the bodies moved. When the bodies are still there, it is as if the clearing up has not happened and we are stalled in a journey towards clarity. The semi-preserved but still decaying body, as a site of the memorial act, perhaps ensures that the past is neither cleaned nor clear. Following Verdery's work on *the political lives of dead bodies*, the important property of the dead 'is their ambiguity, multivocality, or polysemy' (1999, p. 27). If 'remains are concrete, yet protean' (Ibid.), perhaps, following Adorno, this form of memorial, a display of unclarity, does less of an injustice to the victims of the genocide.[19]

So there are two approaches to aid an encounter with Murambi: one that insists we are merely a witness to the bodies' suspended state, admitting we are choked on lime rather than able to open them up as evidence of x, or proof of y, and another that suggests that these bodies have a positive status as *uncleared* residues of a genocide that is patently not yet cleaned up. They are overpowering remnants that, in stalling memory work, appear to have suspended resolution of the original event and thus not removed 'something of its horror': 'appear to' because there is an additional part of the analysis of this memorial that throws aspects of this argument into doubt (and will be returned to below). The argument to come affirms the significance of discovering means of discussing the 'affective force' of this site, but introduces a note of warning about how affect is managed and potentially manipulated. It concerns how visitors to memorials might have an opportunity to 'change from spectator/bystander to witness and to become performers in the event of understanding and remembering' (Patraka, 1999, p. 11) and reintroduces Emmanuel. However, this analysis must come after introducing a second major memorial in Rwanda: one that develops the argument about the management of the memorial process and the problematic execution of the nationwide history-writing project.

Strategic memory – Kigali Memorial Centre

The main national genocide memorial, in the Rwandan capital Kigali, was again built in a partnership between the Aegis Trust and the government and provides a stark contrast to Murambi. Borrowing from Simon, Rosenberg and Eppert's concept of a 'strategic practice' (which is in turn linked to de Certeau's *strategies* from Chapter 1), the approach used at this centre will be called 'strategic memory'. Here it will be argued that the practice of memorialisation is marshalled for a particular purpose as part of a strategic political project.

The Kigali Memorial Centre is on the side of a hill in the Gisozi area of the capital. It was created on the burial site of around a quarter of a million victims of the genocide and stands as a memorial, to quote from the Aegis Trust, that preserves 'the past without excessive intervention [...] to provide public spaces for remembrance and education' (Aegis, 2006b). To quote further from Aegis:

> The Kigali Memorial Centre comprises a main historical exhibition, a Children's Memorial exhibition and an exhibition on comparative genocide, called Wasted Lives. It also has over four acres of memorial gardens containing ten mass graves, as well as the National Genocide Documentation Centre. (Ibid.)

Two parts of the memorial will be discussed here: first the overall shape of the main exhibition and second the Children's Memorial display. The analysis is necessarily comparative because, walking through this site, one becomes acutely aware of the differences between Kigali and Murambi. Reflections on Kigali are, therefore, done through the prism of Murambi. In addition, an important aspect of any commentary is that the international visitor to this venue is a very specific, target audience. The Kigali Memorial Centre is the site that international dignitaries, tourists or NGO staff members are most likely to visit when they arrive in Rwanda.[20] It is, therefore, part of the national response to the genocide that is particularly aware of a desire to impress a certain narrative upon non-Rwandans. It is perhaps here, more than in any other place in Rwanda, that the re-imagining project discussed at the start of the chapter is most explicitly displayed for the international community. Pottier notes that 'rewriting history [...] must be done on many levels and in different contexts' (2002, p. 47) and the Kigali Memorial Centre was one such place. The primary audience was 'newcomer academics, diplomats and aid workers' and this memorial was, therefore, constructed with people like myself very clearly in mind.

After moving through the foyer of the Centre, you descend into a circular room around the edges of which a particular presentation of the pre-colonial, colonial, post-independence, post-1959 revolution, pre-genocide, genocide, post-genocide and then 'reconciliation' phase of a national history is laid out. It is meticulously presented in a circular narrative around a dark corridor with videos, push-button slide shows, maps and backlit displays. It is detailed and offers an impressive mix of authoritative historical description and first-person accounts. There is a momentum, maintained by the need to walk around the circle that moves from stage to stage, to the awfulness of the genocide that is literally and metaphorically *around the corner*. We see the introduction of the ID cards by the Belgian colonials that institutionalised and made permanent the division between Tutsi and Hutu in 1933, the stoking of hatred by publications such as *Kangura* and the signs of planning that the international community ignored. The scope, viciousness and horror of the genocide are then laid out in devastating detail: video interviews with survivors; cabinets with knives and machetes; pictures of lost or orphaned children. Once you have walked past the displays on the actual genocide, you move through the sections on justice, reconciliation and the present day. There is even a small picture of Emmanuel, who, the caption explains, is one of the survivors of the Murambi massacre. In my journey around the exhibition, although Pottier's disparaging words about 'newcomer academics' were on the tip of my tongue and the smell of lime still fresh in my nose, I developed a genuine sense of anger at what was presented as a preventable genocide in the context of a culpable international community. As a western visitor, I felt indicted and chastised.

However, without doubting the care of those responsible for writing and constructing the display, the smoothness of the story, coupled with the memory of Murambi, meant that I also yearned for a 'Proust effect' – I wanted smell to trouble my nose. Not for any putrid pleasure it gave (there was none) but because, while taken by an anger, I felt too little troubled by it. However appalling the history that was presented in this site, there was a movement that was inevitable – one step led to the next – and it was a narrative that writers such as Pottier and Prunier have indicated is far from the only route through Rwanda's past.

Murambi had a children's room where small crumbling bodies were laid back to back, in intimate rows. Kigali's Children's Memorial Exhibition, on the other hand, was a series of rooms above the main thoroughfare narrative of Rwandan history. Around the walls were large photo images of children – backlit like church stained glass with story epitaphs under each one. The mini-narratives included the following:

David Mugiraneza
Age 10

Favourite sport:	Football
Enjoyed:	Making people laugh
Dream:	Becoming a doctor
Last words:	UNAMIR[21] will come for us
Cause of death:	Tortured to death

Arianne Umutoni
Age 4

Favourite food:	Cake
Favourite drink:	Milk
Enjoyed:	Singing and dancing
Behavior:	A neat little girl
Cause of death:	Stabbed in her eyes and head

These are undeniably moving to read but in many ways this was a narrative device similar to that deployed in the wider memorial. One section took us on a dark circular walk with a single historical narrative ending with stories of the present, the other shone light through quasi-religious panels of innocence condemned. However, both had an inevitability structured through them and used light as an 'illumination' of the pain presented. Light in the wider narrative journey revealed insights, knowledge and discoveries that, if accepted, would prevent genocide returning. Each poster-sized picture was backlit, the displays glowed in the gloom and the videos shone. Light was clarifying and made the display come to life. Light in the children's panels transformed each into an icon that we looked up to – an image of someone whose death should not be in vain. History in this memorial was given a clear structure – progressing to the present – and the individual children's deaths were transformed into messages or warnings ('lest-we-forgets', 'never-agains') in the service of a particular project of not forgetting and rebuilding a 'better Rwanda'.

Disquiet at this memorial, and at the way it seemed to resolve the genocide into a project of national reconciliation, is directly comparable to the way that Murambi seemed to prevent, pause or delay resolution and keep the problem of genocide present. To develop this comparison, it is important to consider the notion of 'strategic memory' in more detail. The argument aims, in effect, to suggest why an initial reaction to Murambi might see it as a site from which to develop a case for a form of critical performance practice more readily than the memorial in Kigali.

Memory theatres

The distinction between a strategic and a suspended memory can be further examined in light of the work of Feldman on what he calls 'memory theaters' and the work of Simon, Rosenberg, and Eppert on pedagogy and historical trauma. Feldman's use of Raymond Williams's differentiation between 'archaic' and 'residual' historical practices is echoed in Simon and colleagues' differentiation between memory as 'strategic practice' and alternatively as a 'difficult return' (see Chapter 2). In referring to the Kigali centre as a strategic memory practice I am specifically borrowing from Simon. There is a direct similarity between 'archaic' and 'strategic' practices in these definitions. By way of example, Feldman's words on what he calls the 'museum format' are worth repeating:

> Does this prescriptive plotting 'archaicize' terror, creating museums of suffering? The museum format freezes the past, transforming it into discrete units of time, and petrifying it within classificatory labels, all of which situate the past as an object of spectatorship, no matter how empathic this gaze may be. The spectator in the museum-archive of suffering is also a witness, but this is witnessing at a remove: in controlled conditions, and within spatial divisions between life and death, viewer and the observed, now and then. (Feldman, 2004, p. 165)

Although he is perhaps in danger of universalising one museum format into the approach of all, this could be a description of the Kigali museum. We are still a witness, but this museum creates certain spatial relationships between viewer of history and viewer of child victims that determine our identification with the narrative maker as much as the objects of the narrative. We view history and there is no chance that it will get up our nose. Feldman continues by explaining how Williams understood an 'archaicized past' as 'a convenient signifier that has been too neatly stitched into the dominant ideologies of the present, and which does not disrupt, but enforces the linearity of historical time' (Ibid.). This is a linearity that was all too evident in the Kigali version of Rwandan history. Similarly for Simon, Rosenberg and Eppert a strategic practice is where:

> Formations of memory [...] are efforts to mobilize attachments and knowledge that serve specific social and political interests within

particular spatiotemporal frameworks [...] there is a long history of deploying remembrance practices on such terms that bolster hegemonic, emergent, and, at times, insurgent nationalisms and ethnocultural identifications. (Simon, Rosenberg and Eppert, 2000, p. 3)

With the bodies in Murambi, with no helpful trilingual[22] notices, it was difficult to make out the mechanism of that deliberate mobilisation or deployment. In the Kigali centre, however, you became all too aware of the stitches, whereby the micro-line narrative of the individual children's deaths was seemingly tacked into the wider story that the current government of Rwanda wanted an international audience to learn ('UNAMIR failed to come'). The Kigali Centre was, in the very way it moved you through its structure, an act of mobilisation toward a particular form of identification, 'bolstering' a certain historical vision of Rwanda. Simon further notes that a 'strategic practice' is in effect 'consolatory' in that it is 'the provision of images and narratives against which the future is defined as different' (Ibid., p. 4). Again this resonates with the Kigali Centre, where the images of the bright children's panels, with their terrible conclusion in the death of the child, provided a narrative device that consoled you that the death was clearly something of the past. The very presence of the bodies at Murambi, however, seemed to make the past evident in the present and, because the 'what is to be done with them' question seemed to go unanswered, the bodies offered no consolation that the future would be transformed. In the future perhaps these bodies would still be there, slowly decaying.

An alternative model offered by Feldman (again via Williams) is referred to as a 'residual practice'. This has striking similarities to what Simon calls a 'difficult return' or 'a remembering that humbles any design to master the past' (Ibid., p. 7). This humbling, in turn, echoes the notion of Derrida humble before Celan's poem and illustrates why these are useful frameworks for further analysis of Murambi. This is not, however, to 'clear up' an initial reaction to the site, but to question further why it might have been both troubling and ultimately more challenging than the Kigali Centre. Simon, in rejecting 'strategic practices', hopes for memorials where the past is not neatly resolved in acts in the present but where we learn to live with 'disquieting remembrance' (Ibid., p. 4). Projects of the 'difficult return' endeavour:

To bring forth into presence specific people and events of the past in order to honor their names and to hold a place for their absent presence in one's contemporary life. (Ibid., p. 4)

Feldman's use of William's idea of 'residual memory' is defined in the following way:

> The residual historical fragment is an event or a collage of events, artifacts, and accounts about events that are not easily integrated into such master narratives as the idea of progress, collective reconciliation, or evolution to human rights equity [...] [Residual memory] reserve[s] the right to recall and make public irreconcilable residual historical content that bears upon a present that cannot fully consume or dismiss its problematic past. (Feldman, 2004, pp. 165–6)

A residual practice is therefore one that brings forth the dead or past events into presence in such a way that their integration into problematic, contemporary political projects is made difficult. It is making public a content that bears upon the present, without being fully consumed by it – so that it remains, in the words of Derrida, 'exceptional and extraordinary' (Derrida, 2001, pp. 31–2). The crux of the argument here is that this might be both a clue to how memorialisation might 'honour' those that have suffered and an indication of a framework from which participatory or applied theatre might develop a more critical practice.

The bodies at Murambi were residual or more properly *residue*. They were the remains of dead bodies that gave off residue in the air and in their smell. Therefore, they were fragments in a more direct sense than the quotations above perhaps anticipated. They held, viscerally, the absent present. By their being on open display, an awful past could bear upon the present – they were paradoxically 'live'. Perhaps the only equivalent, again drawing this example towards theatre and performance, might be the live body of a performer who is both of the past and in the present and has the power to 'bring forth specific people'. The Murambi bodies seemed to operate as a *difficult return* because they explicitly held a place in the contemporary life of both the guide Emmanuel and also those who took their smell away with them. They bore down by acting upon those that witnessed them – and making sense was not done in the neat narratives of official history but in the vortex of emotions, recollections, and half-understandings that each person would bring and take away. These bodies could be tied into a master narrative (as is discussed below) but, paused between digging up and reburial, the problematic past also hung suspended as problematic past.

Continuing with the hanging theme, the mud and blood-caked clothes draped on the Murambi line (see cover) also acted in the present, almost bringing forth their wearers. Not in a strict sense of names but in their careless hanging they suggested a present still tangled up with the past. There were cleaner clothes in Kigali stretched across neat wires creating body shapes in one of the rooms that merely hinted at people. There we witnessed the aesthetic decisions of the display creation, not the sense of the act of murder. The dead were long since gone. The clothes in Murambi were matted with the death-residues of their owners and draped hurriedly in such a way as to suggest the act: they were pre-sorting, pre-washing. It felt as if the activity they suggested had only just happened – and because they were mid-process they were not yet incorporated into a master narrative of 'collective reconciliation, or evolution to human rights equity' that felt well settled in the Kigali museum.

In front of the classrooms at Murambi, as mentioned at the beginning of this chapter, is an impressive new building that will be the official memorial at Murambi. It was empty in 2005 and the content still disputed in 2006, but clearly plans are afoot for the Aegis Trust to open it as another major site of genocide memorialisation and education. The new building dominates the top of the hill, and the school with the bodies is merely a collection of nondescript classes behind it. It is a visual reminder of a creeping archaic practice that almost seems to hope to frame the residual or 'difficult return' offered by the locked rooms behind. The bodies appeared to escape in these first reflections upon them, but gradually it appears that the site will be incorporated into a strategic project. Residues need clearing up if bodies are to support the work of 're-imagining'. To quote Elaine Scarry:

> At particular moments when there is within a society a crisis of belief [...] the sheer material factualness of the human body will be borrowed to lend that cultural construct the aura of 'realness' and 'certainty'. (Scarry, 1985, p. 14)

So perhaps tours around Murambi might soon come to their end as the new Aegis Centre eventually opens and borrows those bodies to give a clear sense of what has happened in the past and how Rwanda should now face its future. The 'progress' of the new memorial is, however, still unresolved at time of writing.

Back to the protean bodies

As hinted at earlier in the chapter, it is important to return to the bodies at Murambi, to add a warning or caveat to the argument presented here.

There is a problem with the analysis that is linked to the borrowing of bodies that Scarry warns of in the previous quotation. If the bodies of the dead are 'protean', to use Verdery's term (1999, p. 28), we may find that they are 'borrowed to lend' legitimacy to a whole range of ideological positions and strategic initiatives. They may appear suspended, and I may be reluctant to start a process that seemed paused, but this stillness may be partially illusory.

During the tour around the Murambi site, the survivor Emmanuel talked about his experience when we were in one of the rooms and again towards the end when we were standing between two classrooms. He told the story of the attack, the killing, how he was shot and escaped. At the end of his account, he took off his hat to reveal a hole in his forehead. Surrounded by the dead bodies with their visible injuries, we were shown a living wound as the conclusion of a story. The narrative ended with the visible scar standing for the authenticity of the account, replaying a familiar literary theme of the body as the site of truth. Feldman has argued that 'the witnessing gaze descends into memory and the evidentiary depths of the body for biographical truth' (Feldman, 2004, p. 191) and I cannot deny my gaze was drawn to Emmanuel's bullet-hole wound at this moment. Although this might not seem immediately problematic, this process is linked to the oppressive use of bodies to extract truth. Feldman offers two examples, first in the way that the abolitionist would present a 'live' slave to her or his audience and encourage him (it was usually him) to strip off his shirt to show the wheals of abuse and second, more brutally, in the torturer's extraction of 'truth' literally from the body of his or her victim. The slave who removes the shirt (Ibid.) was reperformed directly in Emmanuel's hat removal and, therefore, in that instant those watching were positioned as the beneficiaries of the location of truth in the wound of a victim of violence. This meant that there was a 'trace of mastery and subordination' in this Rwandan 'theater of witnessing' (Ibid.). Feldman goes on to conclude:

> The audience of witness and the perpetrator share the same visual culture of victimage. They both attain their subject position and relation to the victim through the display of pain, and they both use the marked body of the victim to construct memory, to restage truth. (Ibid., p. 192)

Although Emmanuel was using his own body to authenticate his story, the international visitors to this site, simply by being there, were in danger of becoming part of that 'culture of victimage'. The broader worry is that, like the quotation from Wainaina about the use of 'rotting dead bodies', it could be argued that in this writing I construct a subject position for myself that relies on the display of pain for its authority. In effect, what I am suggesting is that, in concentrating too specifically on the actual bodies and their affect, it is important not to miss the guiding that did take place at this site. There was no ordered route through the displays and there were no signs or explanations – but there was a guide. Rather than the visitors being invited to be humble witnesses, it could also be argued that the proximity of the dead to our own bodies, the way they were laid out on slatted beds, waist height in front of us, engaged the visitor in a particular way. We were being *invited to use*, to borrow, almost to touch those bodies, as part of our own projects of explanation – and if we did not have a script for that account we were given one by Emmanuel. Ushered into classrooms that appeared mid-dig, we were being asked to take on the roles of the diggers, the investigators. It was paused but it was a pause waiting for us, and we were supposed to become, aided by Emmanuel's scar-authorised truth, those academic scriptwriters discussed by Pottier. This is in no way to disparage the generosity that Emmanuel displays to those who go to Murambi, or in any way to deny or minimise the horror of what happened there, but to note that, while there was a form of suspension of the memorial impulse, there was also a sense that the site invited visitors to become performers in the process of discovering what happened. In its presentation as a forensic dig, anyone visiting could slip into the mantle of the investigating authority – and, in a country where answers are offered as part of a national policy of history writing, my nauseous anger inhaled at the sight could easily become attached to the first and most easily expressible narrative. So we might hold onto the pause, and resist the desire to 'tap at the bodies to make them bleed', but the very shape of the displays, which pulled our bodies towards them, enrolled us in a forensic project. This meant that the *difficult return*, which appeared to be finely balanced, could, with the help of the international visitor–scriptwriter, be tipped into being part of the strategic project of creating a particular reconciliation or memorial narrative. Phelan provides a vivid account of this dilemma in the following:

> When writing about the disaster of death it is easy to substitute interpretation for traumas. In that substitution, the trauma is tamed by the interpretative frame and peeled away from the raw 'unthought' energy of the body. The unworded is sentenced to meaning. I am

trying here to hear the body and its symptomatic utterance, that which always remains its most intimate echo, even while admitting that my hearing is pre-determined by the interpretative frame that limits any encounter with bodies. (Phelan, 1997, p. 17)

While the previous chapter will have indicated my concern with her use of the word trauma, this does prompt a question as to whether in Murambi we could continue to hear the echo of those bodies. With a subtle yet real interpretative frame offered by Emmanuel, could we resist the political manipulation of the disaster of death, and create encounters with this crisis that remained intimate and untamed? Can the relationship between images of suffering or performances of crisis, and those who witness them, be one that allows them to remain difficult – not to be reduced or tamed to be part of the show of a resolved or consoled past? This is, of course, a question for theatre and performance as much as a question for memorial practices – and a tentative affirmative response is part of the task of this book.

The argument here has sought to link the anxieties about theatre projects, which struggle to escape the dominant and over-simple version of history and reconciliation that is being promulgated across Rwanda, with the troubling power of the bodies at Murambi. The debates in this detour to memorials – in particular in the search for a residual, difficult practice rather than one that is 'strategic' – are presented as directly relevant to the applied theatre or activist performance community and aim to parallel the validation of *tactical* practices in Chapter 1. The affective response to Murambi provides – at first sight – a space that is polysemic and inspires a sense of outrage that is not then resolved into a discourse that favours certain problematic configurations of the past. A performance realm and discursive register that focus on affect can, perhaps, counter many of the problems of the manipulations of the communicative instinct (which, I would argue, is behind much applied theatre) so that, rather than taming the past in a strategic project, performance can maintain its difficultness, its incompleteness, in the present. What I hope is shown here, and will be developed in the chapters that follow, is that affect is an important site of enquiry that, simultaneously, does not deny a concurrent potential for manipulation. It is, as Phelan suggests, always limited to a degree. While this will be discussed at length in Part II of the book, this chapter will end with two more examples, which will be used to illustrate forms of memory practice beyond obvious 'relations of power' (Khalili, 2005, p. 30): two brief moments that might perhaps have resisted, or might be summoned to forge further chinks, in the systematic and overwhelming interpretative frame that is governing the creation of the new Rwanda.

Both the examples return us to the prison in Kigali. The first is about the prisoners themselves and the second concerns a fleeting moment from the theatre workshop programme. Prisoners in Rwanda live in cramped and overcrowded conditions but they are often allowed to work beyond the walls of their institutions. In their frequently well-tailored pale pink uniforms, they can be seen around towns, working on building sites and harvesting in fields. As mentioned above, there were 60,000 in 2007 in a country of approximately eight million people. Many of them, but by no means all, are either convicted or still untried *génocidaires*. The comment here is not on the system of justice that is imprisoning them, the overcrowding in the prisons or the *gacaca* courts that are trying many. Each of these is tied into sanctioned systems of reconciliation in different ways. Here, however, it is their scattered peripheral presence around the town of Kigali, and occasionally in other towns I visited, which will be commented upon. It would be very difficult to tell – certainly not without considerable further study[23] – how Rwandans view them. I saw non-prisoners in the street holding their hands, chatting with them in a friendly animated way, and I saw them ignored. I heard the story of someone who said she was afraid when she saw them. The point is that they are within sight, but not the main sight; they are spread through the population and are glimpsed. They have an uncertain presence – their pink uniforms flicker peripherally and, assuming their number diminishes over the years, they will gradually fade away. It is impossible to guess what memories they kindle, what Rwandans see, but they are walking accidental reminders that could be heartening for some, appalling for many, or nothing at all for others. It cannot be denied that the prisoners are controlled by the government and are perhaps a sign of the diffused power of the state. However, that person chatting, holding the prisoner's hand in the street, seemed to suggest that they are also part of a daily reality that is only partly determined. They are seen, but they are not the main *site*: they are not a special cordoned place where memory work happens, that can, therefore, be marshalled and controlled. Both Murambi and the Kigali centre were quiet. In the former there were maybe three people plus Emmanuel, all non-Rwandan. In the Kigali Centre there was one other family at the time I visited. These were largely not places *of* Rwanda and Rwandans but *from Rwanda to others*.[24]

To return to the person-in-pink holding the hand of a passer-by in the street. This was a moment utterly beyond prescription; it was perhaps not something anyone should do, it was simply being done. It made me, to use Adorno's word, 'shudder',[25] not because it horrified in any way, but because, like breathing the air of the Murambi bodies, it touched me physically. I could not know what memories were staged, awoken or forgotten in this moment but I was captured by the perplexity and informality of it. It might have been a glimpse of what Das and Kleinman hoped for in projects of reconciliation when they asked for 'the small local stories in which such communities are experimenting with ways of inhabiting the world together' (Das et al., 2001, p. 16). To someone who had had the history of genocide continually explained by official and semi-official processes since my arrival in Rwanda, the accidental or casual was a strange relief. This seemed to be, once again to use Das and Kleinman, a moment where 'reconciliation is not a matter of a confession offered once and for all, but rather the building of relationships by performing the work of the everyday' (Ibid., p. 14). This touch, pink to non-pink handholding, staggered me – it appeared 'exceptional' and 'extraordinary' and was over in a flash. It was unremarked: there was no call to explain.

The second moment to introduce happened during a lunch break in the prison theatre project – and here arguments about applied theatre and memorialisation coincide directly and deliberately. One of the participants had come in with a battered guitar and, as others were chatting informally, he started to sing. It took a few seconds to realise, through his strong accent, that it was a rendition of 'Redemption Song' by Bob Marley. *Emancipate yourselves from mental slavery, none but ourselves can free our mind [...] 'Cause all I'll ever have, redemption songs, redemption songs'.* Did he understand the English? Did the irony of a man standing accused of genocide singing about redemption register? Did he seek some form of forgiveness? Was redemption an intentional theme or objective of the workshop? 'I doubt it' is the answer to each of these questions, yet the impact remained. Following Frith's lead the 'exhilaration' seemed to come from 'the singer's failure to integrate musical and semantic meaning' (Frith, 1998, p. 182). The meanings spiralling from this moment were rich and staggering, and yet my argument now is that we must resist the urge to interpret. Allocating meaning, in Rwanda, seemed to be part of the problem. If 'words are sounds we can feel before they are statements to understand' (Marcus cited in Frith, 1978, p. 14), by holding onto the feeling generated in this moment, we could perhaps resist the pull of the interpretive frameworks discussed earlier. By permitting this to remain a private scene, in much the same terms of the *private* applied theatre discussed in Chapter 1, we celebrate an incident that, while not immune to the world outside, is at least momentarily untamed. Derrida has argued 'there is always a strategical or political calculation in the generous gesture of one who offers reconciliation or amnesty' (Derrida, 2001, p. 40). Here, however, in the two 'scenes of repentance' (Ibid., p. 28) I have described, there seems to be a potential to slip off the strategic coil. In the handholding because it was informal, unnoticed and intimate and in the singing because it evoked smiles and warm responses from those listening, without being endowed with intent. The redemption song was exhilarating because it was allowed to exist as an instance of pleasure, without being determined as a product of a certain 'a political strategy or a psychotherapeutic economy' (Ibid., p. 50). It was outside the formal structure of the workshop, was outside the narrative format of the theatre developed up to that point and, instead, it was appreciated as a joyous, small-scale performance: one that permitted this singer, in a brief instant, to escape the appalling narratives in which he was intertwined – and in front of which this writer could only stand humble. I gave myself permission, to repeat the words used above in relation to Murambi, to *yield before a site/sight that I did not want to make bleed.*

Derrida asks for a form of forgiveness that is perhaps impossible – one that is 'unconditional but without sovereignty' (Ibid., p. 59). I would translate this into a form of performance practice that seeks *an unconditional meeting between people not based on an exercise of the power to forgive, reconcile or heal.* A meeting that is no longer part of a strategy of communication, but a holding onto the difficult affect of presence. Perhaps *the end of effect* is found in performance practices – be they based on people's suffering, crises, memories or desires to forget (or engagement with the beautiful as outlined in Chapter 5) – that seek to operate outside the demands for certain regimes of forgiveness, truth telling, history making or psychotherapeutic healing. This is of course 'apparently impossible' but worth aspiring to as a 'dream of thought' (Ibid., p. 60). Instead of 'tapping' on our practice to see where it bleeds, or using the raw performed pain and narratives of oppression as proof of their truth, I am looking for a performance of the *difficult return* – those times where 'the abject collapses in a burst of beauty that overwhelms us' (Kristeva, 1982, p. 210). We are searching for the 'exceptional and extraordinary that interrupts the normal', to paraphrase the epigraph from Derrida. As a theatre person I search for these moments in the repeated actions of performance – and maybe the handholding and the redemption song here were such bursts. And if writing about these acts should 'touch a kind of madness' (Phelan, 1997, p. 11), and true forgiveness is a type of madness, perhaps there is a link between critical writing, beautiful performance and unconditional forgiveness. Perhaps, therefore, 'this madness is [...] not so mad' (Derrida, 2001, p. 60).

Towards Part II

A theatre workshop working with history, myth and narrative forms *could only* snag equally problematic official and counter-narratives of terror. Explaining the workshop was similarly implicated in the discourses of reconciliation, forgiveness or memory that circulated Rwanda or were assumed to offer an appropriate home for theatre making in post-conflict societies from the broader performance literature. After visiting the memorials and considering affect as a source of inspiration and non-interpretation as a necessary resistance to an overwhelming strategic re-imagining process, the theatre project could be re-examined. Rather than hoping for the generation of understanding from narrative effects, or the resolution of mistakes of the past through restaging of them in the present, the workshop was perhaps best understood for its evocation of affect. This suggests a non-interpretative ethics that validates the singing of the redemption song as a vital, affective moment, over which meanings are kept deliberately murky.[26] This is a dream of resisting the easy absorption of the work of applied theatre and community-based performance into the discourses of forgiveness, reconciliation and historical cause/effect.

Participatory theatre should focus on affect rather than effect. This would seek to avoid the anticipation or extraction of meaning as the primary impulse of an applied theatre process (both in execution of projects that communicate or teach and in the interpretation of those projects that report on effects, problems solved and things learnt). Working with affect awakens individuals to possibilities beyond themselves without an insistence on what the experience is – what meanings should be attached. The private moment of the workshop from Chapter 1, the multiple performance forms advocated in Chapter 2 and the affective response to music and bodies in Chapter 3 will now be tied to discussion of performance affects, performances of beauty and the performance of care and intimacy in Part II.

Part II
Performance Affects

4
Performance Affects:
A Kind of Triumph

> The truths which intelligence grasps directly in the open light of day have something less profound, less *necessary* about them than those which life has communicated to us *in spite of ourselves* in an impression, a material impression because it has reached us through our senses.
>
> (Deleuze, 1964, p. 161. Italics in original)

> That is my mission in this book: to speak seriously of the largely ignored and perhaps incommunicable thrill of the group deliberately united in joy and exaltation.
>
> (Ehrenreich, 2007, p. 16)

> And if it became clear again that sitting together at a table for dinner [...] is *not only about communication*, not only about 'exchange information,' then it might indeed become important and helpful – not only for some romantic intellectuals – to have *concepts that would allow us to point to what is irreversibly nonconceptual in our lives.*
>
> (Gumbrecht, 2004, p. 140. Italics in original)

This chapter starts a process of pointing to what is 'non-conceptual' in the work of applied theatre – of finding what, I will argue, is the important, overlooked 'in spite of' quality of much that takes place in numerous examples of community-based performance. It seeks to draw proper attention to those bits of practice that, echoing Ehrenreich above, are largely ignored, or certainly fit less comfortably into a regime of action and analysis that insists on particular effect and certain means of accounting for it. These 'bits of practice' are the aspects that practitioners and participants might relish, such as joy, fun, pleasure or beauty, but rarely appear in the articulated intentions, funding applications or evaluation reports that surround the field: they are, in the words of Dolan, the 'stunning, nearly prearticulate insights' offered in many experiences of performance (Dolan, 2005, p. 8). Following on from the end of the previous chapter, I will argue that these areas are the vital *affective register* of participatory arts that should not be accidental or peripheral but need to be central to the purpose and thinking about the work, so that, following Deleuze, what has reached us through the senses becomes foundational to the practice and crucially *politics* of applied theatre.

This chapter will build on the chapters from Part I to suggest that they each demonstrated a shift from effects to affects and a discussion of the rationale for this shift will be presented here. This will be followed with an outline of different contemporary theories of affect, particularly seeking to articulate a non-hermeneutic approach to both the practice of and writing on applied theatre. This will be followed by an argument for the politics of affect, countering the assumptions that the affective realm is one that avoids or denies political action. The chapter ends by making the case for a concentration on the affective as a key to the aesthetic and political force of participatory and community-based performance practice.

From effects to affects

In an area of arts practice often reliant on funding from non-arts bodies, applied theatre has inevitably both designed and described its repertoire in terms of social impact. This is not necessarily a narrow set of objectives or outcomes, and has included the effect of participation in theatre projects on a sense of achievement, personal behaviour, confidence, access to human rights, knowledge of curricular and non-curricular issues, involvement in campaigns for social justice and the diminution of the propensity to become involved in a range of 'anti-social' activities.[1] Participation, or engagement with the arts more generally, is said to do things – to have certain identifiable effects. These claims, and the research mission to back them, have been the dominant framework for organising and developing the work. In addition to this focus on theatre's impact, a linked tendency has been to see these arts programmes as revelatory. A play or process not only communicates information about issues or ideas but is also understood to *show* something of the truth of the lives of those involved. It documents a story, displays the real-world oppression of a particular community, or replays the effects of trauma. With their problems revealed, a group can reflect upon them and hopefully they can be changed. Although there is critique of this revelatory/communicative direction within the field of applied theatre, there has been little systematic attempt to frame an alternative. Perhaps the most notable exception is the excellent work of Joe Winston, who has articulated a case for 'arts beyond utility'. His work will be discussed further in Chapter 5, but for now it is his criticism that the 'marginalisation of the arts has not been countered through any re-framing of aesthetic argument but rather by embracing issues of social utility as central to their purposes' that is important for the case to be made here (Winston, 2006b, p. 287).

'Embracing issues of social utility' has borne results for the applied theatre field. It has led to increased funding and to projects in diverse locations and with numerous communities. However, it also has led to a certain atrophying of the practice that now needs to be countered with, what I am calling, an *attention to affect*. Colebrook, in her work on Deleuze, suggests this in the following:

> What we can acknowledge is that art is not about knowledge, conveying 'meanings' or providing information. Art is not just an ornament or style used to make data more palatable or consumable. Art may well have meanings or messages but what makes it *art* is not content but its *affect*, the sensible force or style through which it produces content. Why, for example, would we spend two hours in the cinema watching a film if all we wanted were the story or the moral message? (Colebrook, 2002, pp. 24–5)

The same question can, of course, be asked about applied theatre, where practitioners know intuitively that the work is always 'about more' than just the story or the message. However, the focus on purpose, effect or utility is still dominant. The negative impact of this orientation has, in different ways, been demonstrated by the examples from Part I and it can be divided into three areas – on the artistic activity itself, on the research connected to the field and, finally, on the work's political direction. All chapters in Part II of *Performance Affects* are, then, seeking to reanimate the practice, research and politics of applied theatre through what has been called elsewhere an *affective turn* (Clough, 2007).

In terms of practice, a sole concentration on social utility is in danger of abandoning the terrain of sensation: of the aesthetic concerns for beauty, joy, pleasure, awe and astonishment. These attributes are often still present in projects but are seen either as means to an end, by-product, wonderful extra or hook to the *real work*. Artists know the excitement or sense of fun that exudes from the best work but, in many contexts, they seem to be denied the right to celebrate or elaborate upon the inspiration it provides. At worst, this can lead to a field dominated by practitioners with great knowledge of the issues to be communicated or awareness of the problems faced by the participants, but with little capacity, paraphrasing Ehrenreich, for uniting a group in joy.

For research, the concentration on utility has had a similar draining effect. When studies of community-based arts activities have been required to measure impacts and outcomes, they can be in danger of bleaching accounts of the substance and complexity of the work. People become clients, theatre workshops inputs and performances are outcomes. While I doubt the clarity of many claims made in empirical studies of arts processes,[2] the point here is that they rarely have language for dealing with what is one of their most dynamic features – their capacity for affect. The future behaviour of the group ('they will no longer take drugs') is anticipated, or the truthful, and thus curative, quality of the story is commented upon. The *affective turn* for research, therefore, is a demand for an engagement with programmes that neither reduce complex experiences to indicators of effect nor read performances as simplistic diagnoses of the problems faced in people's lives. It is also, following Chapter 3, an argument for a method that questions the 'mastery' that can be present in attempts to interpret and challenges the ease with which an investigator who 'digs for the truth' can become the proponent of certain problematic narratives and discourses.

Finally, the social utility focus for applied theatre has reduced the scope of its politics. This point has been partially explored by Neelands in an article that claims that 'pro-social' forms of applied theatre have perhaps 'tamed the political' (Neelands, 2007, p. 306). My argument here is that attention to affect can be the basis of an ethical focus for applied theatre that, rather than taming the political, can, in fact, become a generator of its radical intent. This will be explored further in Chapter 6, but the basic connection between affect and politics will be outlined here. I make no apology for starting from the 'minutes of happiness' (or Dolan's 'exquisite moments', 2005, p. 5), somewhat disparaged by Neelands (2007, p. 316), as the powerful, and, for many living within contexts of appalling violence, inspirational driver for the politics of applied theatre. We can lay claim to a 'practice of freedom' (Ibid.) but need to articulate carefully in what context, and how, it can be instigated or shared. Safety, protection and care (particularly when translated to situations of conflict) are not a retreat from some imagined politics of freedom, but the heart of its radical vision. Ethics and politics are intimately combined in this formulation, and I start from the premise that, following political philosopher Simon Critchley, 'if ethics without politics is empty, then politics without ethics is blind' (2007, p. 13).[3]

Defining affect

There has been a surge of interest in recent years in sensation and the passions within the social sciences (see, for example, Fisher, 2002; Heller-Roazen, 2007 and Tambornino, 2002). *Affect* has been a crucial concept within these debates and Thrift has warned commentators about the difficulty in defining, and the dangers in using, the term (Thrift, 2007, p. 19). If it refers to a 'a substrate of potential bodily responses, often automatic responses, in excess of consciousness' (Clough, 2007, p. 2), then that *excess* means that he is right to ask 'who can truly say that they fully understand the forces we tag as "affect"?' (Thrift, 2007, p. 19). The emphasis taken here is that affect refers to emotional, often automatic, embodied responses that occur in relation to something else – be it object of observation, recall of a memory or practical activity. Sedgwick explains this in terms of attachment. Expanding on the work by Silvan Tomkins, she writes that 'affects can be, and are, attached to things, people, ideas, sensations, relations, activities, ambitions, institutions, and any number of other things, including other affects' (Sedgwick, 2003, p. 19). While this notion of attachment is important, it is perhaps too static for the argument here and misses something of the active or generative nature of the affective response. Clough in the following indicates a greater dynamism:

> Affect refers generally to bodily capacities to affect and be affected or to the augmentation or diminution of a body's capacity to act, engage, and to connect, such that autoaffection is linked to the self-feeling of being alive – that is aliveness or vitality. (Clough, 2007, p. 2)

Affect, for Clough, is connected both to a capacity for action and to a sense of aliveness, where it is that vitality that prompts a person's desire to connect and engage (perhaps with others or ideas). It is not a field of particular communicative content, therefore, but rather of capacity and intensity. Healy argues that it refers to 'a certain intensity of sensual, emotional and embodied experience' (2006, p. 231) and, although there is clearly the possibility that an affect can be minor, there is a tendency in the literature to speak of its strength. The 'self-feeling of being alive' is stimulated by a certain power of affect that is *more than* the moment.

Lack of focus on affect (in research or in anticipating the purpose of an arts project as discussed above) denies a large proportion of the experience. Bennett, in her book on affect, trauma and contemporary art, argues that 'affect, properly conjured up, produces real-time somatic experience, no longer framed as representation' (2005, p. 23) and, for her, certain art projects are concerned with, and can only be properly understood in terms of, the production of that experience outside the frame of representation. Affect is then an expansive term, not a simple alternative or opposite to what I am calling the realm of effect, but an augmentation of what should be understood, hoped for and considered in relation to any experience. Following the epigraph from Gumbrecht, there is more to the dinner than what we hope to communicate to our family or guests. Thrift calls these 'nonconceptual' realms 'complex, self-referential states of being' (2007, p. 221) and emphasises the expansive claim made by the term affect by arguing that it is a sensation produced in an encounter between body and event that is 'registered but not necessarily considered in that thin band of consciousness we now call cognition' (Ibid., p. 236). Attention to affects, therefore, extends the contemplation of (and, for the argument here, participation in) arts processes beyond that thin band. In doing so, it aims to register what at times is already there (art work that produces powerful affective sensations) and to encourage a shift from a sole focus on cognitive/representational issues to ensure that the vitality of the art process is not lost.

Theories of affect

The definitions of affect above come mostly from writers inspired by the work of Gilles Deleuze, and, while his work is foundational to the theory of affect used here, there are two other writers who are used to construct this framework. The first is Hans Ulrich Gumbrecht and his work on 'nonhermeneutics' (2004) and athletic beauty (2006) and the second is Barbara Ehrenreich and her entertaining 'history of collective joy' (2007). An outline of their work will be offered here, and I will then return to Deleuze, to argue for a particular 'political' reading of Gumbrecht (one that he disavows). Gumbrecht has argued that 'intellectuals, East and West, have lost not just a tone of writing but an affective disposition, and both are hard to recover' (Gumbrecht, 2006, p. 21) and in a sense his mission in both books considered here is to make the intellectual argument for a recovery of that 'tone'. Gumbrecht is interested in countering the tendency in the Humanities to concentrate only on interpretation – on finding the hidden, beneath the skin, meaning within the material world. While his is a particularly contemporary account, anxiety about interpretation has been evident in writers on the arts for a number of years (see for example, Sontag's 'Against Interpretation' (2001) written in the early 1960s). Gumbrecht traces the intellectual history of the emergence of the purely 'eccentric' or metaphysical orientation to the world and how it fails to permit recognition of what he calls 'presence effects'. He wants to move beyond an 'exclusively meaning-based relationship to the world' (2004, p. 77) so that people come to feel 'in-the-world in a spatial and temporal way' (Ibid., p. 80). Although he does not use the term 'affects', he posits a 'presence culture' against a 'meaning culture' whereby the former allows people to acknowledge 'the immediate physical "touch" of cultural objects' (Ibid., p. 8). He is not seeking to replace meaning with presence but to allow the latter a place in the academy, so that the 'oscillation' between them is properly recognised. He plays particular attention to poetry in this regard, where he notes that 'the institutional dominance of hermeneutic dimension could never fully repress the presence effects of rhyme and alliteration, of verse and stanza' (Ibid., p. 18). In the terms used here, poetry has certain affective qualities that are experienced but overlooked if an interpretative register remains dominant.

It is important to note that Gumbrecht's project is an intellectual one, in the terms of developing a language for analysis of presence within an academy dominated by meaning, and an aesthetic one, in his desire to encourage a form of appreciation of the arts and sport that is not reduced to *what it is done for*. This echoes my concern that *performance affects* is about developing a 'non-hermeneutic' means for researching and analysing applied theatre as well as an argument for an aesthetics of practice. Gumbrecht sums up his academic mission in the following:

> What would it mean – and what would it take – to end metaphysics? It can certainly not mean that we would abandon meaning, signification, and interpretation [...] I think that the 'beyond' in metaphysics can only mean doing something in addition to interpretation [...] It would mean to try and develop concepts that could allow us, in the Humanities, to relate to the world in a way that is more complex than interpretation alone, that is more complex than only attributing meaning to the world (or, to use an older topology, that is more

complex than extracting meaning from the world). The effort it would take us to develop noninterpretative in addition to hermeneutic concepts would therefore be an effort directed against the consequences and taboos coming from the enthronement of interpretation as the *exclusive* core practice of the humanities. (2004, p. 52)

The argument for the academy is about the exclusivity of one approach and a desire for new methods. Although he asserts that this is about opening up the complexity of the world, I would argue that this can be framed as an ethical objection to the limits of interpretation ('extracting meaning from the world') and an inherent politics that emerges from my argument in the previous chapters and is developed further below. The aesthetic vision springs from this position, as he articulates a desire to see the arts 'play a much more prominent role' (Ibid., p. 95) in teaching but also how appreciating artistic qualities can be a valuable end in itself. His enthusiasm for presence effects, and what I would call the affective, is expressed eloquently in the following:

> I wanted my students to know [...] the almost excessive, exuberant sweetness that sometimes overcomes me when a Mozart aria grows into polyphonic complexity and when I indeed believe that I can hear the tones of the oboe on my skin [...] the joy I feel when the quarterback of my favourite college team [...] stretches out his perfectly sculpted arms to celebrate a touchdown pass [...] I want my students to join in that promise of an endlessly and eternally quiet world that sometimes seems to surround me when I get lost in front of a painting by Edward Hopper. (Ibid., pp. 97–8)

It is very easy to see how this can be equated to the 'self-feeling of being alive' quoted above as a central definition of affect. While Gumbrecht is making an argument for a philosophical orientation of importance across the Humanities (what he calls a horizontal rather than vertical engagement with the world), the arts are central to his vision. An engagement with aesthetic questions is what connects the work of Gumbrecht to Ehrenreich's. Where he accounts for the demise in attention to presence in a history moving from the Enlightenment to the present day, Ehrenreich maps this transition as the gradual decline and growing suspicion of collective joy and celebration. Ehrenreich's argument is valuable here because it starts to suggest why attention both to appreciation and to participation in group-based artistic endeavour is important. The paradox is that, in constructing an argument for affect

and for borrowing Gumbrecht's assertion of the philosophical importance of presence (against the concern for communicable meaning), we
start to assert the utility of artistic experience outside a framework of
utility or purpose. For Ehrenreich, it is the rise of rational 'man' (and
Gumbrecht's hermeneutic project where we could conceive of ourselves
as outside the world) that dealt a deathblow to the participatory arts.
While she does not deny the achievements that the sense of autonomous self might have brought, the flip side, she argues, 'is radical isolation, and, with it, depression and sometimes death' (Ehrenreich, 2007,
p. 140). What Gumbrecht 'wants his students to know', therefore, is a
propensity without which, according to Ehrenreich, we will be condemned to a life of misery. In her argument, she pays particular attention to the rise of Protestantism in Western Europe:

> Protestantism, serving as the ideological handmaiden of the new cap-
> italism, 'descended like a frost on the life of "Merrie Old England,"'
> as Weber put it, destroying in its icy grip the usual Christmas fes-
> tivities, the maypole, the games, and all traditional forms of group
> pleasure. (2007, p. 101)

And an 'epidemic of melancholy' is what emerges in its place. Ehrenreich,
then, posits widespread isolation and depression as a consequence of
the triumph of the hermeneutic project. This was not only an affect felt
within Europe but, importantly, was a cultural project that transferred
a dread of collective joy into the violent policies of cultural repression
in various colonies:

> Europeans may have learnt very little about the peoples they visited
> (and often destroyed in the process) – their deities and traditions,
> their cultures and worldview. But they did learn, or imaginatively
> construct, something centrally important about themselves: that
> the essence of the Western mind, and particularly the Western male,
> upper-class mind, was its ability to resist the contagious rhythm of
> the drums, to wall up in a fortress of ego and rationality against the
> seductive wildness of the world. (Ibid., p. 9)

A demand to break open the fortress of rationality, to permit and take
seriously the play of affect, is then, in Ehrenreich's terms, a desire both
to end the frost-like effect of Protestantism and to resist the destructive
dismissal of other cultural practices encountered by colonial officials: a
dismissal that is repeated by the trauma industry discussed in Chapter 2,

where the counter-argument sought to assert the importance of multiple forms of cultural expression in places of crisis. Participation in ritual, dance and other festivities was and is vital for the health of a community in this conceptualisation, in a way that is beyond its ability to communicate or have particular effects. When 'sweetness overcomes' Gumbrecht he is articulating the loss of self that Ehrenreich argues needs to be experienced so that radical isolation is countered and new forms of interconnection are developed. This is a realm of experience outside what Thrift called the narrow band of consciousness that is cognition, and that in times of 'grinding hardship and oppression is a considerable accomplishment' (Ibid., p. 179). And, while some might minimise these moments of happiness as tangential to proper politics, I follow the enthusiasm of Ehrenreich when she argues that their very existence is, to use the subtitle of this chapter, 'a kind of triumph' (Ibid., p. 179).

Deleuze's philosophy, spanning concerns from psychoanalysis and cinema to post-structuralism and anti-capitalism, is closely associated with notions of affect, particularly in the idea of the 'encountered sign' (which comes from his early work on Proust) and his focus on 'expression' rather than communication. For the purpose of the argument here, it is writers working from Deleuze in the fields of art theory and communication who are particularly useful. The 'encountered sign' is a term for what the epigraphic quotation calls the 'material impression reached through the senses'; it is used to denote the sign 'that is felt, rather than recognized or perceived through cognition' (Bennett, 2005, p. 7). Although similar to the presence effect of Gumbrecht in that what the sign expresses 'is not concerned with the communication of information but with the genesis of the definite' (Massumi, 2002, p. xxxii), the central difference in Deleuze is that this is tied closely to what Bennett calls 'critical awareness' (Bennett, 2005, p. 10). For Massumi, perhaps the writer who has developed Deleuze's work on affect most systematically,[4] refiguring 'communicational models of expression', requires an understanding of how signs can produce a *shock to thought* (Massumi, 2002, p. xiii). There is not necessarily an oscillation between Gumbrecht's presence effects and meaning effects, but one shocks the other into existence. For Deleuze, what we find is not that art can be considered within either an affect or a meaning register but that the very definition of art is 'its capacity to sustain sensation' (Bennett, 2005, p. 18). Where Gumbrecht and Ehrenreich have slightly different rationales for moving against an interpretative norm, for Deleuze it is only in affect that the force of art can be understood. Affect therefore disrupts an easy relationship between events or experiences and the words used to describe them. Affect thus:

> far from foreclosing on thought, it agitates, compelling and fuelling inquiry rather than simply placating the subject. In its capacity to stimulate thought, the *encountered sign* is [...] superior to the explicit statement, for it is engaging at every level. (Ibid., p. 36)

Artistic experience and practice are here best understood for their capacity to agitate at the level of sensation, and it is this force that propels a demand to know more. The communicative model of art – the focus on the impact, message or precise revelation – is countered with a notion that the stimulation of affect is what compels the participant to thought and to be engaged *at every level*. Returning to the opening argument in the chapter, the impact of the work of participatory theatre cannot be distilled to the messages, story content or words, but must be opened up to the sustenance of sensation and the subsequent fuelling of inquiry. In this register, the effects are not foretold, but the affects stimulate – and being overcome by joy (with Gumbrecht) or dancing (with Ehrenreich or Goldman) might loosen the icy grip of certain oppressive visions of how we should be in the world. Deleuze, and in particular his disciple Massumi, allow us to consider the encounter in the arts process as the key terrain from which to consider its power – and its radical potential.

Affects and the political

The argument above has already suggested several ways that affects can lead to forms of political focus. However, it is important to emphasise that the affective turn can easily be characterised as one that avoids or dismisses the political. This is particularly evident in the work of Gumbrecht, who specifically champions presence effects for what they are and not for any 'edifying qualities' they may have. He also proposes the presence culture as one less disposed to change compared with a meaning culture, where the interpretative zeal is said to urge people to imagine how the world could be different. It takes an 'eccentric' orientation to the world, according to this position, to understand it as subject to change. What I want to do here is to suggest that within Gumbrecht's anti-politics there is an implicit critical edge that must be acknowledged and perhaps, paradoxically, can provide the source of a political reading of affect. The different ways that affect might be the starting point for a renewed radical politics of applied theatre will be touched on here and then further developed in Chapter 6.

Gumbrecht makes it very clear that the appreciation of an intense aesthetic experience should not be valued for its 'edifying' nature. It is for the moment and it does not allude 'to any values beyond the intrinsic feeling of intensity that it can trigger' (Gumbrecht, 2004, p. 97). In his eulogy to athletic beauty, he insists that he is not 'pursuing intellectually (or even ethically) edifying ends' because he simply enjoys 'the moments of intensity that such events provide' (2006, pp. 31–2). However, the question that his denial prompts is: why do we desire these moments if they are fully purposeless; why should we search them out? Gumbrecht answers this and, in doing so, provides a vision that can only be understood as a demand for protection on the one hand and transformation on the other. Within the peaceful environment of Stanford University, where he is a professor, this might be a casual respite from daily life, but, translated to other less consensual or more violent worlds, his demand for 'the euphoria of focused intensity' that goes 'hand in hand with a peculiar quietness' (2004, p. 55) might prove to be far more radical – and a restatement of the 'art as bunker' proposal from the Introduction. His understanding of presence effects is that they offer an experience that, I would argue, can only be compared with the world in which a person is living. And, in that comparison, the world will inevitably be found wanting. He explains that 'what attracts us without being accompanied by a clear awareness of the reasons for this attraction, is always something that our everyday worlds are not capable of offering us' (2006, p. 100). There is a comparative edge to this proposal that indicates implicit social critique. This is even more clearly an opposition to a certain type of world in the following:

> Once we understand our desire for presence as a reaction to an everyday environment that has become so overly Cartesian during the past centuries, it makes sense to hope that aesthetic experience may help us recuperate the spatial and the bodily dimension of our existence; it makes sense to hope that aesthetic experience may give us back at least a feeling of our being-in-the-world, in a sense of being part of the physical world of things. (Ibid., p. 116)

While many people in more troubled regions of the world will be only too aware of 'being-in-the-world', the dominance of the Cartesian, meaning-based culture means that the realities of suffering are often prevented from being given their embodied character. Worse, in places of violence, the affective impact of events is minimised in the blizzard of information, justification and strategy that forgets that actual bodies are damaged. In this context Gumbrecht's onslaught against an 'insuperably consciousness-centred' world, where 'rather than having to think, always and endlessly, what else there could be, we sometimes seem to connect to a layer in our existence that simply wants the things of the world close to our skin' (Ibid., p. 106), appears to be a demand for protection and a moment of care. And while being 'at peace' (2004, p. 55) might seem a passive state to some, being alive and feeling safe are a radical starting point for many. Gumbrecht provides a vision of what he calls 'focussed intensity' that withdraws a person from the world in a way that can only develop his or her sense of critical dissatisfaction with it. In the smallest sense this might be a protective feature, where the world, with its 'multiplicity of potential distractions' (Ibid., p. 52), is excluded temporarily from the moment. However, in a broader sense, this is a place from which a critique of the world beyond can emerge. From this perspective, an intense awareness of presence, an aesthetic experience which makes Gumbrecht 'drawn into an openness toward the material world' (Ibid., p. 56), can pull a person into critical engagement with his or her surroundings.

What interests me in this potential is that the content for the critique is not given. There is an intensity of experience that can both protect and yet draw people into the world around them – without insisting on the terms of that engagement. As was argued at the end of Chapter 3, this seeks to resist the absorption of the work into problematic discourses (its *taming*) and keeps meanings 'deliberately murky'. There should perhaps be an acceptance of 'pointlessness' so that purpose can emerge through a commitment generated by a new openness toward the 'material world'. And, echoing the paradox mentioned above about the utility of the lack of utility, apparent pointlessness can be one of art's most powerful points. Ehrenreich takes this up in the following:

> Even supposing that the danced rituals and religions with which people worldwide responded to enslavement and colonialization were entirely frivolous, nonthreatening, and politically pointless, who are we [...] to judge them? If the oppressed gained nothing more from their ecstatic rituals and cults than a 'psychic benefit' [...] we must still concede that – to people who have lost their traditions, their land, and often their freedom – a psychic benefit is no small thing. (Ehrenreich, 2007, p. 178)

Once again, that 'no small thing' must be acknowledged as a 'kind of triumph' rather than be dismissed as not sufficiently radical or robust. Those of us who are lucky enough to live within the comfort of communities such as Stanford (or, for that matter, many areas of Manchester) should be wary of critiquing the political ambition of those who live in vastly different contexts: no small thing is *no small thing.*

While Gumbrecht might dismiss the 'combination of aesthetics and ethics' because 'to adapt aesthetic intensity to ethical requirements means to normalize and ultimately dilute it' (2006, pp. 102–3), my argument is that the aesthetic intensity is in itself the propellant of political action. It is, far from being a retreat, a place of safety from which 'critical inquiry' (using Bennett's phrase) or Massumi's 'shock to thought' can develop. Following Dolan, this approach endorses her 'faith' that 'emotions might move us to political action' (2005, p. 15). Ironically, when Gumbrecht asks 'for what, after all, would be the point of politics and potential transformations without a vision of a more enjoyable life?' (Ibid., p. 140), my reply is that the creation of a 'more enjoyable life', in its most infinitely demanding sense, is exactly the point of politics. This might be focused on a collective joy that can overcome the isolation fostered by our 'insuperably consciousness-centred' world; the protective space created by aesthetic experiences; the dances that stamp out a community's survival in spite of what surrounds them; or the desire for 'some sort of celebration' with 'no religious, ideological message, or money to be made' (Ehrenreich, 2007, p. 261). However, it is as likely to be the fostering of an energetic commitment to protecting the environment, campaigning against poverty or for social justice. Affect ensures that there is a passion that imbues, that oscillates with (to use Gumbrecht's phrase) the more programmatic. The fact that, in and of itself, affect has no point is its critical point of departure, and if the fact that there 'is no point to it' offends those who seek clear prescriptions, end goals or fixed visions the response must be that no change is possible without enthusiasm, commitment and a passionate sense of the possibility of a better life.

Theatre, performance and affect

It is perhaps somewhat amiss that I have reached this far in the chapter and not mentioned the person in theatre history for whom the oscillation between affect and meaning is most significant – Bertolt Brecht. Although his ideas on the merits of 'education' and 'entertainment' are familiar and not to be repeated here, the relationship between the poles of fun and edification continue to reverberate in a number of contemporary debates within theatre and performance studies. The task here is not to expand on these debates in detail but to outline how I see *affect* fitting into some of their parameters. Gumbrecht has referred to the relationship between meaning effects and presence effects as one of tension or oscillation, and this echoes the relationship between Brecht's 'theatre for pleasure' and 'theatre for instruction'. While for the argument in this chapter it might be easy to suggest that Brecht overlooked affect in favour of meaning and interpretation, this would be a simplification. The joyless caricature that might be witnessed in modern-day renditions of 'Brechtian' theatre seem to miss the point that Brecht himself knew that 'the contrast between learning and amusing oneself is not laid down by divine ruler' (Brecht, 2003, p. 920). It is revealing that Walter Benjamin's description of Epic theatre, where the actor's style was 'intended to purge them of the sensational' (Benjamin, 1999, p. 145), in fact alluded to sensation strongly:

> Instead, the art of the epic theatre consists in producing astonishment rather than empathy. To put it succinctly: instead of identifying with the characters, the audience should be educated to be astonished at the circumstances under which they function. (Ibid., p. 147)

I would argue that, rather than a replacement of affect with cool detachment, what Benjamin outlines is the very 'shock to thought' discussed by Massumi. 'Astonishment' is only possible if the experience makes something familiar extraordinary, and while certainly Brecht anticipated this at the level of thought, I would argue that, when he explained that 'what is "natural" must have the force of what is startling' (Brecht, 2003, p. 920), he is alluding to an impression that must be felt. To hope for astonishment, for that startle, the sensation of the aesthetic experience must be sustained and, once again, cannot remain within that 'thin strip' of human capacity called consciousness. When Brecht asserts, therefore, that 'there is such a thing as pleasurable learning, cheerful militant learning' (Ibid.), we can perhaps suggest that he is describing an interaction of both the effective and the affective register under discussion here.

That said, the affect here is still the adjective to the noun. The pleasure eases the learning (it is not learnt cheer) and therefore the relationship indicates an order to the tension between affect and effect. My argument is that, rather than a hierarchical relationship, it is better to insist that 'meaning culture' or the act of interpretation is a stratum of affect. Astonishment contains a range of interrelated embodied responses, one of which is the activity of the mind. These perhaps interact with intensity, but not in the strictly dialectical way that the opposition between presence effects and meaning effects, pleasure and learning, suggests. Affect might produce a 'shock to thought', but that thought cannot be simplistically detached from the affective realm. This argument can be refigured within another set of terms familiar to the performance studies community. Richard Schechner has outlined the history of performance as one that moves between, or exhibits the interrelation of, entertainment and efficacy. This 'braid' is a 'basic polarity' where performances that effect transformations are compared to those that entertain (Schechner, 1988, p. 120). Again, it would be a caricature to suggest that Schechner does not appreciate the complexity and instability of the interaction between these two ways of understanding performance, and the earliest account from his book, *Performance Theory*, acknowledges that 'no performance is pure efficacy or pure entertainment' (Ibid.). However, the notion of affect is designed to disturb the opposition that these two words suggest. The critique above of applied theatre practitioners concentrating on effects implies that the work has become firmly located within one plait of that braid. A focus on affect insists that the lines between efficacy and entertainment are impossible to draw. Fun – and its many corollaries in delight, awe, or astonishment – should not be disentangled from what inevitably becomes the more commendable purposefulness of efficacy; it should not be the mere adjectival flourish to the dominant noun of effect. Affect tries to turn a braid into a mesh of felt responses that do not relegate or promote certain threads of the aesthetic experience against others. Learning is an affective, felt state – comprised of many elements of awe, fear, love and intrigue – that is only diminished in its banishment to that part of the body called the mind.

If I am trying to blur the distinctions between entertainment and efficacy, or pleasure and instruction, what *force* for theatre and performance is suggested? I have already argued that the focus on affect is, in fact, not a departure from a sense of purpose or political ambition for the practice of applied theatre. Whether it be Schechner or Brecht, there is a strong tradition within the field of performance studies for a communicative model of theatre. For many, theatre is perhaps the communicative art form *par excellence* – with its ability to speak about the broadest range of issues, across and between diverse audiences and participants. I am not dismissing what might be called, somewhat anachronistically, 'consciousness-raising', but rather locating that power to affect in what I believe is a richer, more complex and yet ultimately more promising zone. Deleuze is again instructive here:

> [Theatre] forges alliances here and there according to the circumstances, following the lines of transformation that exceed [theatre] and take on another form [...] It is truly a matter of consciousness-raising, even though it bears no relation to a psychoanalytic consciousness, or a Marxist political consciousness, nor even a Brechtian one. Consciousness-raising is a tremendous strength but one made neither for solutions nor for interpretations. When consciousness abandons solutions and interpretations, it thus acquires its light, its gestures and its sounds, its decisive transformation. (Deleuze, 1995, p. 243. Also cited in Thrift, 2007, p. 132)

The decisive moment of transformation is found in an abandonment of 'solutions' and 'interpretations' and a location of consciousness in gestures and sounds. Consciousness is not raised in a straightforward fashion but in a context-specific way that moves beyond the moment of the theatre, through a series of, what Deleuze calls, alliances. This is not a communicative model, therefore, but, borrowing from Bennett, a *transactive* view of performance processes. Rather than providing a set of information or communicating 'the "secret" of personal experience' (Bennett, 2005, p. 7), the formal qualities of the work create a transaction between artist, artwork and those encountering it. There is a relational process, a series of 'affective transactions', that govern the engagement where any dichotomy envisaged between 'sensation and knowledge' is 'bridged by a kind of compulsion engendered by the sign' (Ibid., p. 64). Where Bennett is largely discussing visual art, it could be argued that the affective alliances are forged more dynamically, and in a more heterogeneous way, within the participatory practice of applied theatre. This is not the one-way traffic of 'audience coming to the work' (Ibid., p. 7), but a diversity of encounters, processes and experiences that extend the relationships over time and in different, frequently unusual spaces. At its best, translating Deleuze's 'encountered sign' into the *participatory performance encounter* ensures an engagement that 'propels us into a form of intellectual inquiry through its assault on our senses, emotions, and bodies' (Ibid., p. 64). The entertainment/efficacy braid is, therefore, reconfigured as an overwhelming, affective transaction between individuals, groups and their wider community. This experience includes the joy – the buzz – of the participatory arts as inseparable from the total impact of the event. The sensation is no longer the adjunct, the expendable adjective, but the dynamic texture of the work through which it finds its force.

Affect and method

Chapter 3 presented an account of the struggle to accept and work with the affective impression made by bodies displayed in a memorial in Rwanda. I argued that holding onto that shock was needed in order to find a place for practice, outside the particular 'meaning culture' that dominates in that country. It is important not to overlook, however, that this was very much a debate about method. It was asking: if we are to move from effect, and take bodily sensation seriously, how do we continue to write and research? In that chapter, the lead was taken from Phelan's writing on the 'interpretative frame that limits any encounter with bodies' (Phelan, 1997, p. 17). It is easy to see how close this is to Gumbrecht, with Phelan's warning that acts of interpretation can ensure 'the unworded is sentenced to meaning' (Ibid.), echoing his aversion to an over-reliance on hermeneutics. Phelan's objection to interpretation can be located within a postmodern critique of representation and an interest in trauma as a force that somehow transcends its limits. Her position on trauma, considering the concerns I have already expressed about the term, can, however, be usefully translated into a focus on *affect* (as a broader and more inclusive term). Her critique of 'sentencing experiences to meaning' provides, therefore, an ethical starting point for a method for researching *performance affects*. When she notes that Derrida fails in an act of interpretation where usually he would tap 'on the silent black-on-white words until the colors bleed' (Ibid., p. 9), the violent imagery insists that hermeneutics has blood on its hands. Once again, Gumbrecht's argument that his preference for an attention to presence effects cannot be political must be countered with an assertion that he seems to forget the often brutal history of the extraction of truth to which his desire for presence is an alternative. Accounting for affect-focused performance work, therefore, requires an intimate means of re-staging the force of that affect in our critical work that avoids scratching at it until it bleeds.

There are at least three ways through which this method might be realised. The first is related to time and the latter two are connected to place. Gumbrecht, in a chapter called 'To Be Quiet for a Moment', provides a temporal warning that I believe is a powerful starting point for any critical engagement with applied theatre practice. Echoing the *poise* in Bernardi's art discussed in Chapter 2, he urges a pause 'before we begin to make sense' (Gumbrecht, 2004, p. 126). It is in this moment that we will feel the force of affect, and if we can hold onto this experience we are more likely to do it justice in any account. For Gumbrecht, 'if we then let ourselves be caught by an oscillation where presence effects permeate the meaning effects' (Ibid.) we will more readily acknowledge them. In a sense, this is similar to that stammering moment from Chapter 2, where uncertainty demonstrates the continual play of affect within the person. If Gumbrecht argues that 'in the teaching of literature and culture we should pause, from time to time, and be silent' (Ibid., p. 134), I would urge that the transaction of affect between the event and the critic's body should continue in the tension of the stammer in the writing. Silence may hold the complexity of affect within the body of the person, but, rather than being resolved, its troublesome quality needs to spread across the page.

In terms of place, there are two concepts from which I think applied theatre method should take its cue. The first is intimate and based on Sedgwick's concept of 'besides', and the second is more expansive and will be called here *horizontal method*. Sedgwick explains her approach in the following, taken from her beautiful book *Touching Feeling*:

> I have tried in this project to explore some ways around the tops of depth or hiddenness, typically followed by the drama of exposure that has been such a staple of critical work of the past four decades. *Beneath* and *behind* are hard enough to let go of [...] Instead, as its title suggests, the most salient preposition in *Touching Feeling* is probably *beside* [...] the irreducibly spatial positionality of *beside* also seems to offer some useful resistance to the ease with which *beneath* and *beyond* turn from spatial descriptors into implicit narratives of, respectively, origin and telos. (Sedgwick, 2003, p. 8)

Besides provides an ethics of the position of the inquiry. Once again there is a distinctly political critique here of the 'drama of exposure' (an echo of Narrative *Exposure* Therapy) and, rather than searching for a truth within, the method proposed here is for research that coexists alongside experiences, processes or objects of interest. Being next to, of course, is very close – practically touching the 'object' – and this, therefore, means that the affects, the sensations of the work, will course across our skin. Our shudder or stammer comes from this proximity, this intimacy, and we are to acknowledge that affective transaction in our engagement and criticism of the work. *Besides* insists that affect is replayed through us, and is not forgotten or denied. Similarly, a method of research based on being next to the work ensures that we are only ever collaborators, co-inquirers, experiencing the work in an entirely valid but never superior way.

An emphasis on being 'beside the work' is, of course, a horizontal position on an axis. We are not above, beyond or looking over, but next to and with. In his critique of the vertical axis or 'science of the hidden', Rancière has proposed an approach concerned with horizontal relations:

> I always try to think in terms of horizontal distributions, combinations between systems of possibilities, not in terms of surface and substratum. Where one searches for the hidden beneath the apparent, a position of mastery is established. (Rancière, 2004, p. 49)

Rather than being masters of the work, insisting on a horizontal method for researching performance affects ensures an examination of 'systems of possibilities' rather than assertions of certainties. Standing (or sitting for that matter) beside colleagues, co-participants, audience members and other members of our communities and pausing to acknowledge the affective resonance of any art practice, therefore, provides the starting point of a method of enquiry. We are not the 'disembodied observer and the world [...] an assembly of purely material objects' (Gumbrecht, 2004, p. 27), but part of a transaction between people who coexist within the same world. We can make no claims to know the effect of the moment on others, and will often only be beside through an act of invitation, but we will always feel the affect that propels people's engagement with the artistic process and will in turn ripple through our body.

Conclusion: Back to bewilderment

In many ways this chapter has taken me back to a previous interest in the notion of bewilderment (Thompson, 2003). It has made the case for a shift in emphasis from effect to affect, to demand an attention to the play of sensation across different projects of applied theatre. It has also configured *performance affects* as a reminder, to the researcher, of the importance of holding on to the affective impression of the work. Brecht's *startle* or Benjamin's *astonishment* are thus both the *affect* of the work and the starting point of a critical inquiry into it. Affect opens the field to the *perruque* suggested in Chapter 1, and the multiple performance forms from Chapter 2 that cannot be contained in the prescribed notion of trauma. Considering affects permits an awareness of how the best work stimulates in those who produce it, and those who are beside it, a 'shock to thought' that is a precondition for critical engagement with the world. Focused intensity generated by presence cannot be unwoven into competing strands of the pleasurable and the educational, but must be understood as a totally absorbing moment in itself: a moment that is also potentially a propellant to a passionate commitment to social change.

In this chapter and the proceeding chapters, the motivational character of affect has been emphasised. A focus on the affective realm is productive for the creative work of the art project itself, for founding a more ethical position from which to conduct research and, as will be expanded upon in the final chapter, a more productive site from which to imagine a radical politics for applied theatre. Affect is the bodily sensation that is sustained and provoked particularly by aesthetic experiences. It is the force that emerges from attention to pleasure, astonishment, joy, and beauty. Of course, as has been deliberately overlooked here, that force can also be connected to experiences of pain. Fear, despondency, jealousy and despair are all affects. In many ways my critique of the overuse of the concept of trauma finds its alternative in the notion of affect. The 'affect' of many terrible events can be profound – but importantly this just suggests a somatic reaction without dictating the nature of the impact on a person or how it will make them respond in the present or the future. The point to conclude, however, is that while the 'affective realm' is one dominated by a concern for broadly 'positive' sensations stimulated by aesthetic processes, recognition of the relationship between pleasurable and undesirable affects is needed. Gumbrecht's focus might have been the pleasure of 'the tones of the oboe on his skin', but what if the performance caused a shudder of terror across his chest? If the claim is that an intense feeling of joy can be central rather than peripheral to an applied theatre practice, could a similar argument be made for an aesthetic sensation of fear? These are directly the concerns of Chapter 5, where one particular and complex affect (beauty) is compared with an 'aesthetic of injury' or performances of pain.

5
The Call of Beauty:
An Affective Invitation

When we come upon beautiful things [...] they act like small tears in the surface of the world that pull us through to some vaster space.

(Scarry, 1999, p. 112)

On the one hand, something does not need to have a purpose in order to be beautiful. But on the other hand, whatever we find beautiful looks as if it has a purpose.

(Gumbrecht, 2006, p. 44)

For me it was the *beauty* of the experience that mattered most.
(Winston, 2006a, p. 293. Italics in original)

The general attention to affect proposed in Chapter 4 is narrowed in this chapter to a more specific focus on the notion of beauty. The aim here is to raise the concept as one worthy of serious consideration in any performance work that aims to contribute to social justice. *The call of beauty* makes the case that, rather than being a distraction from radical politics, beauty can be positioned as central. The claim is that asking participants to create something they understand to be beautiful engages them in a quest that has powerful and potentially positive results. Beauty is, of course, a term with a complex and contested genealogy and, while the intricacy of that history will be touched upon, the focus is how certain theories of beauty can be developed to make a case for it as a *force for good*.[1] The aim is to acknowledge the place of beauty in broader discussions of aesthetics, but also to argue that it is not a mere analogy for them.[2] The chapter hopes to enhance a number of related arguments from Part I and is, therefore, connected to the playfulness of the term *perruque*, the focus on multiple cultural forms as an alternative to the singularity of storytelling, and the performance of the difficult return, the 'burst of beauty', suggested in Chapter 3. *The call of beauty* starts by outlining how the term has returned to critical attention, seeking a definition that corresponds to the argument for affect rather than defining it in terms of what are described below as either formalist or cognitivist schools of aesthetic theory (see Graham, 2000, p. 45). This will then be followed by a comparison between beauty and pain. As mentioned at the end of Chapter 4, the focus on affect should not be restricted to the aesthetically pleasing. Pain, and more broadly human suffering, have been pivotal concerns in the history of performance and this account of beauty, therefore, seeks to examine the possible relationship between performances of pain and performances of beauty without reducing them to mirror images of each other.

The second half of the chapter will concentrate on the relationship between beauty and 'goodness' and focus, in particular, on what I will call its non-autonomous aspects. This is where beauty makes demands upon us, or 'pulls us' to use Scarry's words, to make particular connections with others. These affects of beauty will lead to an argument for an end to what I believe is the uncritical affirmation of 'ephemerality'. The common assertion that 'of course performance is ephemeral' needs to be examined as perhaps a case of *protesting too much*: something does remain once the show is over. Finally, I will conclude with a demand that the bias in the literature on beauty towards the 'beholders' is replaced by a commitment to those who seek to make or create the beautiful. As I say above, the emphasis here is on those who are asked to make what they consider to be beautiful. This commitment sets up the arguments for the final chapter, where the hopes and desires of those producers are linked to a particular politics of applied theatre.

It needs to be emphasised that the approach here is *normative* in the sense that I am not describing a theory of art making, but making a proposal for what its focus could be. I am arguing for a particular emphasis and a way that the process could be valued. I do not intend to offer a close account of every twist and turn in the history of beauty's place either within or beyond a philosophy of art, but to make an inevitably partial plea for one way that beauty may be considered. A comprehensive overview of theories of beauty is, therefore, beyond the scope of this chapter. Instead, I hope to convince readers of a particular approach, but, as with any normative proposal, there is no claim that the values on which it is based are timeless. Rather, they exist firmly within the acknowledged cultural context, tastes and perspectives of the author. There are numerous definitions of the concept of beauty that might make my use somewhat unusual, but I offer it as a way into understanding and validating the many moments of joy, pleasure and awe that are (or could be) experienced when participating in applied theatre projects.

Beauty makes a comeback

As was mentioned in Chapter 4, Winston has made a convincing case that beauty 'is worthy of serious attention' (2006a, p. 299) and the pages of the journal *Research In Drama Education* have seen a debate about the place of beauty in community-based performance work (Ahmed, 2006; Thompson, 2006; Winston, 2006b). Although my contribution to that debate was focused on performance in war zones in particular and the argument here seeks to make a more general case, it should be noted that it was the research on performance and war that generated a concern for beauty in the first place. Artists from immediate sites of conflict, during interviews conducted as part of the *In Place of War* project, frequently expressed a demand not for what Skloot has called a 'theatre of atrocity' (1996, p. 53) but for a 'theatre of beauty'. This is most dramatically illustrated in the work of Al Rowwad, a theatre organisation offering informal education and a range of cultural activities in Aida refugee camp near Bethlehem. They describe their work as an effort to provide opportunities for 'beautiful resistance' and insist that this is a powerful alternative to the dangers of violent resistance (see Al Rowwad, 2008). So, while writers on beauty might argue that 'the vocabulary of beauty has been banished or driven underground in the humanities for the last two decades' (Scarry, 1999, p. 52), it has flourished in the most unexpected locations. Rather than, as argued by Sartwell, beauty appearing 'frivolous and politically suspect' when the world is 'beset by war, genocide, and nuclear holocaust' (Sartwell, 2004, p. 13), it is in fact in those very worlds that beauty is of relevance. This is not to diminish its suspect nature or to suggest that it is beyond critical appraisal, but to note that its 'return' is not purely a whimsical interest from some place of academic comfort. I agree with Richmond that 'for many people at the level of ordinary life – in human relationships, arts activities, and love of nature, for example – beauty never really went away because beauty is a source of pleasure and well-being that we cannot help wanting' (2004, p. 78). I would emphasise that when that 'ordinary life' is most beset by the horrors of war and violence the *want* can become particularly strong. If 'beauty seems to be making a comeback' (Ibid.), perhaps this is because we are living at a time when violence is more prevalent, ugly and devastating. This perspective accepts that there are areas where the concept of 'beauty' never went away (for example, beauty as it is expressed in global marketing campaigns and certain racialised and gendered notions of perfection). Here, however, I am claiming an alternative reading, which, while recognising the very real power of the 'beauty industry', seeks to delineate a radically different set of experiences. So, following Winston, the argument here does not 'place beauty beyond argument and analysis' (Winston, 2006a, p. 299), but insists that we should focus our concern on how and why it might emerge from the very spaces in which conventional wisdom suggests it is least expected.

There are two more related arguments to support beauty's 'comeback' and these are more my attempts to rehabilitate the term than evidence of a wider cultural tendency. One is related to what I believe is a default assumption about the 'proper form' of applied theatre and the second is the particular place of beauty in the order of affects. In her article on 'an erotics of injury' Salverson has noted a certain 'aesthetic of injury within theater (*sic*) for social change' (2001, p. 122). As will be discussed below, it is frequently assumed that the starting point for a 'theatre for social change' is the oppression of an individual, group or community. While this is not to dismiss the importance of acknowledging suffering, the argument of *Performance Affects* is that sole attention to 'violation and violence' (Ibid., p. 119) can not only exclude many performance forms (see Chapter 2), but also restrict the potential power of the work. This is, therefore, a reiteration of the demand for a shift from *effect* to *affect*, and further advocacy of Goldman's *beautiful radiant things*. Salverson seeks to examine the assumptions behind this focus, but does not go far enough. She asks 'why is the pain of injury considered more accurately translatable, more faithful to grief, than the complex terrain of laughter, of the imagination, or the pleasure of encountering another person in the touching of worlds that is testimony?' (Ibid., p. 124). This is an impressive shift but still relies on testimony and 'personal stories' (Ibid., p. 119) as the core material. My critique of storytelling has already been made, but here the concern is that the demand from Salverson that 'those of us who practice theater that engages with people's accounts of violent events must articulate the nature of that contact' (Ibid.) should perhaps be even bolder. It is not only that the 'nature of the contact' should be scrutinised, but we must also question whether 'theatre for social change' should even focus on those accounts in the first place. Why must laughter, imagination and pleasure return to that testimony?

Why can we not collaborate in creating something beautiful as the very point of departure for this type of performance work?

The focus on beauty, its 'rehabilitation', is also a necessary part of the shifts urged in the wider framework of affect. I would argue that the sensations connected to an experience of beauty (which are a small subset of affects more broadly) are archetypal for the argument made in the previous chapter.[3] Their qualities and ambiguities enhance the case made for the importance of attention to affects in both art making and research, and a focus on beauty can, therefore, capture much of the radical potential for the proposed affective turn. Eco, in his virtuoso treatise on western philosophical theories of beauty, presents a decidedly Kantian definition of the term as a place where 'both the intellect and reason give up the supremacy they respectively exercise in the cognitive and moral fields, and come into free play with the imaginative faculty' (2004, p. 264). Beauty, in this formation, is, then, a central concept in challenging the dominance of what Gumbrecht called a 'meaning culture'. It is no accident that Gumbrecht's book arguing for a non-hermeneutic philosophy was followed by his monograph on athletic beauty: beauty becomes the emblematic example of his case for 'presence affects'. Here, therefore, beauty becomes my emblematic concept for performance affects. It is my term for that moment of pleasurable, world-stopping sensation created through observing and, more particularly, participating in artistic activity. This is not to argue that the different 'ends of effect' articulated in Part I find a simple resolution in a search for beauty, but rather that beauty is one place where the benefits of the shift to affects can be illustrated. While Eco might argue that Kant was not too disturbed by the 'presence of the non-rational phenomena in the system' (Ibid., p. 365), my argument is that beauty's power to disturb is crucial and has important, rarely acknowledged, political power.

A troublesome term

An interest in beauty may be due to the strength of its 'affective invitation' (Richmond, 2004, p. 84), or how it provokes a 'quality of heightened attention' (Scarry, 1999, p. 81) but these indications that it provokes embodied responses, and therefore is at home in an affective register, do not help determine what 'it' is. Of course, even a cursory glance at the Eco edition indicates that this is precisely the fraught question that has concerned a western philosophy of art from the Greeks onwards. While there are many impressive accounts of the shape of these debates (both in general aesthetic theory that contains discussions of beauty such as Graham (2000) and work that focuses solely on beauty such as Armstrong (2004)), there are two caveats to offer before a brief outline of some key features of the field will be given. First, most philosophical discussions in English concentrate on debates within a western tradition. Two notable exceptions would be *Six Names of Beauty* by Sartwell (2004) and the edited collection on global aesthetic theories by Feagin (2007), both of which examine definitions of beauty cross-culturally. Any discussion of the different views of beauty, therefore, must acknowledge that there are numerous traditions that exist outside the debates and sources that dominate the account here. In raising 'beauty' as an important concern, I still endorse an ethnographic disposition for applied theatre and, therefore, I make no claims to map all the objects that fall within its definition or the sensations that emerge in its encounter. The point here is not to say what beauty is, but to suggest the importance of asking different groups what beauty might be. Second, many discussions of beauty emphasise their incompleteness and, in fact, acknowledge that the inadequacy of any definition is a permanent and necessary feature of all attempts to grapple with it. Rather than see this as a weakness, however, the struggle to understand beauty, and more particularly the experience of beauty, is an important part of its appeal. It stimulates a desire to know what it is (a sense of enquiry for an applied theatre project perhaps), at the same time as resisting any finality in that search. Being surprised by the performance of young people on stage, or sharing the joy of play during a workshop, are sensations frequently acknowledged but often hard to define. Armstrong indicates this in the following:

> It would be a mistake to suppose that such an elusive notion as beauty [...] could be made completely lucid and brought into the clarity of daylight. Our comprehension of such things might become dim just when it becomes serious. (Armstrong, 2004, p. 162)

I would argue that being perpetually out of reach is one aspect of what Armstrong calls the 'secret power of beauty' and might here be labelled the force of its affect. Its elusiveness at the point of comprehension is, perhaps, the place from which its power to stimulate engagement with the wider world starts. So while 'any theory of beauty is inadequate to its examples' (Shaviro, 2002, p. 19), experiences of beauty continue to demand more theories (why is that beautiful?) and further experience (where else can we have this feeling?). Although I agree with Eaton, who describes a process that links beauty to a precise definition as a 'philosophical folly' (Eaton, 2006, p. 40), her bold attempt to steer a path between the 'beauty as the property of the object' (formalist) and 'beauty as a response of the mind' (cognitivist) frameworks is echoed in the approach here. The best definitions, therefore, 'enlighten without providing a litmus-test' (Guyer, 2005, p. 333) and also offer a cumulative set of ideas about beauty from which certain theoretical patterns and further questions emerge.

Armstrong's book, *The Secret Power of Beauty* (2004), is one of the best examples of this cumulative approach to definition. Rather than dismissing any particular tradition, explanations are layered throughout his work, showing a series of overlapping and contradictory concerns, many of which appear to hold an element of truth. So historical deliberations on finding the essence of beauty in the object (broadly *formalist*), either in the move of its curves (Hogarth) or in the harmony of its lines and shape (Pythagoras), cannot be dismissed with the arrival of the consideration that beauty lay in a judgement of taste in the late eighteenth century (broadly *cognitivist*). Although there is now popular consent to the idea that beauty lies in the 'eye of a beholder', this common sense is frequently challenged by our feeling that beauty exists beyond our body. We may theoretically accept that an appreciation of beauty is determined by context and the judgement of the person, but seeing it as part of the formal property of an object or event is difficult to resist entirely. As Kirwan notes, 'for, though to say that beauty is relative is quite easy, to feel that beauty is relative is impossible' (Kirwan, 1999, p. 26). This tension, between the saying and the feeling, is crucial to the debate that follows, and central to shifts in aesthetic theory that have understood beauty as form, expression of a form and also as judgement of that form. It may be easy to accept the transition marked by Hume, and then Kant, where 'the debate about Beauty shifted from the search for the rules of its production [...] to a consideration of the effects that it produces' (Eco, 2004, p. 275), but harder not to hold onto earlier accounts where 'in poetry it is expressed by that enchantment that makes men rejoice, in sculpture by appropriate measure and symmetry of the parts, and in rhetoric by the right rhythm' (Ibid., p. 41). In applied theatre terms, we might know that the delight in the workshop is the subjective response of the participants, but feel it is a product of the combination of games and exercises. As a subset of aesthetic theory (but not contained entirely by it[4]), beauty can be constrained by this dualism: between a search for beauty's essence in human judgement and its location in the material properties of the object. While the approach here seeks to blur this distinction, the existence of beauty within and between these frameworks, as discussed below, is one of its powerful features.

Beauty can, then, for the purpose of the argument here, be understood as an intense affect generated by an object or experience that is felt by the person, but simultaneously located beyond them. We see the beautiful field of flowers and appreciate it as beautiful, but knowledge that this is a subjective feeling does not prevent us from continuing to train our gaze on that field. Or, more appropriately for this debate, participants create an impressive, well-crafted scene and, although we know its beauty is appreciated 'in the eye', we still want to see it again. This is, in turn, linked to the idea that we do not experience the pleasure of the scene, game or song in order to achieve another end. It is (borrowing from Kant) a 'disinterested pleasure' – a concept that is central to arguments that beauty has no intrinsic use and also, paradoxically, the key to the case for its value. While the beauty of the scene, person or melody is not dependent on, nor can it be reduced to, what they are for, this does not diminish a sense of its importance. Beauty may have 'no external purpose' (Richmond, 2004, p. 80), but, following the epigraph from Gumbrecht, 'it looks as if it has a purpose'. The proposal that is made here, therefore, is similar to the one developed in Chapter 4: the intense affect of beauty suggests significance without the specific contours or content of that significance being revealed.

For Kant, the fact that beauty is a *judgement of taste* did not mean that a relativist position left each assertion of beauty as equally valid. His understanding of judgement still made a claim to universality, as explained in the following from Winston:

> Rather than this leading to any relativist position, however, he insisted that such judgments make universal claims to validity. It logically follows, therefore, that, if there are such things as valid and invalid judgments of taste that are universally applicable, then one duty of education is to identify what good taste is and to educate the young into it. (Winston, 2006a, p. 288)

Kant's position implies the morally worthy bringing the young towards a particular standard of taste and is a dubious basis for a consideration of beauty at the heart of a practice of radical performance. However, his notion of universality and duty cannot be dismissed outright. What is useful is the relationship suggested between an awareness of beauty's subjectivity and the trueness of the belief that what we appreciate as beautiful *is* beautiful. This is the path steered by Eaton mentioned above and the broader desire not to be drawn into a binary distinction between formalist and cognitivist schools.

When we see, feel or become aware of beauty, we are making, and subject to, a universal claim. I do not look at a particularly impressive moment in a participatory performance and have an immediate inclination to say 'of course it may not be beautiful to you'. Instead, I would urge a partner, friend or anyone present to see what I see. This is not necessarily a Kantian duty to edify, but a desire *to share affect*. How many of us have played a piece of music to try to convince friends that it is the best song ever, or pressed people to go to a play that has overwhelmed us? Who has not, with co-participants in a theatre project, energetically reminded each other of those moments we *know* were the best. We accept beauty is in our eye, but we are desperate to locate it in an object (workshop, performance, song) and share that feeling with others. This antinomical feature of beauty is, then, central to an argument linking beauty to ethics that is developed below. Shaviro explains:

> On the one hand, the judgement of beauty is entirely singular. There is no concept to determine it. On the other hand, we see such a judgement as universal, and we demand assent from others regarding it. (Shaviro, 2002, pp. 12–13)

The two classic positions on beauty therefore meet in this definition. It can be located in the object or experience – formally in its shape, sound or grace – but these qualities are *felt* individually and provoke the desire to convince others of their validity. Although Sartwell has suggested that this is a 'call on us to yearn impossibly, to yearn for an object that is always slipping from our grasp' (2004, p. 4), the argument here is that the deep yearn can be an affective impulse towards engagement with others. And, as will be developed below (and in Chapter 6), this desire to share a response ensures that an individual experience becomes communal.

The yearning produced by beauty, whether it is the forlorn version of Sartwell or the assent-demanding account of Shaviro, is also central to the definitions of beauty produced by Scarry in her seminal book *On Beauty and Being Just*. The section below will outline the relationship in Scarry's work between beauty and pain, and between beauty and justice, but first it is important to explain the two ways in which Scarry's work connects to the contradictory subjective/objective impulses discussed above. The first is the notion of replicability and the second refers to beauty's expansiveness. For Scarry, the basic urge prompted by an encounter with beauty is our desire to reproduce it. We see a beautiful object and the feeling is so precious we want to hold, draw or describe what we have seen. According to Scarry, 'it seems to incite, even require, the act of replication' (1999, p. 3). There is an energy in this account of beauty that is less a yearning, and more an encouragement to act. There is a 'kind of urgency as though one's life depended on it' (Ibid., p. 30) and an increased 'desire to bring new things into the world' (Ibid., p. 46). The point to emphasise for the argument here is that the 'things' in Scarry should perhaps be reconfigured as relational. While she offers a convincing case for the 'urgency' prompted by the beautiful, she tends to posit an isolated artist or observer who, on seeing the beautiful palm, retreats to the solitude of her or his studio to reproduce it. Although the experience may be felt internally, I would argue, as discussed above, that the urge to repeat is also an urge to share, communicate and offer other people the same sense of pleasure. So when we see that palm we could retreat and sketch it, but equally we might enthusiastically bring it to the attention of others. Beauty in this formulation is a stimulus to collaborative work – it is an invitation to participate.

This slight reworking of Scarry's account of the desire to repeat is directly related to her notion of beauty as a phenomenon that 'fills the mind' (Ibid., p. 29). The argument above that beauty urges an engagement with others is connected to a suggestion from Scarry that an experience of beauty cannot be contained within the person. In many ways the formalist/cognitivist distinction is blurred here as beauty 'breaks all frames' (Ibid., p. 23) or has 'a forward momentum' (Ibid., p. 46) that almost suggests that beauty spills from the object and beyond the body. As we experience beauty intensely as both internal affect and property of an external event or object, the boundaries of the body become unclear. Scarry allows us to think of the incitement of beauty as increasing our sense of interconnectedness, or being-in-the-world, where that desire to repeat is in fact a desire to maintain and share a heightened sense of presence.

In highlighting Scarry's assertion that beauty has an expansive effect, however, the argument also turns to her previous work on pain. If beauty 'fills the mind', pain is 'experienced spatially as either the contraction of the universe down to the immediate vicinity of the body or as the body swelling to fill the entire universe' (1985, p. 35). The repetition here of the word 'fill' indicates a complex interrelation that makes necessary a comparison between pain and beauty – between what will be called, borrowing from previous writing, performances of pain and performances of beauty (Thompson, 2006).

Performances of pain

I have already explained that this chapter is focusing on the 'affect of beauty' as an alternative to the 'aesthetics of injury' that has come to dominate applied theatre and many different forms of radical performance. However, to make the case for an attention to beauty, the nature of those aesthetics, particularly the problematic notion of 'pain', needs to be examined. This next section will start, therefore, with Scarry's account and particularly the idea of pain's lack of referent. This, I believe, connects to how pain can be used and misused in performance. Definitions of pain will be returned to in the final part of the chapter, where a different account, from the anthropologist Veena Das, will be used as an alternative way of conceptualising the link between pain, beauty and ethics.

If Scarry's beauty is expansive, her central argument about pain is that it is constrictive. She anticipates her later work on beauty in the book, *The Body In Pain*, when she gives the following description of pleasure:

> It has tended to be understood as a *bodily* state in which something other than pain is experienced: [it is] the feeling that accompanies the expansive, outward movement into the world [...] it is a condition associated with living beyond the physical body. (Ibid., p. 355)

Pain, on the other hand, reduces the person to the boundary of her or his body so that the world beyond it is lost. Scarry vividly explains this in the simple example of hitting your finger with a hammer. At the moment of the strike, the world is forgotten as the pain swells to occupy the whole of one's body and consciousness. This is then the basis for her argument that pain destroys language, and that, at the moment of its infliction, it cannot be shared:

> Whatever pain achieves, it achieves in part through its unsharability, and it ensures this unsharability through its resistance to language [...] Physical pain does not simply resist language but actively destroys it, bringing about an immediate reversion to a state anterior to language, to sounds and cries a human being makes before language is learned. (Ibid., p. 4)

This argument resonates with the debate in Chapter 2 about how trauma is resistant to language or representation, but it should be emphasised that Scarry is not talking about psychic pain or the failure of representation in any literary sense. The failure is explicit in that at the moment of hitting your finger you tend not to speak (you may scream, of course). This does not mean that pain remains unspoken but only that, where initially beauty might be expansive, pain is, in the first instance, reductive. The contraction, however, once the 'sounds and cries' have died down, can prompt a return to language. Scarry argues that pain 'has no physical voice, but when it at last finds a voice, it begins to tell a story' (Ibid., p. 3). Although, as argued earlier, rather than viewing this process as inevitable, the emphasis should be that, depending on context, pain can either stay with the individual or lead to an urgent need to communicate the experience. Where that urgency does exist, there is a link to beauty, because it too can prompt a form of engagement with others. However, if beauty is specifically connected to things beyond one's body – objects, events and other people – pain is characterised by its lack of objects. Unlike other feelings, it does not refer to something beyond itself. So where jealousy has its lovers, and thirst has its drink, pain may 'begin to tell a story' but the metonymic connection to that story is not automatic. Importantly, both pain and beauty are affective states that cannot be easily resolved or sated. You might want pain to go away and beauty to continue indefinitely but the former will not be straightforwardly accomplished through the availability of an object and the latter does not automatically gain longevity through the attribution of purpose.

The significance for the argument here is that pain's lack of referent means that it is liable to have an object assigned to it. And a similar process emerges in beauty's relation to its sense of importance. When Scarry asserts that 'the human attempt to reverse the de-objectifying work of pain by forcing *pain itself* into avenues of objectification is a project laden with practical and ethical consequence' (Ibid., p. 6. Italics original), it could be argued that giving apparently purposeless beauty intent is a similarly difficult enterprise. What this means for pain is that the sensation can cause a search for objects or symbols that might express the reality of the suffering, but just as easily exploit it. Those objects (stories, people, ideologies) can be given added pathos, legitimacy or validity by their association with the suffering. This is exactly the argument made in relation to the bodies in Murambi (Chapter 3) and it is worth repeating (in full) the quotation from Scarry used in that context:

> At particular moments when there is within a society a crisis of belief – that is, when some central idea or ideology or cultural construct has ceased to elicit a population's belief either because it is manifestly fictitious or because it has for some reason been divested

of ordinary forms of substantiation – the sheer material factualness of the human body will be borrowed to lend that cultural construct the aura of 'realness' and 'certainty'. (Ibid., p. 14)

Although Scarry does suggest elsewhere that pain can be 'brought into the world in such a way that the pain itself is diminished and destroyed' (Ibid., p. 51), it is unclear how we can ensure when objectification is 'borrowed' to give cultural constructs an air of certainty and when it is used to help reduce the suffering of a person or group. One person may view the staging of pain as an attempt to legitimise a contestable political position, while another may view the same event as a profound statement of the suffering of a particular community. The community might feel that pain is diminished in the experience, but they could just as easily feel that their suffering has simply been 'borrowed'. This is the crux of the argument against a sole reliance on a 'theatre of injury'. It may aim to offer an opportunity for people to articulate suffering beyond the moment, to find symbols that take pain out from the boundaries of the body, but this process could also be a process of lending their pain to validate the power of some other.

This argument is relevant to a chapter whose main focus is beauty, because, as hinted above, similarly problematic 'uses' of beauty can be made. It is easy to see how beauty too can be 'borrowed to lend' ideological positions a certain aura. Beauty's search for purpose is, therefore, comparable to pain's search for objects. This would suggest that the performance of beauty is a somewhat poor alternative to my wariness about the easy manipulation of the aesthetics of suffering. If pain searches for objects – and in being attached to them serves to give them 'realness' – can beauty, in searching for purpose, be similarly attached to both noble and vile intentions? The history of the aesthetics of Nazism, as well my experience of performances in more contemporary war zones, suggests that the answer would be an unequivocal 'yes'.

This dilemma frames much of the argument in the rest of this chapter. However, the starting point for countering the inevitability of that 'unequivocal yes' is to examine the different relationship that pain and beauty have to objects. If pain has no immediate referent, beauty has them in abundance – and I mean 'objects' in the broadest sense here to include the literal (flowers, pictures, jewels) as well as people, experiences or processes. The tendency in performance practice, and much therapeutic practice, has been to give pain its objects as a means of giving exterior shape to suffering through which it can be diminished, drawn out of the body or reflected upon. Pain is relocated to an object as something that can stand for it – be it a play, an art piece, or a memorial. A question to ask is: what would happen if, rather than thinking about objectification as creating something that refers to or stands in for the pain, it was understood as a process of providing a place, experience or object of disassociation? Perhaps performances of beauty could be understood not as separate or distant from performances of pain, but as a different starting point – a different way of relating to pain itself. So the beautiful becomes an experience/object that pain is searching for not as a representation, but as a distraction or displacement. There is no claim that the pain is taken from the body, but that the overwhelming nature of pain within the body is given an experience through which the totalising presence of that pain can be equalled by another intense range of sensations. This is not to suggest that the beautiful cures, destroys or heals – but it places 'objects' before pain that can overlay one sensation with another. A person in pain may be pulled from an overwhelming experience in a way that gives respite. Beauty, following Scarry, might tear at the surface of the world of suffering and pull us through to some vaster, non-pained space. Performances of beauty could become a means for overcoming suffering (perhaps momentarily) that does not rely on drawing pain from a body as part of a process of exhibition (and perhaps exploitation). So here 'purposeful' involvement in creating or experiencing what an individual or group themselves define as beautiful provides a layering above, rather than a representation of, the sensation of pain. While this does not end the problem of beauty being located in ends that may be far from positive, it is mitigated by beauty being assigned its purpose in relation to suffering. Beauty might be made to *mean* many things that include the vicious or pernicious (the flower becomes the symbol of the racist group and the beautiful melody the anthem of a tyrant), but an experience of beauty is rarely able to make one *feel* anything but a series of positive sensations[5] – and when these are drawn up alongside (or experienced in the context of) suffering or pain, they can, perhaps, deflect it.

So is beauty good?

It is commonplace in arguments about beauty (particularly following Kant's notion of *disinterest*) to disavow any sense that it has intrinsic moral value. This follows, and can be linked to, Gumbrecht's denial of any positive or transformative potential in a focus on presence or, what I am calling, affect. Although there are some excellent counterblasts, most notably from Winston and his use of Iris Murdoch (1991), the dominant wind blows against beauty having any intrinsic moral value. Shaviro, for example, reworks Kant to assert that beauty 'is as free from any notion of goodness or perfection as it is from any notion of utility' (2002, p. 12) and Armstrong similarly endorses Kant's assertion of the 'independence of beauty from moral and political demands' (2004, p. 61). Kirwan makes this argument particularly firmly and emphasises the point made above about beauty's 'purpose' being decidedly promiscuous. Beauty, for Kirwan, 'holds no more promise of freedom that it does the threat of suppression', and he asserts that 'as value itself beauty is neutral' (1999, p. 80). The purpose of the next section is to make some tentative nudges in the opposite direction: not to argue for beauty's inherent value but that there is an overwhelming potential for the positive. I have already argued that beauty could displace the painful, and this argument is further developed below. Whatever Kirwan may say, I cannot get away from the fact that participating in a theatre process rarely induces in me a sensation that can helpfully be described as *neutral*.

The starting point for answering the question of whether beauty can be called 'good', and whether, then, an attention to beauty in performance has both good intentions and outcomes, is the problematic relation to pain discussed above. Where pain, in overwhelming the body and perhaps spilling outwards in forms of expression, can become symbolised in objects and give them a validity or sense of 'realness', beauty spills beyond the body (and from the object) in provoking a search for something else. This 'something else' – for Scarry a repetition, for Kant a 'look of purposiveness' (Richmond, 2004, p. 80) – is unnamed and therefore can as easily become a commitment to building the Third Reich as a desire to campaign for social justice. The argument above, however, suggests, by bringing a search for beauty into a context of pain, that the 'sensation of goodness' can displace that feeling. The 'something else' is not left to chance – beauty's value or purpose becomes experienced *in relation* to pain. The response to the question 'is beauty good?', then, focuses on beauty's relational or comparative properties.

The sensation of beauty has an intimate relation to the context in which it is experienced[6] and, as with affect more broadly, this is in both the history of the person who meets with that sensation and the social situation in which it takes place. While there is a division in aesthetics between those who argue for a concentration on form (for example, Bell, 1987) and those that assert that beauty must be understood in relation to a particular context (a sociological position exemplified by Wolff, 1988[7]), the point to emphasise here is that, even when giving context its due, there is often an implicit norm that seems to posit the experience of beauty as it is encountered in calm galleries or tranquil English gardens. Accepting that context (and of course, more bluntly, a marketing economy) affects the appreciation of beauty, however, does not prevent theories being constructed from an assumed setting of harmony or peace. Gumbrecht's claim that the beauty of athletic sport has no political intent or moral purpose, for example, universalises his context of appreciation and normalises, and thus ignores, the relation of beauty to its surroundings. Scarry refers to context in a somewhat individualised way, so that beauty in fact stimulates a rapid reflection on both the past experiences of a person and his or her current situation: it prompts what she calls a 'search for precedents and parallels' (1999, p. 30). Armstrong, however, gives a more social version of beauty's comparative urge and his analysis suggests that it is beauty's relationship to the possible ugliness of its context that may be a clue to its power. It is not Scarry's internal workings of the mind but the place of the encounter that is crucial:

> It is not necessarily in the art gallery or in the lecture theatre or even curled up on the sofa with a book that we gain what may be our deepest insights into our need for beauty. Perhaps this is not surprising. For needs are revealed most acutely not when they are satisfied but when we suffer deprivation. (Armstrong, 2004, p. 135)

So beauty is most intense when it is experienced in a place of deprivation, and, more significantly, here we have a sense that beauty reveals, and perhaps fulfils, a need. Far from being valueless, beauty in being positioned within (or against) a site of suffering can be partly involved in heightening our awareness of it. Beauty is not irrelevant to a troubled social context but can be part of its critique. In certain galleries, beauty may feel independent from social concerns, but in other less calm places it gains value through its difference. It actually 'draws upon dissatisfaction' (Ibid., p. 85) and 'makes the ugliness of existence all the harder to bear' (Ibid., p. 85). This is far from neutral in the context of, for example, violence or the suppression of human rights. It is perhaps a source of comparative impulse that can stimulate the critique of 'ugliness' and a desire to create a better world. Beauty is not, therefore, 'merely another nice thing' (Ibid., p. 137) but in *certain* contexts can be experienced as a source of inspiration. In asking a group to create something beautiful, you may be asking them to implicitly critique the situation in which they live. The beauty in Al Rowwad's *beautiful resistance*, therefore, has a force in relation to the context in which they proclaim it. The poppy in a vase in my house is certainly somewhat beautiful, but in the fields in Flanders, at the end of a brutal war, it was beautiful in a startling way because it *compared critically* with the terror of the battles that were fought there.[8]

In turning to beauty, Scarry's argument does not start from a comparative impulse that I believe can be located in the social context of its occurrence. Her premise for beauty's connection to *being just* is linked to a notion of fairness. This concept, however, does ultimately bring beauty into relation with its surroundings and once again can be a source for the argument that beauty can prompt a critical engagement with the world. Scarry argues that the etymological connection between fair–just and fair–beautiful suggests that the properties of beautiful things can be linked to a desire for justice. As I have written elsewhere, for Scarry 'fairness prompts an appreciation of balance and ultimately fairness in personal and social relations' (Thompson, 2006, p. 49). In some ways Scarry's position here appears to repeat formalist accounts of beauty (returning, for example, to Aquinas and Pythagoras) where the symmetry of parts and balance of composition – 'rightness' – were connected to correct behaviour. Scarry's 'fair' can perhaps be replaced by 'right', so that right angle and right action mirror her connection of fair–beautiful and fair–just. However, the connection between the proportions of an object and 'the sense that virtuous actions bring about correctly proportional words' (Eco, 2004, p. 88) takes on a less didactic tone in Scarry so that 'beautiful things give rise to the notion of distribution' or a sense of 'a symmetry of everyone's relations to one another' (1999, p. 95). It is not a justice of the right thing done, but of interrelations. I still have some doubts about the fairness argument, both from an aversion to the implicit colour of justice it suggests (the history of slavery indicates that the fair were far from just) and to a personal knowledge that I have found things wildly out of proportion profoundly beautiful. However, it is perhaps redeemed by its final emphasis on comparison. Scarry argues that in societies where there is no justice, either because the notion is not yet conceived or because it has been withdrawn, beautiful things 'hold steadily visible the manifest good of equality and balance' (Ibid., p. 97). My gloss on this would be that it is not necessarily a vision of equality that is understood but more basically a sensation of goodness: that there is something better than the feelings associated with the absence of justice.

The idea of 'something better' is felt only in the context when beauty is made to compare. Surrounded by what one understands is a good world, beautiful things and processes will perhaps only be analogous to the context in which they occur. They will lack any force or compulsion. Scarry's argument continues with an emphasis on the importance of context and comparison and this strengthens her overall insistence on a connection between beauty and justice:

> When one term ceases to be visible [...] then the analogy ceases to be inert; the term that is present becomes pressing, active, insistent, calling out for, directing our attention toward, what is absent [...] beauty is a call. (Ibid., p. 109)

Beauty is, therefore, a call to what is absent and, following the earlier discussion, we reply with an appeal that is made to others. The idea that beauty prompts us to this communication, to sharing our belief that what we have experienced should be understood universally, is now connected to this additional assertion that beauty, in certain contexts, has a critically comparative edge. The combination of these two strands of the argument brings us to the place where beauty most directly meets questions of ethics.

When the body is called upon to do something, there is immediately a challenge to a sense of individual autonomy. We are no longer the self-organising rational and independent being, but the scope of what we can and cannot, should and should not, do is subject to limiting forces. An argument for non-autonomous subjects (what Critchley calls 'heteronomy', 2007, p. 37) counters the belief that political action is motivated by the realisation of an individual sense of personal freedom, with an alternative view that it is our interrelations, our dependence on others, that is most important. It is the limits of our autonomy, and thus our *limitless* responsibility to others, that I believe should be at the heart of an ethical practice of applied theatre and the starting point for its politics. While this idea will be further developed in the next chapter, the point here is that the experience of beauty is one occasion in which our lack of autonomy can be realised. Beauty might be in the eye of a beholder, but we cannot help feeling that it is beyond us. We do not subjectively move through the world making decisions about what we will and will not find beautiful. We are faced by beauty, sometimes when we least expect it, and we cannot prevent the pleasure it gives. I do not decide to find a moment of a performance beautiful and, therefore, the experience limits my sense of myself as a free, rational subject. Beautiful things, people or events therefore make a call upon us that we cannot help but respond to – and that response is tied to an awareness of the limits of our own autonomy. Beauty's call has a hold on us and, because the call is experienced as true (I do not doubt my belief in the performance's beauty), in sharing our encounter with others, we are making a universal claim to some form of good. Intellectually we may know that beauty is subjective, but, in wanting others to agree with our perspective, we are entering a relation with others that has ethical implications. We are motivated to start a debate about what we understand is good, and in many contexts this will be a comparison with circumstances that are experienced as unjust. We have, therefore, propelled ourselves from a consideration of beauty to the terrain of politics.

The autonomy-limiting call of beauty is, however, also somewhat modest. It is rarely a loud insistence but more often a quiet and intimate claim. It might be the squeeze of a partner's hand to pass on your appreciation of the beauty of a piece of music, the gentle yet infectious applause started by one participant who is particularly moved by an improvised scene, or the young actors' urge to share their joy of performing with their friends. We know that something is beautiful – and therefore make the claim to others – but at the same time we are aware that this claim can never command obedience. Guyer has noted this in his belief that the call of beauty produces recommendations rather than instructions:

> There is a more modest conception of the judgment of taste: while I may not reasonably *command* that you like an object, I can certainly commend it to you [...] To commend something is to perform a speech-act, thus in the realm of practice, and at least in principle subject to the constraints of morality. (Guyer, 2005, p. 340)

Our squeeze, applause or commendation to friends is subject, as Guyer says, 'to standards of responsibility' (Ibid.) and brings us into relation with others in a particular way. We want to share something that we think is good, but we know we cannot insist upon it. The universal claim, which ensures a political engagement with others about 'goodness', has a self-limiting feature because of the paradoxical nature of beauty. This, I would argue, creates a political space that is alive to assertions of what is right, but with the arrogance of righteousness structurally tempered. And this is the political space central to a vision for community-based performance developed in the next chapter.

'Good' as an affective sensation, rather than a rationally formulated programme, can be a vital counterpoint to a situation of pain and suffering, and therefore the compulsion provoked by beauty can become a compulsion to overcome the suffering of another (or at least offer them a place apart from it). While this may start as a political engagement between one person and another, based on beauty making us aware of the limits of our personal autonomy, it would be wrong only to conceive of this as a simple dialogue. It is, of course, more properly a plurality of commendations. Objects are encountered across groups and beautiful events are often experienced in large numbers – and in applied theatre projects deliberately so. Guyer notes that 'shared pleasure in an object' is 'commendable precisely because of the additional bonds of sociability it creates within a particular community' (Ibid., p. 344) and he, therefore, provides a positive description of this extended process. I would shift emphasis, however, and argue that the creation of those 'bonds of sociability' is in fact an exercise in *the intimate politics of sharing the affect of the beautiful* and an opportunity for fostering a powerful protection from, and perhaps alternative to, suffering. When Spivey writes that 'art keeps us going in our wounded state' (2001, p. 19) or Scarry argues that beauty is 'life saving' (1999, p. 24), I believe that, while the individual sense of being taken beyond our bodies is important, it is the engagement with others that provides the ballast to this affect. Beauty may make 'life more vivid, animated, living, worth living' (Ibid., p. 25) but this is a call towards engagement in a process that must be comparative and relational: beauty is better than something else, and I want you to believe me (and I accept your life history might make you disagree).

The argument that beauty is a call, and Spivey's use of the word 'wound' when discussing art more generally, return us to theories of pain but in a slightly different manner. A case has already been made for how performances of beauty might support a form of disassociation from pain and how they, therefore, offer an alternative to an automatic resort to an 'aesthetics of injury' in 'theatre for social change'. However, there is another aspect of pain, drawing on the work of Das, that is important to consider because it connects to the limits of autonomy discussed here. For Das, pain does not destroy language, in the way conceived by Scarry, but instead makes a claim for acknowledgement (1997, p. 70). The phrase 'I am in pain' is another form of call that, even if denied by the person to whom it is addressed, forms an ethical claim upon them. Even when there is not the literal statement, the vision of the pain of the other makes a demand on us; it 'touches us viscerally' (Bennett, 2005, p. 48) and makes an appeal that has ethical implications. This is another form of 'affective invitation' to act where, according to Das, 'denial of the other's pain is not about the failings of the intellect but the failings of the spirit' (1997, p. 88). It is a call made not in a cognitive but in an affective register. So, if both beauty and pain make this call, why the emphasis here on beauty as a source for political engagement rather than the call made by 'I am in pain'?

First, it is important to emphasise that the argument in this chapter is not a rejection of one process in favour of another. I am seeking to offer an alternative to a *default* preference for a 'theatre of injury' rather than a wholesale replacement of it. That said, many performance processes that start from the pain, suffering or oppression of a community do not conceive this as premised on a call to the observer for an ethical response – or a call to action. Rather, it is framed within a commitment to individual autonomy, so what is staged is said to permit a form of self-realisation. Revealing pain becomes about one's right to self-represent and be relieved of suffering, with the audience being free to accept or witness that event as equal partners in the process. My emphasis on the *call* is that, in fact, we are not equal – our autonomy is restricted in this process and the call of beauty or pain limits our subjectivity. Das's 'failure of the spirit' is in fact a failure to recognise how watching the pain of others compels us to act and binds us to them. Radical performance might therefore choose to work from pain, but I would hope that this is understood as a call for an interrelationship between people – where we become aware of the limitations of our sovereignty. My proposal for working from beauty, however, aims to provide scope for a similar interrelation, but, I would argue, particularly in contexts of suffering or violence, it provides a safer route through. Beauty can overlay pain or stimulate a critique of it, but in the process profound pleasure or delight is experienced. Maybe in the calm and peace of certain situations, urging an engagement with suffering of others can be an overt and explicitly performed process, but in a diverse range of more troubled contexts – contexts in which, I believe, applied theatre should be working – performances of beauty might be ultimately more rewarding.

Limiting the ephemeral

The argument that the call of beauty places a limit on our subjectivity – I cannot stop finding that moment beautiful of my own volition – provides, finally, an opening for a debate about the notion that performance is an ephemeral practice. In a very literal sense, of course, performance is ephemeral. It does last a short time, disappear once it is over and then our critical work starts as a response 'to the loss of the object' (Phelan, 1997, p. 3). However, the concept of beauty and the notion of affect suggest that assertions of ephemerality may deny as much as they reveal. The argument of this chapter is that the beautiful object is both over there, on stage, and also experienced within – and, because of the compulsion to share, *between* people. Beauty is in my eye, coursing through my body, and in front of me. Affects can start from outside a person, but they are real sensations – we blink, sweat and cry. They cannot be easily compartmentalised between cause-objects and effect-objects, but instead shift back and forth across moments of experience. Performance is, therefore, only ephemeral if you believe that bodies on stage are radically separate from those watching: once they have gone, they have gone. A consideration of performance affects, and the attention to beauty developed here, suggests otherwise.

The notion of non-autonomy and affect refigures the performance event as a moment within and between the bodies of the beholders, the actors and participants so that the 'it' of the experience is not solely located in a physical presence on stage or in the workshop room. The event does not pass or finish that easily because it is not only a time-bound phenomenon. Affects last beyond the event and, to repeat a term I have used before, they can *linger* (Thompson, 2005, p. 235). The term 'lingering' implies that affect does not have to happen at the moment of the performance but can either be sustained beyond it or occur at a different time. Guyer confirms this in his discussion of pleasure, where the feeling 'need not be synchronous with the activity that produces it – it may linger on after our encounter with the object is over' (2005, p. 331). This echoes Dolan's desire to discover 'utopian performances' that 'rather than ending with the curtain call [...] ripple out into other forms of social relations' (2005, p. 34). Affects, and particularly the sensations associated with beauty, do not, therefore, disappear once the object is withdrawn. The quality of the experience is not only reliant on, or reducible to, the presence of the actors on stage. Anyone who has met the joy of young people off-stage, after finishing a play, must know that their effervescence is real in the moment and no less intense because the object, their on-stage performance, has passed. The play is not there anymore but the force of affect continues dynamically – and dismissing performance as ephemeral in this context seems to disparage these children's delight.

Giving affect 'serious attention', therefore, intentionally extends the range of a performance event. Something is only ephemeral if we agree to an autonomous version of subjectivity with participants and audience members independent and separate. The version of beauty developed here, and affects more generally, disrupt this – they insist that the performance is happening between people, and can remain with them, sometimes long after the moment. Affects linger, stretching performance across time and space, in a way that assertions of ephemerality seem to miss. The practice of performance, and a search for its *ends* (particularly where it makes a claim to be a 'theatre for social change'), must track the contours of that extended reach: a contour, of course, shaped according to the histories, geographies and differences in culture, gender, sexuality or disability of participants. Performance affects continue to happen – to linger – and we should be focusing on the shape and intensity of that sensation in our planning, execution and analysis of what is necessarily an elongated performance moment. This means mapping a potentially larger political terrain, which escapes the black box and presents expanded and complex questions for a broader ethics and politics of applied theatre practice – a discussion that is taken up in detail in Chapter 6.

Conclusion: Beholder bias

It is perhaps unsurprising that the majority of accounts of beauty concentrate on those who see, witness or confront beauty. Art historians, theorists and audiences tend to write more than the artists themselves. When Armstrong asks for an 'account of beauty that takes the beholder seriously' (2004, p. 79), he demonstrates his failure to pay similar attention to the person who makes the beautiful. Some of the problems with beauty discussed in this chapter come from this *beholder bias* and a failure to take the perspective of the maker seriously. The assumptions of ephemerality are most devoutly uttered by performance critics, and are less frequent in the discourse of actors who hold a performance within them for many months both before and after that small moment of the 'performance event'. The relational and comparative potential of beauty is similarly known acutely by the artist who has to touch the clay or hone the melody. The danger of the beautiful being 'borrowed to lend' legitimacy to dubious ideologies is less noteworthy if we are considering beauty from a creating/experiencing rather than an observing/ experiencing standpoint. The process might be a struggle, but the person or group confronted with the challenge of making something beautiful are debating personally or between themselves the structure of joy and pleasure. They are working to create something that they will unequivocally feel is good. Of course, the sense of making something greater than themselves might inspire them to move in unpredictable directions, but the sensation will be a positive alternative in the first instance. And, where the beholder might invent purpose from a beauty that appears without purpose, a maker or a participant has his or her own sense of purpose welded to the action of creating the object or event from the outset.

A shift from beholder bias to an emphasis on the maker is, of course, another way of advocating a turn away from a view of art making as something done by others. Applied theatre is less about beholders and more about participants co-creating work, from their own desires, delights or inspiration. In certain circumstances this might be from a sense of pain or anger, but here an alternative has been suggested that starts from an invitation to create something that is understood by the makers to be beautiful – something a group might hope to share with others, be they audience members or other participants. This is a process that can allow people to displace the worst aspects of their lives in a moment of joy but that can also encourage a critical disposition to an unequal or unjust world. The work of creating the beautiful engages participants in a debate about what is good, and presents a place where the truth of that position is gently asserted. In this process all involved become political actors – making claims for new, better, more beautiful worlds that they want to linger as an ongoing inspiration for social change. Affect, and emblematic beauty, become a political force – and the shape and aspiration of that politics are the subject of the final chapter.

6
About Face: Disturbing the Fabric of the Sensible

> The dream of a suitable political work of art is in fact the dream of disrupting the relationship between the visible, the sayable, and the thinkable without having to use the terms of a message as a vehicle.
>
> (Rancière, 2004, p. 63)

> By the time of the landing in France – June 6, 1944 – photographs of anonymous American casualties had appeared in a number of newsmagazines, always prone or shrouded or with their faces turned away.
>
> (Sontag, 2003, p. 63)

> Right or wrong, reading the face was here to stay as a type of irreducible folk wisdom of popular culture.
>
> (Taussig, 1999, p. 230)

Part II has attempted to offer both broad and specific approaches to applied theatre that emerge in response to the different ends of effect proposed in Part I. A particular priority for the argument has been to explore the potential political grounds for a community-based and participatory performance practice that, while working often in small, private settings, understands and connects with wider *public* actions. The intimacy of that hidden moment, however, was not to be forfeited in favour of a stronger avowal of more visible practice, but rather the care exhibited in those settings becomes linked to a particular ethics, and in turn politics, of applied theatre. A politics that, I believe, is in danger of being lost in the eagerness to apply performance *at the service* of the various institutional, social and discursive regimes that surround and contain the communities in which the practice takes place. The notions of affect and beauty, outlined in the previous two chapters, started to suggest a sensate and aesthetic focus that, I argued, can be linked to notions of social justice. The discussion here will open with an account of ethics that in turn will be connected both to this concern with affect and subsequently to a particular political aspiration for applied theatre. The debate will draw at first on Levinas's notion of the *face*, borrowing from discussions of the term in Butler and Critchley, and subsequently suggest how an account of the face-to-face encounter within performance can draw from these arguments. The call of the face, much like the call of beauty, becomes a further motivational force in this account. The structure of the performance encounter will then be taken as a starting point for an ethical and radical politics of practice that intervenes in what Rancière has called the 'distribution of the sensible' (2004, p. 7).

Facing the other

The face has become particularly controversial in relation to recent world conflicts, with the images of prisoners, 'terrorists', veiled women and war-dead occupying prime positions in different media. Although 'turning the face' is discussed in Sontag's work on early war photography, more recent articles on the hidden face of Afghani women (Whitlock, 2005), the lip-sewn faces of Australia's refugees (Pugliese, 2002) or newspaper images of the faces of the Bali bombers (Philpott, 2005) have brought the problems associated with seeing the face to a new form of critical attention.[1] While acknowledging the arguments in these articles, this chapter returns to an earlier concept of the *face* from Emmanuel Levinas, presented in detail in his book *Totality and Infinity* (1969, pp. 194–219) but also developed across his philosophical work, to explore how meeting the face of the other can be the source of a particular ethics and politics of practice.

The face, for Levinas, is used both literally as the face of the other and more conceptually as a term for the limit of our ability to know the other. In the face of a person, we see something of who they are and yet we are also made aware that they are not fully knowable. Appignanesi and Baum refer to this as a vision of the face that is 'bewildering, beyond anything we or the philosophers can pin down, explain, understand' (2006, p. 92), linking the concept to the arguments in previous chapters for the importance of *difficultness* and my earlier concern for *bewilderment*.

Levinas himself explains the face in terms of resistance:

> The face resists possession, resists my powers. In its epiphany, in expression, the sensible, the graspable, turns into total resistance to the grasp. (Levinas, 1969, p. 197)

The epiphany becomes the realisation that our 'grasp' is inevitably limited: a sense that Levinas argues is 'not a reasoning' but an '*en-ergy* [*sic*] in the vision of the face' (Ibid., p. 196. Italics original). Already hinted here is that the face can be conceived of as having a force that operates at the level of affect, and one that suggests, or makes us feel, the restriction of our capacity for understanding. The depth of our unknowing (Levinas's *infinity*), however, makes us uniquely beholden to that other: it acts as a 'moral summons' (Ibid., p. 196). For Levinas, the resistance 'does not do violence to me, does not act negatively; it has a positive structure: ethical' (Ibid., p. 197). This structure, I would argue, has a similar shape to that proposed in the discussion of beauty. The face makes a summons – a call – that urges us not to do harm to that person whom we recognise as human like us but cannot fully understand. The humanness we acknowledge in that specific meeting, then, has universal significance. In arguing that we cannot hurt the other, we simultaneously assert that we can harm no other: by saying 'I cannot kill you', we announce, 'thou shalt not kill'. There is a generic ethical commitment in the intimacy of the one-to-one encounter that Reynolds refers to as 'the paradox of responsible behaviour' (2001, p. 33), and, I believe, is one key in a search for what might motivate responsible action.

The ethics proposed in the concept of the face is not one deduced by inquiry – it is not 'the conclusion of an argument or the product of rational deliberation' (Perpich, 2005, p. 115). It is instead prior to consciousness, in the sense that it is the result of the experience of being confronted by the presence of another. It is the felt relationship of coexistence, which, while visible in what Levinas calls the 'contours of its form in expression' (Levinas, 1969, p. 197), is also the experience of being with others who are 'in society with us' (Perpich, 2005, p. 108). It is, therefore, intimately connected to the encounters we have, but does not necessarily become constituted in the actual moment of looking between the eyes of another person. The face of Levinas, for the argument I am making here, is the acute awareness of the body of the other as it impinges on our sense of self. It is the feelings that flow between people as they share space: sensations that exist in one body as a result of the care (or animosity) it feels for the other. And the unfathomable aspect of a person (and of that feeling) multiplies the depths of the responsibility I have towards him or her – and makes that responsibility, almost overwhelmingly, infinite.

An alternative to Levinas's vision of the face can be located in the 'science' of physiognomy. In many ways, if Levinas's concept works within what Gumbrecht would call a culture of presence effects, physiognomy is the classic disposition to the face within a culture dominated by meaning effects. Levinas's face belongs within horizontal research practices and physiognomy within vertical: it seeks to read what is hidden beneath the skin. This is touched upon here as it relates to theatre and performance practice, and a certain scepticism to the other common in everyday life that might temper the claims for the face's automatic 'affect' (discussed in detail below). Taussig has referred to 'physiognomic prejudice' that sees the face both as a mask or a 'window on the soul', so that the viewer encounters it either as a dishonest obscuring or as a transparent revelation of a true nature (Taussig, 1999, pp. 224–31). Either way the observer is given the power to know the other as a means of affirming or denying his or her 'truth'. This is, of course, an ethics – but one based on a relationship of power to define or disregard others. Taussig takes this as an explicitly artistic process, so that the 'physiognomic prejudice' is

> now honed to ever greater skills by the arts of cinema making *and viewing*, these everyday arts of reading the face, of defining the human, the inner being, not to mention the insalubrious arts of making through such reading racial and gendered types and subtypes, in short, the great cast of characters stalking the human stage in modern times. (Ibid., p. 231)

I would argue that this prejudice is very apparent in forms of performance or theatre, where participants, facilitators or audience members engage with others as an opportunity to see behind their faces in such a way that they are understood as evidence of some inner condition. We diagnose a history, a need or vulnerability from the wrinkles on a forehead, from the depth of a frown or the crease of a smile. Similarly, the engagement is premised on doubting the person, whether actor or collaborator, and assuming that he or she is merely presenting a mask to his or her true self. The metaphors of theatrical processes, where 'the mask slips' or someone 'puts up a front', where the stage character reveals or hides something of the actor, all hint at a tendency to physiognomy. While these acts of interpretation, at their best, can be dispersed across a group of participants, they are too often located in the 'seeing powers' of an audience, facilitator or director (or, for that matter, psychoanalyst). Although the tendency to read the face is hard to avoid, the argument here is that this approach fails to acknowledge the presence of the face, and, therefore, the possibility of forming an ethics of practice on a more egalitarian basis. A popular hermeneutic response within the arts cannot be simply switched off, but the less remarked affect or touch of the face should be encouraged as an important starting point for the ethics of participatory arts. What this suggests, and this is significant for the discussion that follows, is that the call of the face in Levinasian terms is not necessarily experienced automatically. I accept that the face of the other makes me 'infinitely responsible' to them, but the aside here on Taussig's 'physiognomic prejudice' reminds us that what commentators might highlight as a preconscious given of our relationship to the other might not always meet with approval: we may not always experience that epiphany, and may instead insist on reading behind the lines.

Before expanding on this challenge to Levinas's concept, it is important to explore the connection between the 'call of beauty' and the demands made by the face in more detail. This will lead to a further discussion of whether the face has automatic or inevitable *affect* below. As mentioned in the previous chapter, Critchley uses the term 'heteronomy' to argue for a form of subjectivity that is non-autonomous. Politics, following this perspective, is not a process of making the individual free or of increasing our ability to act unencumbered by the restrictions imposed by external forces. It is, instead, a process of recognising our direct and felt responsibility to those amongst whom we live. Where beauty helped us recognise that there are times when our autonomy is curtailed by an external demand we cannot refuse, the face is presented as a similarly restricting moment:

> It is this incomprehensibility in ethics that interests me, where the subject is faced with a demand that does not correspond to its autonomy: in this situation, I am not the equal of the demand on me [...] ethics is obliged to acknowledge a moment of rebellious heteronomy that troubles the sovereignty of autonomy. (Critchley, 2007, p. 37)

The relationship between the two people, in this account, should not be understood as equal – or as a movement towards equality. It can be symmetrical only if someone has the power to stand outside and see it from above (Ibid., pp. 59–60). Within the moment, it has to be unbalanced or asymmetrical as you feel the infinite demand of the other constraining you. Our autonomy is challenged and limited as we are confronted with an individual ethical appeal that is transformed into a universal demand as it is made. The face of a homeless person not only asks that we respond, but makes a claim that people should not have to live on the street. We may pass by, but we know that a claim for individual and general ethical behaviour has been made – and we cannot possibly fulfil it in its entirety. In experiencing that claim, I do not feel an equal and opposite claim that the homeless person should be beholden to me. In a similar fashion, the asylum seeker who presents you with their threat of deportation is simultaneously making a claim for personal support and about the general unfairness of the immigration system. We cannot affirm the former without implicitly asserting the latter, and, therefore, we are implored to respond, but that response can never be sufficient. Our autonomy is not only troubled, it is curtailed because in meeting the homeless person or the asylum seeker we do not choose to be affected. Their encounters with us, their respective faces, make demands that we cannot help feeling. This alters the ground of the relationship between people to a point where the asymmetrical affect of the other becomes a motivating force: a force that is a major propellant for political action because it has this implicit universal assertion structured into it. Seeing the face of the homeless person asks me to campaign against homelessness and a personal connection to an asylum seeker fuels a commitment to resisting the injustices of the UK's immigration laws.

Paradoxically, the extremity of the demand is also central to its energising nature. Critchley refers to this as an 'ethics of heteronomy' that is 'articulated through the *hetero-affectivity* of an unfulfillable, one-sided and radical demand' (2007, p. 56), so that the enormity of the request felt in the simple meeting propels one forward into an attempt to fulfil that impossibility. Butler expands this so that we become 'open to narration that decenters us from our supremacy, in both its right – and left-wing forms' (2004, p. 18), giving a specifically political character to the somewhat jargonistic 'hetero-affectivity'. We are no longer the physiognomist here, but a person who is open to an ethical call to action, which is not premised on our ultimate authority. This is the starting point for a politics that has an inbuilt ethics of humility, where we are 'implicated in lives that are not our own' (Ibid., p. 28).

Political affects

The face-to-face encounter, as explained here, provides a motivation for ethical behaviour that now needs to be more firmly connected to its political implications. Critchley posits this encounter as a 'meta-political ethical moment' that is 'at the heart of a radical politics' and for the argument to proceed it is important to discover the shape of that moment (2007, p. 119). This will be done by exploring Butler's notion of bringing faces to the public, by a consideration of the problematic concept of 'approval', and finally by suggesting that the overwhelming nature of the political demands of the face can be made bearable by a reiteration of the arguments for a focus on the beautiful.

Although the premise of Levinas's argument is that the face makes the demand as a preconscious auto-affect that is an inevitable result of the relationship between the self and the other, it is important to question again whether this force is definite or desired. Is Levinas making a case for ethics based on what should be, or simply on what is? I would argue that Critchley's account of the 'meta-political' indicates that he believes it is the latter: that there is something inherent in an encounter with the other than ensures we are dynamically responsible to them. Although, as will be discussed below, it is important to question his reliance for this position on the idea of 'approval', the account of the physiognomic disposition above indicates that I tend to the former (that we need to explore the notion of the ethics proposed here as a *what should be*). This perspective can be further illustrated using Butler's idea of the distribution of *grievable* faces (Butler, 2004).

While the reader might concur that the vision of the suffering of another catches them and forces them to act, or even feel guilty for not acting (which is still an example of heteronomy), I believe that it is harder to insist that this is an inevitable or universal response. Where the work of Butler helps is that she suggests an economy of the face, whereby the visibility of certain faces marks out an acutely political terrain of the acceptance or dismissal of particular groups. The distribution of the face, and which face can make claims – and ultimately which person can be mourned or grieved – demonstrates certain constructions of who is worthy within any specific community. The presence of a face, or an image of a face, does not ensure that it is understood as human but can just as easily mark out its 'defacement' (Taussig, 1999). Butler, therefore, creates an urgent task, which is the acceptance of various faces that have had their humanity reduced by contemporary cultural frames that designate certain people as less than human. Levinas's ethic of the face is not a given, but understood as 'useful for those cultural analyses that seek to understand how best to admit the "faces" of those against whom war is waged into public representation' (2004, p. xviii). What she is proposing is a question of both quality and form.

The use of the human face – for example, in mug shots, wanted posters or 'face of evil' tabloid exposés – 'effaces' its potential to be the source of an acknowledgement of the precariousness of the other. The face becomes mediated in such a way that the *quality* of an affective encounter is replaced with an image that stands in for a preordained limit to its humanity. Similarly, she urges that 'certain faces must be admitted into public view, must be seen and heard for some keener sense of the value of life, all life, to take hold' (Ibid.), suggesting a political project to ensure not only an intensity in the quality of engagement, but also that new *forms* of the face are part of a public realm: new *people* become present, participate and are valued. This, I believe, demands a particular type of meeting with the face and, while Butler presents this as a process whereby 'dominant forms of representation can and must be disrupted' (Ibid.), she does less to articulate the shape of that disruption. My suggestion is that it might be constructed through a careful mediation of the encounter with an image, but it is most *affectively* done in the face-to-face encounter. The political project of 'admitting' faces suggested by Butler is potentially located within a series of interpersonal engagements. When Critchley argues that 'resistance can be intimate and can begin in small affinity groups' (2007, p. 114), I would emphasise that it is in this space that the demand of the face *is more likely* to be felt. And, of course, this is the firm ground on which participatory performance operates.

As an alternative, therefore, to the idea that the face provides a given or automatic call, this suggests that there is a way of conceiving of the concept as a willed part of a process or project. The importance of this shift, from the inevitable to the planned, is also demonstrated through the problematic notion of *approval*. Critchley asserts that the demand of the face 'is only felt *as* a demand for the self who approves of it' (2007, p. 18. Italics original) but then proceeds to construct a general theory to overcome 'indifference' to suffering from what I am arguing is not the universal result of seeing the face of the other (Ibid., p. 25). Ethical experience requires a subject who in meeting a face is affected by 'the approved demand of its good' (Ibid., p. 23), but there is little understanding as to how that approval will be generated. Again, there is an assumption that this is inherent in the structure of the meeting rather than simply desired. Critchley sums up his political position in the following, interestingly borrowing heavily on Butler:

It is this meta-political moment that propels one into facing and facing down a wrong or confronting a situation of injustice, not through sovereign legal norms backed up with the threat of violence, but through an ethical responsiveness to the sheer precariousness of the other's face, of their injurability and our own. An ethical politics flows from our constitutive powerlessness in the face of the other. (Ibid., p. 120)

While I admire the intention here, there appears to be little aware-ness of the possibility that we may not feel that powerlessness – and the 'flow', therefore, might become blocked. The political project in this account becomes how to maintain the motivation of those who approve of the demand, rather than discover means for ensur-ing approval. Many, however, to use a theological metaphor, walk on the other side of the road with no sense of connection to the person they pass. Unfortunately, in a cruel, super-individualised world, rather than the conscience nagging 'you must really go over and help', it may in fact think 'what a loser'. The distribution of encounters with the face happens within a social framework that may permit you to see the precariousness of others' lives but not necessarily feel impinged by them. We live in a time where a glance into the face of the other can lead to a mocking disregard more quickly than deep appreciation. So while *one might approve* of the demand of the other, there needs to be a process for encouraging that approval. The 'meta-political ethical moment' needs, therefore, to be reinterpreted as a contested rather than inevitable experience. The concept of the face allows us to develop an understanding of the structure of its ethical call and the demands that it is *ideally* seeking to make – but this is an ideal for which we need to work.

It is here that the starting point for a connection with a participatory performance practice can be made. In a project we do not say 'look into the face of the other', but sit beside people who are both similar and different from you and feel them as real people who have needs that act affectively upon you. Shifting from disregard to limitless regard requires a movement over time where the defacing effect of contem-porary culture becomes transformed into the vision of fundamental responsibility hoped for in the work of Levinas. And this is a process that requires close collaboration and is central to the argument for the politics of performance made here. The 'affect' of co-creating theatre (or other arts) could, therefore, be one means of moving people from an 'anaesthetised' (Rockhill, 2004, p. 1) reaction to the face of the other to feeling the demands that those faces make upon them: it could become the means of creating *approval*.

Becoming 'sensitised' (*aesthetised*) to the other through a collaborative, artistic process could be based on a gradual recognition of the suffering of another and, in turn, appreciating the precariousness of her or
his, and your own, life. In Butler's terms, in her discussion of contemporary wars, this is a process of disrupting a context in which only certain lives are deemed worthy of mourning. The face becomes a marker
to suggest that our own humanity is diminished by designating some
lives to be of less value than others, or less important than our own.
This is a resource for a radical politics because, once we refuse to accept
a particular designation of the worthy and non-worthy, we can only, for
example, resist wars (which are constructed around ideas of who can
be killed and cannot be mourned) or campaign against poverty (which
insists the famine within one community has no bearing on the health
of another). The small act of accepting that another person makes an
ethical demand, as outlined above, extends to a universal. This is, to
quote Žižek in his discussion of Israeli Defence Force members who refuse to serve in the Occupied Territories, 'the miraculous moment in
which eternal Justice momentarily appears in the temporary sphere of
empirical reality' (2002, p. 116).[2] The applied theatre practitioner, in
working in a prison with inmates John and Jane, must simultaneously
be making the claim that all prisoners deserve, at minimum, humane
treatment. The artist working on a project with disabled colleagues
must be making a statement about the rights of all disabled people. The
particular is not particular if the work seeks to encourage an acceptance
of the notion of the face proposed by Levinas.

One of the problems of the leap from the intimate to the inordinate is
that responsibility can overwhelm. By insisting that the particular call
of the face can be experienced as infinite and ultimately as universal, it
is easy to see how the subject of that demand can be weighed down by
it. We might work with some street children in a short-lived project but
the experience is *felt* as a demand that all children should have the right
to a decent place to live. It is almost structurally impossible to work
in that context and not believe the universality of this claim.[3] This
belief, however, in its enormity, might lead to a sense of powerlessness.
Our work feels like a 'drop in the ocean' and our response is doomed
to be experienced as forever inadequate. Critchley notes this explicitly
when he asks, 'how can the extremity of the ethical picture I have
described be borne without crushing the ethical subject?' (2007, p. 69).
His account, however, responds by advocating our inevitable failure 'to
fulfil the radicality of the ethical demand' not as the source of 'dejec-
tion or disaffection' but 'as the condition for courage in ethical action'

(Ibid., p. 55). The very tension between the specifics of the moment, and the universality of the claim that it makes, sparks the motivation to continue to campaign for social justice.

Even with that spark, however, the 'crush' of felt responsibility can remain, and this is where this vision of an ethical demand connects with the previous arguments about beauty. By working with those street children, I will struggle not to believe strongly in a much broader demand for children's rights, and it is a common result of many projects that participants and facilitators articulate an energetic enthusiasm for and commitment to *something beyond* the immediate concerns of the particular initiative. In a context of extreme suffering, and where the thematic material for the project has drawn from those conditions, it is easy to understand how that enthusiasm can quickly shift to despondency. Critchley's answer is to suggest an 'aesthetic reparation' where the subject of the demand avoids being destroyed by it through submitting himself or herself to self-deprecating humour (Ibid., p. 69). The aesthetic for Critchley provides a screen that avoids the 'direct glare' (Ibid., p. 74) of responsibility, and allows us to hold onto our commitment. It is maintained through a gentle mocking of our own failures and provides a resource that ensures we are not crushed by our limits. It is easy from this perspective to see where his admiration of the carnivalesque anti-globalisation protests emerges. The frustration of the size of the political task becomes channelled into a joyous, mocking humour – and this stimulates ongoing commitment to what might otherwise seem an impossible, and perhaps demotivating, task.

For the participatory or community-based arts, however, this model is not sufficient. Although protecting the enthusiasm of facilitators by ensuring that they are trained to mock their own ambitions with gentle humour is certainly welcome, the overall stimulus to political action across a group of participants is also in danger of being overwhelming. I would argue that it is not in humour, but the previous debate about beauty, that secures a more rewarding screen from the 'direct glare'. This can be understood in two slightly different ways. First, the place of beauty can be within the boundaries of a project itself. It may be that, appropriately, the focus for participants is painful issues in their lives or broader issues of oppression within their community. In this case, attention to delight, beauty or joy, as an integrated or preparatory aspect of the work, can actually awaken individuals to each other's needs and perspectives. As suggested earlier, it is conceivable that the call of the face is far from automatic, and openness to its affect might be as much aspiration as precondition. Attention to beauty – to aspects of play, dance, or joy – could be the act of creating an intense 'meta-political' moment that prepares people for recognising the face of the other as an appeal that they cannot refuse. Beauty creates both the capacity for being affected (it 'aesthetises') and an openness to a call from beyond one's body, but it does so within an framework of pleasure and therefore the feeling of responsibility is less likely to overwhelm. Delight experienced within this broader process might temper despair at the size of the political task and, therefore, energetic commitment for tackling a problem can be propelled and sustained.

Second, in a context of great suffering, the project itself can be understood as the 'screen'. The pain beyond the immediate vicinity of the performance project might already make huge, perhaps debilitating demands on the participants. In this situation, a project that focuses on pleasure or celebration might be protective. Attention to beauty might distract or provide a respite, but here it is conceived as providing the means for infinite responsibility to be borne in such a way that a struggle for an end to suffering can continue. Critchley's self-deprecating individual who says 'I can bear the radicality of the ethical demand because I can laugh at myself' (Ibid., p. 86) becomes the group or community who bear the trouble of their situation because they have the capacity to dance, sing and enjoy themselves (an echo of Ehrenreich's 'kind of triumph'). The struggle for beauty is the struggle for the resource not to be crushed by the injustice of troubled lives. Although, as suggested in the previous chapter, in certain contexts the 'glare' might not be sufficiently strong to require the protection of the beautiful, in many beauty could, to repeat the words of Scarry, be life-saving: hedonism, once again, might just be that bunker.

Face to face in performance

The use of the term 'face', while shifting between the actual eyes, noses and mouths of others and the conceptual impenetrability of those others, takes literal form in many examples of performance. It is important to consider this briefly before ending with a broader argument to link the ethics of the face with a politics of intervention in Rancière's 'distribution of the sensible'. Being faced with an actor on stage, a co-participant in an improvisation or a survivor in a testimonial performance, a person can be attuned to responding in particular ways. It is clear from previous arguments that I would see this encounter as one where the communication of information is often valorised above the shared sensation of affect. The point here is to emphasise that, even considering the moment as affective, there is a danger of transforming the face-to-face encounter into one with an imperative structure. This links specifically back to the notion of the 'imperative to tell' in Chapter 2, where the observer of the performance becomes a witness to the necessary revelation of the other. The popular terms for dealing with suffering hint at this compulsion, and connect this argument explicitly to the face (for example, we are told we must 'face up to our responsibilities' or 'face our troubles'). The face within these terms is given an authority that is disciplinary and revelatory. Within this model the performance becomes a means to tell the truth or 'infect' others with it, in a way that Leys makes explicit in the following:

> The basic model for that transmission is the face-to-face encounter between a victim, who enacts or performs his or her traumatic experience, and a witness who listens and is in turn contaminated by the catastrophe. (2000, p. 284)

This is an account of the face that this chapter has sought to argue against. I would contend that the word trauma here should be replaced with affect, and, as has already been argued, that its transmission is poorly explained within a model of contagion because it fails to recognise that the sensation is transformed in the relationship that emerges between people in performance. While I do not accept that personal hurt is transmitted in this way in the first place, the idea of performance as infection is a dubious basis for a radical 'social change' orientated practice. Rather than 'I feel your pain', the model I would suggest is 'I accept the feeling of responsibility you provoke in me'. In addition, to argue that the presentation of a person on stage reveals something of the performer's *true nature* once again returns us to the audience as physiognomist. I would argue that coming face to face with others in performance is a moment of shared affect – the presence of the other produces a range of affects within me – and this instigation of a relationship between people makes ethical demands, without necessarily revealing 'truth'. Faced with someone on stage, I am urged to recognise their presence as a call to respect their humanity, rather than sit in judgement on the accuracy or integrity of their story. The face – in the terms I am using it – must, therefore, paradoxically include the right to turn away, to avert the eyes and refuse the interrogatory gaze of the 'witness'. If the dead had their faces turned away in the photographs described by Sontag, the argument here is that the living must have the same right. The face as a concept delineating the contours of an ethical meeting must permit the literal face not to show itself. This is a repeat of the earlier assertion that the audience and fellow participants in applied theatre projects operate an ethics of being *beside* the person – and that people have the right not to tell or 'face up to' a story. Two people might, in fact, be looking forward, in the same direction but not eye-to-eye, while still being physically aware of the demands made by 'approving of' the other's presence. Face-to-face is also, therefore, side-by-side.

The fabric of the sensible

In the argument so far a person's encounter with the face of the other is understood to be the source of inspiration for both a responsibility for that other and also an infinite responsibility to campaign for social justice. The face, then, becomes another emblematic concept in performance affects, drawing people to a form of ethical engagement with each other and their wider worlds.[4] However, in asserting that the ethical encounter stimulates political action, the shape of the political terrain needs to be elaborated in more detail. While I am comfortable with the assertion that 'politics is an ethical practice that arises in a situation of injustice which exerts a demand for responsibility' (Critchley, 2007, p. 92), this does not explain the relationship between that initial response and the political field in sufficient detail. The question remains: how does an awareness of the struggles of those street children transform into political action? Critchley provides a half-answer in his belief that the intimacy of work in small groups can be drawn together, 'weaving cells of resistance' (Ibid., p. 114) so they are combined in a broader political project. This, in turn, leads to an enthusiasm for what he calls the contemporary anarchism of street theatres, carnival-style protest and other acts of civil disobedience. To a certain extent, his is a perfect model for the questions raised in Chapter 1 concerning the necessary interrelation of the small-scale private 'tactical' practice of applied theatre and more public acts of radical performance. While I would endorse this enthusiasm, and believe there are vital links in artistry and politics between applied theatre and these movements, this cannot be the only location of practice after the *end of effect* proposed in the book's subtitle. My dissatisfaction is that it ultimately leaves us with two spheres of activity that we could call *the intimate* and *the street*. This, in turn, demands a theory for moving between the two – from the particular or private to the universal or public. This move, I would argue, suggests a shift in both time and in value, where one happens before the other, and ultimately one is implicitly of higher status. So the very search for the *political field* articulated above seems to valorise the general over the intimate and the political over the ethical. This is not satisfactory for applied theatre because it makes the workshop or performance only ever pre-political[5] and only ever subservient to an alternative, proper politics of 'the streets'. In terms of the concepts of the *strategic* and the *tactical*, we must instead consider the fluid interrelation of the practices to which they refer and resist *value* being ascribed automatically to one realm. The notion of 'weaving cells of resistance' to construct *full-bodied* radical action needs to be reworked to see the actual practice itself as already an intervention in the 'distribution of the sensible'. This is a refashioning of the political project proposed by Butler, where accepting the call of the face intervenes in the distribution of who can be properly mourned.[6]

Rancière proposes the idea of a 'sensible fabric' (Ibid., p. 64) to suggest that patterns of association and practice are characterised by particular ways of organising who can speak, be visible and participate in society. This is simultaneously cultural, social and economic in its reach. According to Rancière, we live in communities that are drawn together by common ways of acting in a 'shared sensible world' (2004, p. 42) and this shapes his particular understanding of both politics and art practices. It is the interconnection of these two that offers a way through the problem raised above. Politics, for Rancière, 'revolves around what is seen and what can be said about it, around who has the ability to see and the talent to speak, around the properties of spaces and the possibilities of time' (Ibid., p. 13), indicating a realm that cannot be separated between the private and the public or the immediate encounter with the call of the face and subsequent political action. Similarly, artistic activities are 'ways of doing and making' that 'intervene in the general distribution of ways of doing and making' (Ibid., p. 13). Here is a position that suggests there is no temporal or value shift between ethical affect and political act. While the strategic and the tactical are still valid analytical categories, they both operate within this broader fabric. To tie this to the concept of the face used here, on seeing the face of another we are at one and the same time engaged in the politics and the ethical implications of that encounter. The very workshop space, for example, is structured as part of a wider distribution of the sensible, and therefore our actions within it either contribute to the broader system of 'doing and making' or, perhaps, start a process of undoing 'the sensible fabric' in which it is located. Of course, working in any space through the arts can make no automatic claim to be a disturbance of the broader organisation of who speaks, has a part, or is visible, but the argument of Rancière offers a place to suggest that the ripple of affect can be marshalled as a political act. There is no shift here – the whole of an applied theatre event, precisely because of the place of the participants in any distribution, is already engaged politically. The prison or refugee camp – acutely painful examples of abusive distributions – can have their ways of 'doing and making' either disrupted or constituted by sense-based activities.

The following from Rancière, where he discusses how the 'meaningful fabric of the sensible' can be disturbed, sets out the scope of his political–aesthetic project, in a way that makes politics and ethics simultaneous and refuses to valorise the carnivals in the streets over the intimate moment of the theatre workshop. After expressing his dream of a political work of art, quoted in the chapter's epigraph, he goes on to say:

> It is the dream of an art that would transmit meanings in the form of a rupture with the very logic of meaningful situations [...] political art cannot work in the simple form of meaningful spectacle that would lead to an 'awareness' of the state of the world. Suitable political art would ensure, at one and the same time, the production of a double effect: the readability of a political signification and a sensible or perceptual shock caused, conversely, by the uncanny, by that which resists signification. In fact, this ideal effect is always the object of a negotiation between opposites, between the readability of the message that threatens to destroy the sensible form of art and the radical uncanniness that threatens to destroy all political meaning. (Ibid., p. 63)

Here Rancière combines a vision for political art that works strongly in an affective register (it shocks and is uncanny) with a deep suspicion of 'awareness raising' or the meaningful spectacle. He is not dismissing readability entirely, but is suggesting a politics found in what, I would call, a negotiation between *affect* and *effect*. This echoes the meaning and presence 'oscillation' in Gumbrecht and the significance here is that we are presented with a dream of a 'political work of art' that takes the terrain of the 'sensible' seriously. And it is a terrain that does not respect clear divisions between private and public. The distribution of the sensible, rather than having artificial boundaries which operate at the edges of rooms, theatres, child soldier camps or between the intimate and the street, is the sensate organisation of the whole of our social lives. As suggested in Chapter 1, the strategies and tactics

appear within each moment, shaping how the workshop room or theatre is built, how the time is organised and who is present, as much as
the structure of the carnival, street demonstration or activist performance. Therefore, engagement within one site cannot be 'less' political or
'pre-political' – it is only another form of politics that is working within
one particular area of distribution. So when Critchley, as cited in the
previous chapter, announces 'if ethics without politics is empty, then
politics without ethics is blind' (2007, p. 13), he is right insofar as he is
describing a simultaneous process, so that we could have empty applied
theatre projects as well as 'blind' ones.[7] However, we just might have *the
uncanny* – political performances of affect that seek to disturb: events
that, at their best, could fundamentally challenge who speaks, where
they dance and at what time they play – in a way that redistributes the
sensible in favour of those whose faces are excluded or made invisible.

Conclusion: Political passion

About Face has moved from a specific argument about the ethical call of
the face to a claim that certain performance events – whether they are
applied theatre projects or street theatre – can be interventions in a frequently violent or oppressive organisation of the sensible. The concept
of the face has been used to suggest that intimate meetings between
people, the primary ground of much performance practice, can create an
ethical demand on a person that is both specific and general. Although
the classic conception of the face insists that this is a call that cannot be
ignored, I have suggested that, through sensory or aesthetic encounter
with others, we can become more aware of the demand that it makes.
Once this is felt, we are drawn beyond ourselves in such a way that our
autonomy is limited – and, although we may be overwhelmed by the
enormity of this, it can be an energising source of our commitment to
social change. Where the infinite call to act, protect or struggle for rights
does overpower, projects involving the beautiful can offer a screen, respite or protection – from the conditions of difficult lives or the potentially paralysing affect of these monumental political challenges.

In order for performance projects to encourage individuals to see the
face of the other, I have argued that a prejudice towards physiognomy
needs to be countered. We do not see the face in order to be infected
by the trauma it transmits or edified by the story of suffering it reveals.
The face should make an ethical demand for our responsibility to that
person, and, therefore, to all people in a similar situation. This might be
through the story they tell, their smile on stage, their playing of a game

or through shared *perruque*-like acts of resistance. Performance practice following this logic becomes a sensitising process which might include the withdrawal of the face, the right to turn it away, as much as a held gaze between two people. These processes are, then, understood as part of a wider political project – that does not denigrate performance as preparation for the real work of political change, but values it as a purposeful part of an intervention into our sensible world. Applied theatre in this argument is one intervention in the fabric of the sensible amongst many – but one particularly adept at working in sites where the distribution is most inequitable. While the argument suggests that the politics of the street is wrongly valued above the 'ethics of the workshop', the case here is that both are political (and both will fail if they are not ethical). Although applied theatre, and all forms of participatory performance, might appear small and insignificant, without a place in which sensitivity to the face of the other can be nurtured, politics will be drained of its passion and continue to lack its capacity for care. Without the intimacy of meeting others, the universal programmes – for the rights of street children, for the demands of the homeless or for the needs of refugees – will extract the human from the heart of their action, and in so doing forget that social change, while perhaps motivated by a sense of anger at suffering and inequity, is also vitally about the compassion we feel.

Conclusion: Let them slide

In Chapter 5 I argued that performance's ephemeral nature was perhaps asserted too quickly. This was not to deny that the material object of performance slips from view, but to argue that art's capacity to sustain sensation beyond an initial moment (to paraphrase Deleuze) offers a stretched field of enquiry. Performance affects linger in such a way as to create a terrain or, particularly in the case of process-based projects, a shifting patch of sensation deserving of analysis. This is necessary if the various political implications of the *play of affect* are to be understood. Examining this terrain of the sensible, and seeing how aesthetic–political action is orientated to maintain or interrupt a certain distribution of 'who can dance, speak and play', are a priority for assessing the politics of performance practice. When Scarry wrote that 'beautiful things [...] act like small tears in the surface of the world' (1999, p. 112) or Kristeva asked for a 'burst of beauty' (1982, p. 210), we can see demands for actions within Rancière's sensible fabric. But we now need to ask: what is the optimum intervention that we can hope for? Do we stitch or do we tear?

The argument of *Performance Affects* has suggested that beauty, the call of the face, and a broad attention to the *shock to thought* produced by an affective register can be part of an explicitly political and aesthetic project. In making this proposition, it has questioned how certain forms of storytelling or displays of suffering may create a disturbance of the sensible realm, but they could also be marshalled to enhance its powerful inequalities. Similarly, when we consider that Rancière's fabric of the sensible is woven with the feelings of hunger as well as grief, fear and despondency, it is clear that this is a project that cannot be restricted to a falsely distinct cultural realm. These areas of human feeling are also part of the tapestry of a sensate world. Campaigning against economic

inequity, therefore, must be considered to be part of an affective register as well – being without food, drink, or income is felt in ways linked
to objects of sustenance, as well as to the broader senses of anger or
righteous indignation. Goldman in the introduction needed her dance,
Ehrenreich's joy overcame isolation and depression, and Gumbrecht
wanted to feel the tone of the oboe on his skin. These all indicate different emphases on how artistic activity might not only be necessary
for health and well-being – *but be part of the act of redistributing healthi-
ness and wellness.* A struggle against hunger must similarly be part of
this politics of affect redistribution – so that what are conceived of as
cultural projects versus social projects versus economic projects start
to lose their sense of separateness. The readers of this book are more
likely to be those who create performance projects, but our alliances
must also be stretched so that, when seeking to bolster the reach of our
affective work, some of our collaborations will become unpredictable.
For example, the community that is organising against a planned golf
course that will suck up the ground water and thus dry out wells in surrounding villages might be part of a linked sensate project – somewhere
applied theatre practitioners may connect to what is a campaign against
the radically unequal distribution of thirst.

   In the opening chapter, the focus was on de Certeau's idea of the
actions possible for the weak. This was not a reduction of political ambition but an acknowledgement that resistance in certain circumstances
needed to recognise how people must also stay safe. In the disaster and
war zones mentioned in this book, staying alive is perhaps the corner-
stone of the distribution of the sensible: death is the end of affect.
Butler's attention to the rights of different people to be mourned or
grieved demonstrated that we live in a world that distributes the right
to life in a hugely unequal manner. Many lives are considered hardly
worthy of being lived and their demise does not register. The approximately 5.4 million deaths in the war and subsequent humanitarian
disaster in the Democratic Republic of the Congo (1998–2003) (IRC,
2008) are in no way accorded the same status as the 3000 who died
on 11 September 2001[1] in the USA. But, of course, in the family of the
single dead person, his or her loss tears the fabric brutally.[2] Working
to keep people alive, to value their and others' lives, and to announce
proudly that they are worthy of living and being valued for being alive,
is then central to the politics proposed here. And happiness, joy and
celebration are indispensable sensations in this act of redistribution.
There is a frequent note of surprise from people who enter disaster
or war zones and see communities starting to rebuild *all* the sensory

aspects of their lives – not just the walls to keep out cold, or the cooking to stop hunger, but the dancing, singing and playing. While we may struggle to articulate the needs that are attached to these apparently 'cultural' actions, they indicate how new worlds are built in relation to affect – bricks, food and music all connect to sensations. While agreeing with the statement that all have a right to be mourned, celebrating these micro-actions of the assumed-to-be-weak is a similar proposal in an affective register, simply made in a less grandiose key.

The small acts of living against the odds, and having those actions celebrated, should neither be ignored nor disparaged as unworthy of critical attention. They can be usefully linked to the notion of the *perruque* discussed in Chapter 1 – where people *disguise* their resistance to become 'poets of their own affairs' (de Certeau, 1984, p. 34). *Performance Affects* has insisted that, although there are different sites of aesthetic–political action, the mesh of our worlds makes a distinction between the apparently private (for example, the hidden work of applied theatre) and the public (such as the highly visible world of activist performance) difficult to sustain. *Perruque*-like actions criss-cross the affective realm, and are moments that cumulatively might challenge what is, and is not, allowed to be sensed. Pushing back the tables in a classroom and creating a beautiful installation, transforming the prison workspace into a lunar landscape, choreographing wheelchair dances or a ballet in a bombed-out building – all pick away at the inequitable structure of our felt world. These may appear to be tactical interventions, but as demonstrations of the *ethics of tenacity* (Ibid., p. 26) they cannot be dismissed as a retreat or somehow 'frivolous': they are that *kind of triumph*.

In focusing on these *perruques* in the system, it becomes important to examine how they adapt to or counter dominant discourses of survival and redemption. They may fit or contradict, but, importantly, there should be no singular approaches for explaining how people live and resist. Chapter 2 developed this analysis by focusing in particular on how people might both want, and may be required, to construct stories from their suffering. It is important to emphasise that the argument here is not for *an end to storytelling* as a component of radical performance or applied theatre practice. Storytelling is a wonderfully rich, diverse and delicate way of reflecting and mediating our lived experience, but only if it is not cajoled into a simple solution for that narrow band of suffering called *trauma*. The attention to different cultural activities, in their stunning diversity, is part of an ethnographic disposition suggested here, so that the complexity of the organisation of the sensible does not get reduced to patterns of suffering and survival determined in one location and propagated across others. An ethnographic practice is proposed as one that validates the culturally specific responses to suffering and questions how they help people resist and survive within their own terms. It champions different plays of the *perruque* without insisting on their shape, size or scale of ambition. They may include storytelling, they may include the intentionally communicative, but these have no automatic right to higher places in a hierarchy of modes of resistance.

When working within the realm of affect, new alliances between acts of resistance, and an acceptance of different artistic responses to suffering, become necessary. Similarly, this 'realm' demands a reorientation of research methodologies and the behaviour of researchers. The shift from *effect* to *affect*, the acceptance of the non-hermeneutic into the academy to use Gumbrecht's terms, demands a broadening of artistic practice but also requires a debate about how to register the bodily response to material presence in writing and teaching. These questions were touched upon most directly in Chapter 3, where Phelan's desire to 'enact the affective force' of performance in our writing (Phelan, 1997, p. 12) and Adorno's warning about 'clearing up the past' became responses to the ethical problem of interpretation in that context. It is important to emphasise, however, that neither Rancière nor Gumbrecht demand an *end to meaning*, or a wholesale replacement of the interpretative with an advocacy of the sole rule of affect. Rancière's ideal is 'a negotiation between opposites' (2004, p. 63) and Gumbrecht hopes we can 'let ourselves be caught by an oscillation where presence effects permeate the meaning effects' (2004, p. 126). While the demand for 'oscillation' or 'negotiation' is entirely legitimate, the polemical nature of this book has sought to emphasise *affect* against *effect*. This suggests that the tipping point in their interaction is slightly different in the argument presented here. This is evident in two ways in particular. First, to some degree the distinction between what Gumbrecht calls meaning and presence effects is less obvious in a broader notion of *affect*. Although in a number of the chapters they were set against each other, in Chapter 4 it was asserted, somewhat tentatively, that an affective realm contained the effective. This was an insistence that an interpretative disposition to the world is one of many affective responses we can have to our surroundings. Put simply, being cerebral must also be an embodied response to the world. I do not want to press this point too far, because in many ways affective responses (which may start in the gut) are often perceived as different from the more analytical (which may argue with the gut). We may experience that oscillation whether or not the reality of their different origins is as clear as we might presume. Second, the tip towards affect here has been based on a particular ethical commitment. The argument for horizontal method, or the demand for the orientation to working besides others, was made to avoid a position of mastery above the communities in which we work. This is the recognition that interpretation, or finding meaning, is too often aligned with forms of extraction, exploitation and ownership. It is this particular vertical orientation that must be challenged. Clearly reading behind the lines of a poem is hardly the action of a despot, and the work of the forensic anthropologist can scrape and delve to discover truths that are intimately connected to justice. However, too often, digging beneath the skin is done to assert control over people, resources, and a distribution of knowledge. The bodies, returning to Scarry, are borrowed to lend legitimacy to some dubious assertions. Starting from affect does not mean a flight from clear statements or a fierce denunciation of acts of injustice – but grounds it in our humility and lack of superiority. The *pause*, then our *stammering*, can find a voice to condemn or console – but it exhibits a tender, embodied connection to the suffering it denounces, rather than its cool detachment from it. Gumbrecht's oscillation is a disturbance at the heart of the performance that must still be able to take an uneasy yet bold stand: a stand that may be a sign of surety or tentativeness, or even a stamp of pride. But it is a stand made of a body in its encounter with the face of others. This can be followed by an energy that bristles beneath the speaking or writing of these events that researchers must not be afraid to show – so our commitment to justice starts from an *affection for others* and is not afraid to exhibit its passionate desire to see justice done.

The end of the story?

In January 2008, I spent a day as an assistant on a production by young refugees, directed by Janine Waters[3] at the Royal Exchange Theatre in Manchester. The children were aged between 11 and 15, from a diverse range of countries. Their effervescence before, during and after the performance is what provoked the comment about the stretch of performance in Chapter 5: there was no way the *affect* of their performance stopped at the stage door. Sitting next to them as they chatted through their lunch, I could only admire the fact that youngsters, who did not speak like actors would 'normally' speak, were eating the wrong food in the wrong part of the building. During the break some of the younger boys took off their shoes and slid across the stage with a delight that was 'not in keeping' with the theatre. And in the rehearsal they laughed in the wrong places. However, in the performance, they demonstrated a commitment to clarity and energy that was awe-inspiring – from people *who were not meant to be there*: as young people in the Royal Exchange[4], as children on a stage and as refugees in the UK. The whole event disturbed a particular sensible world, layered in many complex ways across that building, the work within it, the social organisation of the education system the children were part of, and the histories of migration and conflict that made them present in the UK in the first place. When their school friends talked with them after the show, they were suddenly the authority – they owned the Royal Exchange stage and the building, and beamed with rightful pride. A *sense* of belonging is an *affect*, not an *effect* – it was woven across the complexity of these children's lives in ways that I cannot understand precisely, but I know were felt at this moment.

And yet what I do understand is that the event intervened in my affective world, as a parent, as a resident of Manchester, as a Royal Exchange patron and as a citizen outraged by my country's hypocrisy in dealing with the displaced.

But there are now more questions. How do we sustain a particular disruption of the 'distribution of the sensible'? How does the patchwork practice of applied theatre bring those reconfigurations of the world into new alliances with each other? How do we make work that is permitted not to promise *effect*? And at what point do I insist the boys put their shoes back on so as not to get into trouble and jeopardise the work – to stop their *perruque*? When does our ethics of tenacity become too quiet?

Shush. Let them slide.

These are questions that might demand a return to some of the points raised in this book, but should also lead to a critique of it. The proposal at the heart of *Performance Affects* can feel the barnacles growing across it before it has even been launched. Hopefully practice will test, challenge and transform many of the ideas offered here. There is no prescription, only an orientation: and it is one that is turned towards beauty, feels the face of the other and is drawn to a radical redistribution of the sensory organisation of our world.

Notes

Introduction

1. The 'evening events' echo Eugenio Barba's concern for barter as the model for theatrical exchange (Bovin, 1988), and Grotowski's interest in the 'paratheatrical' (Mennen, 1975).
2. See Thompson (2005, pp. 124–32) for one example of forum theatre's adaptive problems.

1 Incidents of cutting and chopping

1. This was reported in the English language newspaper *The Island*: 'The President expressed shock at the incident saying that it was an unfortunate incident at a time when she had formed a Cabinet comprising of all communities' (*The Island*, 2000a).
2. Irene Fraser, who continues to run arts projects in Washington DC.
3. I would like to acknowledge the assistance of Amal de Chickera, Ruwanthie de Chickera and Deanne Uyangoda in locating these materials.
4. Shorthand for the Liberation Tigers of Tamil Eelam (LTTE).
5. The ceasefire was signed on 22 February 2002 between the Government of Sri Lanka (GoSL) and the LTTE. While the signing was met with a sense of optimism, after gradual deterioration through 2006 and 2007 the agreement was finally rescinded by the government in early 2008.
6. The LTTE did not claim responsibility for the assassination – but they rarely claim responsibility for such attacks.
7. See Human Rights Watch report titled 'Sri Lanka: Karuna Group Abducts Children for Combat':
    > The Karuna group [...] split from the Tamil Tigers in 2004 and now cooperates with the Sri Lankan military in their common fight against the LTTE [...] 'The Karuna group is abducting children in broad daylight in areas firmly under government control', said Brad Adams, Asia director at Human Rights Watch. 'The government is fully aware of the abductions but allows them to happen because it's eager for an ally against the Tamil Tigers'. (HRWa, 2007)
8. The *Sunday Observer* and the *Daily News* are the English language papers run by the Government-controlled Lakehouse group.
9. This was part of research being conducted with Sri Lankan colleagues as part of a performance project (see postscript) that was being developed in response to the massacre.

2 The end of the story?

1. From Appadurai, cited in Argenti-Pillen, 2003, p. 8.
2. 'Trauma studies' does seem to adapt itself to human disasters wherever they occur. However, it is clearly recognised within Holocaust studies that the

lessons of the Holocaust cannot be simplistically compared across historical examples. The argument here is that it is the terms of the debate that continue to shift across time and space.
3. The Indonesian province of Aceh was the worst hit.
4. I visited Sri Lanka several times in the months after the tsunami and these comments are based on interviews with people working directly within psychological and mental health services in the country.
5. Sri Lanka, with over 20 years of civil conflict prior to the tsunami, has many local agencies working with war-affected communities.
6. Rushika Amarasekera and Ananda Galappatti.
7. This was commonly expressed by many people I met in mental health, relief and arts communities during the first year after the tsunami.
8. Conversations with the author. I would like to thank Premalatha 'Rajitha' Pratheepan for additional information about this example.
9. It should be asked, of course, who writes those 'reports' and in what tradition they were educated.
10. This demands the question 'Which studies?', and why does he transfer the PTSD diagnosis onto all his participants: another fairly blunt *seepage*.
11. Chapter 3's discussion of the Aegis Trust's work in Rwanda is a case in point.
12. Playback Theatre is a form of interactive storytelling developed by Jonathon Fox in New York in the 1970s (see Salas, 1996 and Rowe, 2007).
13. A term used in Canada broadly corresponding to practices that would be considered Applied Theatre in UK or community-based performance in the US.
14. This was with Tamil Hindu communities and is, therefore, not necessarily transferable to the Sinhalese young people in the second *stone*, but it is relevant to the assumptions in the general applicability of 'trauma relief' in Sri Lanka as a whole.

3 Academic scriptwriters and bodily affects

1. The Great Lakes region of Africa is centred on Rwanda, Burundi, Eastern Democratic Republic of Congo, Uganda and western Tanzania. For a detailed reading of the history of the area see Chrétien (2000, 2003).
2. Two of the most famous media outlets were the militantly anti-Tutsi *Kanguru* newspaper and 'hate radio' station *Radio-Television Libre Milles Collines*. Ranck explains their power:
   Both of these sources relied on a melange of rumor, political humor, and traditional cultural forms to criticize and demonize the RPF and other potential adversaries. In a manner similar to the Nazi use of pseudo-historical myths, those Hutu in power used the media to make reality itself a form of theatre. (Ranck, 2000, p. 194)
3. Prunier notes, 'the work of popular singer Simon Bikindi is fascinating. In songs such as "*Akabyutso*" (the small awakening) or "*Bene sebahinzi*" (son of peasants) he kept propagating with a talent a highly confrontational and slanted version of Rwandese history and culture' (1995, p. 210n).
4. Spoken word narration during the performance – translated from French by author.

5. References in this section come from a visit to Rwanda in November 2005. I would like to thank Ananda Breed, who organised the meetings with the groups described here. Ananda was a PhD student conducting fieldwork for a doctoral thesis on theatre in post-genocide Rwanda.

6. *Gacaca* is a form of community court instigated to enable a rapid processing of the huge number of people accused of crimes relating to the genocide – in a country with minimal surviving legal structures post-genocide. *Gacaca* is said to be a recreation of a traditional form of village-based justice.

7. *Ingando* camps are education camps for ex-prisoners returning to their communities and for students who have finished their studies. They include educational classes on the history of Rwanda and cultural activities.

8. Conducted by Ananda Breed and joined by the author in November 2005.

9. I have to thank Ananda for drawing my attention to this.

10. The use of a picture of the hung clothes of genocide victims from Murambi for the book's cover aims to announce the pivotal place of that memorial in the analysis of *Performance Affects*, without pretending that the work is external to the critique of Wainaina.

11. The notion of 'suspended' can also be found in the work of Lambek on the way the Sakalava in Madagascar 'bear' their history (2002) and in Turner's work on 'suspended space' in a Tanzanian refugee camp (2005).

12. At the time of writing, there is still controversy about the content of the Aegis Trust section of this memorial. The Guardian newspaper (UK) reported in 2006 that it was 'mired in controversy' and the director replied later that their 'memorial to 50,000 dead is no empty exercise' (*Guardian*, 2006a, 2006b).

13. Kristeva writes:
    In the dark halls of the museum that is now what remains of Auschwitz, I see a heap of children's shoes, or something like that, something I have already seen elsewhere [...] The abjection of Nazi crime reaches its apex when death, which, in any case, kills me, interferes with what, in my living universe, is supposed to save me from death: childhood, science, among other things. (1982, p. 4)

14. I have chosen not to anonymise the name because it is widely available via web sources and he is named in the Kigali memorial.

15. Figures differ in different records. For example: www.geoffbugbee.com/index.php?id=558, where it mentions 60,000; www.aegistrust.org/index.php?option=content&task=view&id=218&Itemid=222, where it mentions 40,000 (both accessed on 3 March 2006). Then the Kigali Memorial Centre says 50,000.

16. Wittgenstein in the preface of *Tractatus Logico-Philosophicus* famously wrote 'what can be said at all can be said clearly, and what we cannot talk about we must pass over in silence' (Wittgenstein, 2007, p. 7). This is repeated in the final line of the book as 'What we cannot speak about we must pass over in silence' (Ibid., p. 98).

17. See Spivey for an overview of Adorno's 'too loosely bandied' phrase *'Alle Kultur nach Auschwitz [...] ist Müll'* (2001, p. 250n).

18. C. Taylor's work explores the link between the notion of the national body, acts of bodily mutilation and restriction of movement during the genocide:
    In Rwanda of 1994 torturers manifested a certain proclivity to employ violent methods with certain forms. These forms betrayed a

     preoccupation with the movement of persons and substances and with the canals, arteries, and conduits along which persons and substances flow. (2002, p. 158)

19. Paradoxically for true clarity bodies are disinterred before being buried again. The first President Kabila of the Democratic Republic of Congo knew this when he kept forensic anthropologists in Kinshasa while he sent his troops back to atrocity zones to un-bury and burn the dead. They had not properly *cleaned* up and he did not want others' help in *clearing* up the past (see Koff, 2005).

20. An example being George W. Bush in February, 2008.

21. The United Nations Assistance Mission For Rwanda, which was widely criticised as being ineffectual in preventing or intervening in the genocide. It must be questioned how someone recorded David Mugiraneza's last words – and how convenient it is that they condemn the inaction of the international community who are the audience for the display. This is not to deny the culpability of the international community but to highlight the scripted nature of this exhibition. For more on UNAMIR's role see Dallaire (2005).

22. French, English and Kinyarwanda.

23. Considering Gourevitch's comments on the use of the word 'theatre', *ikinamucho* in Kinyarwandan, for 'not telling people what you are thinking', anthropological study has a challenging point of departure (see Gourevitch (1998), p. 258).

24. It needs to be acknowledged that, during the annual genocide commemoration events each April, Rwandans do visit these sites in large numbers.

25. See Young (2004, p. 154) for a discussion of Adorno's shudder in relation to the South African Truth and Reconciliation Commission.

26. The concept of *murky* is taken from Taussig's 'politics of epistemic murk' (1987, p. xiii).

4 Performance affects: A kind of triumph

1. Listing these objectives is, of course, not the same as endorsing them.

2. For an example in the field of communication and arts for development, see Inagaki (2007).

3. Perhaps an unacknowledged reworking of Einstein's famous 'Science without religion is lame, religion without science is blind'. See Dawkins (2006, p. 36) for why this statement did not make Einstein 'religious' in a traditional sense. Also connected to Žižek's rephrasing of Kant and Robespierre in his analysis of *divine violence*, 'love without cruelty is powerless; cruelty without love is blind' (2008, p. 173). I would, however, hesitate before equating politics with cruelty and ethics with love in this way.

4. Massumi is also one of Deleuze's translators (for example, the eclectic exposition of 'nomadic thought' *A Thousand Plateaus* with Guattari, 1987).

5 The call of beauty: An affective invitation

1. The deliberate lacuna in this discussion is the notion of the sublime and its relation to beauty. I would argue that the feelings associated with the

sublime should be part of what Sontag has called the 'register of the beautiful' (2003, p. 67) rather than a separate category, but this is controversial. The
sublime has traditionally been understood as an affect of greater intensity
than the 'merely' beautiful. It is more often associated with awe-inspiring
nature (storms or mountains) than the 'less dramatic' beauty. This discussion warrants more space than offered here and perhaps there is a future
argument for the relationship between sublime performance and beautiful
performance that will welcome, or disparage, what Schiller called the sublime's 'strong arms' and their capacity to bear us 'across the profound abyss'
(Schiller, 1801, cited in Eco, 2004, p. 297). See Eagleton (2005, pp. 42–67)
and Gilbert-Rolfe (1999) for recent discussions of the sublime that develop
both its dangerous and its emancipatory capacity.
2. Beauty, of course, is not only found in art and therefore is not simply a subset
of aesthetics. This echoes Derrida's demand that beauty is liberated from a
purely aesthetic discourse (Derrida, 1990, p. 13).
3. I am interested in the *affect* of beauty and beauty as an affect. This includes
the feelings produced by what is perceived as a beautiful event, object or
person – and by the collective sharing of that moment. The difference
between beauty *producing* affect and beauty *as* affect is blurred because it
should sustain both understandings.
4. It is important to question whether the beauty of nature can be called 'aesthetic' beauty. While what is 'natural' or 'created' is at times blurred (a garden,
for example), the work of the artist raises a different set of questions from an
apparently 'intentionless' natural beauty (depending on your belief or non-
belief in god, of course). On beauty and nature see Graham (2000, p. 170) or
Adorno (1997, pp. 81–101).
5. Again, this might not be the case with the sublime – which can induce both
awe and terror. For a discussion of beauty and terror, where beauty might
link to the terrible, see Korsmeyer (2006) and for a review of the 'contemporary sublime' see Beckley (2001).
6. This point is made by Eaton in relation to the sites in which we appreciate
natural beauty (2006, p. 48).
7. Janet Wolf has written extensively on beauty in relation to Holocaust art and
feminist theory (Wolff, 2003, 2006).
8. This point is reminiscent of, but not analogous to, Baudrillard's comment
on September 11 that 'by the grace of terrorism, the World Trade Center has
become the world's most beautiful building' (Baudrillard, 2002, p. 48).

6   About face: Disturbing the fabric of the sensible

1. Faces have also been used in art projects. See, for example, *Towards a Promised
Land* in Margate, UK, by Artangel and the photographer Wendy Ewald, where
huge images of the faces of young refugees were displayed along the sea front
(Artangel, 2008).
2. While Žižek has argued that 'our duty today is to keep track of such acts, of
such ethical moments' (2002, p. 117), my emphasis on these acts as a source
of 'resistance' would be questioned by his aversion to 'resistance studies'. I
would assert that *resistance* can be validated without being a sign of a retreat
from principled opposition. Žižek's critical review of Critchley's work and

the ongoing debate between them develop this argument (see Žižek, 2007 and Critchley, 2008).

3. 'Almost' because there will be a racist who assumes that just because they work with certain children does not mean that others have the same right, or a misogynist who may believe that the cultural rights of boys are of primary importance.

4. For a related discussion of the connection between 'face-to-face' encounters and ethics see Phelan's review of Marina Abramović's *The House with the Ocean View* (Phelan, 2004).

5. 'Pre-political' might be another way of saying 'rehearsal' and this, therefore, becomes a critique of Boal's 'rehearsal for the revolution' (Boal, 1979).

6. The notion of the political here borrows from Spencer, where an anthropological approach leads to an affirmation of 'a performance of the counter-political' (2007, p. 175): a smaller scale that denotes the blurring of boundaries of where 'the political' is 'properly' located.

7. 'Blind' is in inverted commas to echo the previous quotation but also to indicate disquiet about the use of words associated with disability as negative metaphors.

Conclusion

1. The fact that *Wikipedia* announces that 'there were 2,974 fatalities, not including the 19 hijackers' suggests that some deaths are not even counted as deaths (Wikipedia, 2008).

2. This is not to get 'involved in the obscene mathematics of guilt' (Žižek, 2002, p. 52), and I agree with Žižek that 'the terrifying death of each individual is absolute and incomparable' (Ibid., pp. 51–2).

3. Janine Waters is the inspirational director behind the arts organisation Water's Edge – see www.watersedgearts.com.

4. This is in no way meant to suggest that the Education Department at the Exchange did anything but welcome them. In many ways that department is an exemplary case of a programme of affective/affectionate work that is disturbing the distribution of who can sing, dance and play in the heart of a major UK arts institution.

Bibliography

Adorno, T. (1997) *Aesthetic Theory*, trans. Robert Hullot-Kentor (London: Continuum).

Aegis Trust (2006a) *Welcome to Aegis*, www.aegistrust.org.

— (2006b) 'Aegis in Rwanda', http://www.aegistrust.org/index.php?option=cont ent&task=view&id=37&Itemid=68 (accessed 7 March 2006).

Ahmed, J.S. (2006) 'Negotiating "Theatre (in Place/Instead) of War"', *Research in Drama Education*, 11, 1, 59–75.

Al Rowwad (2008) *Al Rowwad Children's Theatre Troupe*, http://electronicintifada. net/multimedia/arts/al-rowwad/ (accessed 12 February 2008).

Amnesty International (2007) *Rwanda: Human Rights Concerns*, http://www. amnestyusa.org/By_Country/Rwanda/page.do?id=1011229& n1=3&n2=30&n3=979 (accessed 2 November 2007).

A'ness, F. (2004) 'Resisting Amnesia: Yuyachkani, Performance, and the Postwar Reconstruction of Peru', *Theatre Journal*, 56, 395–414.

Appignanesi, J. and Baum, D. (2006) 'Ex-Memoria: Filming the Face', *Third Text*, 20, 1, 85–97.

Argenti-Pillen, A. (2003) *Masking Terror: How Women Contain Violence in Southern Sri Lanka* (Philadelphia: University of Pennsylvania Press).

Armstrong, J. (2004) *The Secret Power of Beauty: Why Happiness Is in the Eye of the Beholder* (London: Penguin).

Artangel (2008) *Wendy Ewald: Towards a Promised Land, Part 2*, http://www.artan- gel.org.uk/pages/present/present_ewald.htm (accessed 21 April 2008).

Azeda, H. (2005) *Interview Conducted by Jenny Hughes as Part of the In Place of War Project*, http://www.inplaceofwar.net/web_db/php/index.php?page=about (accessed 30 January 2009).

Baudrillard, J. (2002) *The Spirit of Terrorism* (London: Verso).

Beckley, B. (ed.) (2001) *Sticky Sublime* (New York: Allworth Press).

Bell, C. (1987) *Art* (Oxford: Oxford University Press).

Benjamin, W. (1999) *Illuminations* (London: Pimlico).

Bennett, J. (2005) *Empathic Vision: Affect, Trauma, and Contemporary Art* (Stanford: Stanford University Press).

Blau, H. (2003) 'Art and Crisis: Homeland Security and the Noble Savage', *Performing Arts Journal*, 75, 6–19.

Boal, A. (1979) *Theatre of the Oppressed* (London: Pluto Press).

Bovin, M. (1988) 'Provocation Anthropology: Bartering Performance in Africa', *TDR: The Journal of Performance Studies*, 32, 1, 21–41.

Brecht, B. (2003) 'Theatre for Education, Theatre for Entertainment', trans. John Willett, in W. Worthen (ed.) *Anthology of Drama* (London: Heinle).

Brow, J. (1996) *Demons and Development: The Struggle for Community in a Sri Lankan Village* (Tucson: The University of Arizona Press).

Butler, J. (2004) *Precarious Life: The Powers of Mourning and Violence* (London: Verso).

— (2005) *Giving an Account of Oneself* (New York: Fordham University Press).

Caruth, C. (ed.) (1995) *Trauma: Explorations in Memory* (Baltimore: The Johns Hopkins University Press).

Chrétien, J.-P. (2000) *L'Afrique Des Grands Lacs: Deuz Mille Ans d'Histoire* (Paris: Flammarion).

— (2003) *The Great Lakes of Africa: Two Thousand Years of History*, trans. Scott Strauss (New York: Zone Books).

Chrétien, J.-P. avec Reporters sans Frontières (1995) *Rwanda: Les Médias du Génocide* (Paris: Karthala).

Clough, T.P. with J. Halley (eds) (2007) *The Affective Turn: Theorizing the Social* (Durham and London: Duke University Press).

Colebrook, C. (2002) *Gilles Deleuze* (London: Routledge).

Critchley, S. (2007) *Infinitely Demanding: Ethics of Commitment, Politics of Resistance* (London: Verso).

— (2008) 'Ignorance Is Strength in Depth', *Harper's Review*, May 2008.

Daily News (2000) 'Shocking Savagery', 27 October 2000.

Dallaire, R. (2005) *Shake Hands with the Devil: The Failure of Humanity in Rwanda* (London: Arrow Books).

Daniel, E.V. (1996) *Charred Lullabies: Chapters in an Anthropology of Violence* (Princeton: Princeton University Press).

Das, V. (1997) 'Language and Body: Transactions in the Construction of Pain', in A. Kleinman, V. Das and M. Lock (eds) *Social Suffering* (Berkeley: University of California Press).

Das, V., Kleinman, A., Lock, M., Ramphele, M., Reynolds, P. (eds) (2001) 'Introduction', *Remaking a World: Violence, Social Suffering and Recovery* (Berkeley: University of California Press).

Dawkins, R. (2006) *The God Delusion* (London: Black Swan).

De Certeau, M. (1984) *The Practice of Everyday Life* (London: University of California Press).

Deleuze, G. (1964) *Proust and Signs*, trans. R. Howard (New York: George Braziller).

— (1995) *Negotiations, 1972–1990* (New York: Columbia University Press).

Deleuze, G. and Guattari, F. (1987) *A Thousand Plateaus*, trans. B. Massumi (London: Continuum).

Derrida, J. (1990) *Writing and Difference*, trans. A. Bass (London: Routledge).

— (2001) *On Cosmopolitanism and Forgiveness* (London: Routledge).

Disaster Mental Health Response Handbook (2000) Centre for Mental Health, NSW Health, NSW Institute of Psychiatry, State Health Publication No: (CMH) 00145.

Dolan, J. (2005) *Utopia in Performance: Finding Hope at the Theater* (Ann Arbor: The University of Michigan Press).

Eagleton, T. (2005) *Holy Terror* (Oxford: Oxford University Press).

Eaton, M.M. (2006) 'Beauty and Ugliness In and Out of Context', in M. Kieran (ed.) *Contemporary Debates in Aesthetics and the Philosophy of Art* (Oxford: Blackwell Publishing).

Eco, U. (ed.) (2004) *On Beauty: A History of a Western Idea* (London: Secker and Warburg).

Edmondson, L. (2005) 'Marketing Trauma and the Theatre of War in Northern Uganda', *Theatre Journal*, 57, 451–74.

Ehrenreich, B. (2007) *Dancing in the Streets: A History of Collective Joy* (London: Granta).

Ehrenreich, J.H. (2001) *Coping with Disasters: A Guidebook to Psychosocial Intervention* (State University of New York: Old Westbury).

Eng, D.L. (2002) 'The Value of Silence', *Theatre Journal*, 54, 85–94.

Feagin, S. (ed.) (2007) *Global Theories of the Arts and Aesthetics* (Oxford: Blackwell).

Feldman, A. (2004) 'Memory Theaters, Virtual Witnessing, and the Trauma-Aesthetic', *Biography*, 27, 1, 163–202.

Felman, S. and Laub, D. (1992) *Testimony: Crises of Witnessing in Literature, Psychoanalysis, and History* (London: Routledge).

Fisher, P. (2002) *The Vehement Passions* (Princeton and Oxford: Princeton University Press).

Franklin, C. and Lyons, L.E. (2004) 'Bodies of Evidence and the Intricate Machines of Untruth', *Biography*, 27, 1, v–xxii.

Frith, S. (1978) *Sound Effects: Youth, Leisure, and the Politics of Rock 'n' Roll* (London: Constable).

— (1998) *Performance Rites: Evaluating Popular Music* (Oxford: Oxford University Press).

Galappatti, A. (2005) 'Psychosocial Work in the Aftermath of a Tsunami: Challenges for Service Provision in Batticaloa, Eastern Sri Lanka', Field Report submitted to Intervention 3, 1.

Gilbert-Rolfe, J. (1999) *Beauty and the Contemporary Sublime* (New York: Allworth Press).

Goldman, E. (2006) *Living My Life*, abridged by M. Brody (London: Penguin).

Gourevitch, P. (1998) *We Wish to Inform You that Tomorrow We Will Be Killed with Our Families* (Oxford: Picador).

— (2001) 'Among the Dead', in M.S. Roth and C.G. Salas (eds) *Disturbing Remains: Memory, History, and Crisis in the Twentieth Century* (Los Angeles: Getty Research Institute).

Graham, G. (2000) *Philosophy of the Arts: An Introduction to Aesthetics*, 2nd edn (London: Routledge).

Guardian (2006a) 'Two Years Late and Mired in Controversy: The British Memorial to Rwanda's Past', http://www.guardian.co.uk/international/story/0,,1946277,00.html (date accessed 9 November 2007). Copyright Guardian News & Media Ltd 2006.

— (2006b) 'Our Memorial to 50,000 Dead Is No Empty Historic Exercise', http://www.guardian.co.uk/comment/story/0,,1952885,00.html (accessed 9 November 2007). Copyright Guardian News & Media Ltd 2006.

Gumbrecht, H.U. (2004) *Production of Presence: What Meaning Cannot Convey* (Stanford: Stanford University Press).

— (2006) *In Praise of Athletic Beauty* (Cambridge, Massachusetts: The Belknap Press).

Gunaratna, R. (1990) *Sri Lanka: A Lost Revolution – the Inside Story of the JVP* (Sri Lanka: Institute of Fundamental Studies).

Guyer, P. (2005) *Values of Beauty: Historical Essays in Aesthetics* (Cambridge: Cambridge University Press).

Haedicke, S.C. (2002) 'The Politics of Participation: Un Voyage Pas Comme Les Autres Sur Les Chemins De L'Exil', *Theatre Topics*, 12, 2, 99–118.

Hamera, J. (2002) 'An Answerability of Memory "Saving" Khmer Classical Dance', *The Drama Review*, 46, 4 (T176), 65–85.

Hansen, T.B. and Stepputat, F. (eds) (2005) *Sovereign Bodies: Citizens, Migrants, and States in the Postcolonial World* (Princeton and Oxford: Princeton University Press).

Harrison, F. (2003) 'Analysis: Sri Lanka's Child Soldiers', http://news.bbc.co.uk/1/hi/world/south_asia/2713035.stm (accessed 4 October 2006).

Hatzfeld, Jean (2000) *Into the Quick of Life: The Rwandan Genocide: The Survivors Speak*, trans. Gerry Feehily (London: Serpents Tail).

— (2003) *A Time for Machetes: The Rwandan Genocide: The Killers Speak*, trans. Linda Coverdale (London: Serpents Tail).

Haugbolle, S. (2005) 'Public and Private Memory of the Lebanese Civil War', *Comparative Studies of South Asia, Africa and the Middle East*, 25, 1, 191–203.

Healy, C. (2006) 'Dead Man: Film, Colonialism and Memory', in K. Hodgkin and S. Radstone (eds) *Memory History Nation: Contested Pasts* (New Brunswick and London: Transaction Publishers).

Heller-Roazen, D. (2007) *The Inner Touch: Archaeology of a Sensation* (New York: Zone Books).

Hinton, A.L. (ed.) (2002) *Annihilating Difference: An Anthropology of Genocide* (Berkeley: University of California Press).

Hoffman, D. (2005) 'Violent Events as Narrative Blocs: The Disarmament at Bo, Sierra Leone', *Anthropological Quarterly*, 78, 2, 328–53.

Hughes, R. (2006) 'Nationalism and Memory at the Tuol Sleng Museum of Genocide Crime, Phnom Penh, Cambodia', in K. Hodgkin and S. Radstone (eds) *Memory History Nation: Contested Pasts* (New Brunswick and London: Transaction Publishers).

Human Rights Watch (2007a) 'Sri Lanka: Karuna Group Abducts Children for Combat', http://hrw.org/english/docs/2007/01/24/slanka15141.htm (accessed 19 November 2007).

— (2007b) 'Rwanda: Events of 2006', http://hrw.org/englishwr2k7/docs/2007/01/11/rwanda14782.htm (accessed 8 November 2007).

Inagaki, N. (2007) 'Communicating the Impact of Communication for Development: Recent Trends in Empirical Research', *World Bank Working Paper* (120).

IRC (2008) 'International Rescue Committee – Congo Forgotten Crisis', http://www.theirc.org/special-report/congo-forgotten-crisis.html?gclid=CKTvlq_I-pECFQ6jQwodIhyWxQ (accessed 7 March 2008).

Isar, R.Y. (2003) *Artistic Activism in Situations of 'Extreme Conflict': The Challenge of Evaluation* (Brussels: Information European Theatre Meetings).

Kadirgamar, L. (2000) 'Address to Winnipeg conference', http://www.satp.org/satporgtp/countries/shrilanka/document/papers/lakshmans_address_in_winnipeg_canada.htm (accessed 1 September 2006).

Kapferer, B. (1988) *Legends of People, Myths of State: Violence, Intolerance, and Political Culture in Sri Lanka and Australia* (Oxford: Berg Smithsonian Institution Press).

— (1991) *A Celebration of Demons: Exorcism and the Aesthetics of Healing in Sri Lanka* (Oxford: Berg Smithsonian Institution Press).

Karp, M. (2000) 'Psychodrama of Rape and Torture: A 16 Year Follow-up Case Study', in P.F. Kellerman and M.K. Hudgins (eds) *Psychodrama with Trauma Survivors: Acting Out Your Pain* (London: Jessica Kingsley Publishers).

Keane, F. (1996) *Season of Blood: Rwandan Journey* (London: Penguin).

Keenan, A. (2005a) 'Making Sense of Bindunuwewa – From Massacre to Acquittal', *Law & Society Trust*, 15, 212, 19–42.

— (2005b) 'No Peace, No War: Have International Donors Failed Sri Lanka's Most Vulnerable?', *Boston Review*, http://www.bostonreview.net/BR30.3/keenan.html (accessed 30 January 2009).

Kellerman, P.F. and Hudgins, M.K. (eds) (2000) *Psychodrama with Trauma Survivors: Acting Out Your Pain* (London: Jessica Kingsley Publishers).

Khalili, L. (2005) 'Places of Memory and Mourning: Palestinian Commemoration in the Refugee Camps of Lebanon', *Comparative Studies of South Asia, Africa and the Middle East*, 25, 1, 30–45.

Kirwan, J. (1999) *Beauty* (Manchester: Manchester University Press).

Klaic, D. (2002) 'The Crisis of Theatre? The Theatre of Crisis!', in M. Delgado and C. Svich (eds) *Theatre in Crisis: Performance Manifestos for a New Century* (Manchester: Manchester University Press).

Koff, C. (2005) *The Bone Woman: Among the Dead in Rwanda, Bosnia, Croatia and Kosovo* (London: Atlantic Books).

Korsmeyer, C. (2006) 'Terrible Beauties', in M. Kieran (ed.) *Contemporary Debates in Aesthetics and the Philosophy of Art* (Oxford: Blackwell Publishing).

Kristeva, J. (1982) *Powers of Horror: An Essay on Abjection* (New York: Columbia University Press).

Kulatilaka, P.H.K. (2001) *Report of the Presidential Commission of Inquiry into Incidents that Took Place at Bindunuwewa Rehabilitation Centre, Bandarawela, on 25 October 2000*, http://www.brynmawr.edu/peacestudies/faculty/Keenan/srilanka/Documents.html (accessed 5 March 2008).

Kuppers, P. (2007) *Community Performance: An Introduction* (London: Routledge).

Kurahashi, Y. (2004) 'Theatre as the Healing Space: Ping Chong's Children of War', *Studies in Theatre and Performance*, 24, 1, 23–36.

Lambek, M. (2002) *The Weight of the Past: Living with History in Mahajanga, Madagascar* (New York: Palgrave Macmillan).

Langford, J.M. (2005) 'Spirits of Dissent: Southeast Asian Memories and Disciplines of Death', *Comparative Studies of South Asia, Africa and the Middle East*, 25, 1, 161–76.

Laub, D. (1995) 'Truth and Testimony: The Process and the Struggle', in C. Caruth (ed.) *Trauma: Explorations in Memory* (Baltimore and London: The Johns Hopkins University Press).

Lawrence, P. (2000) 'Violence, Suffering, Ammam: The Work of Oracles in Sri Lanka's Eastern War Zone', in V. Das, A. Kleinman, M. Ramphele and P. Reynolds (eds) *Violence and Subjectivity* (Berkeley: University of California Press).

— (2003) *The Ocean of Stories: Children's Imagination, Creativity and Reconciliation in Eastern Sri Lanka* (Colombo: International Centre for Ethnic Studies).

Levinas, E. (1969) *Totality and Infinity: An Essay on Exteriority*, trans. A. Lingis (Pittsburgh: Duquesne University Press).

Leys, R. (2000) *Trauma: A Genealogy* (Chicago: Chicago University Press).

Malpede, K. (1996) 'Teaching Witnessing: A Class Wakes to the Genocide in Bosnia', *Theatre Topics* 6, 2, 167–79.

Massumi, B. (ed.) (2002) *A Shock to Thought: Expression after Deleuze and Guattari* (London: Routledge).

Mennen, R. (1975) 'Jerzy Grotowski's Paratheatrical Projects', *TDR: The Journal of Performance Studies*, 19, 4, 58–69.

Miller, N.K. and Tougaw, J. (eds) (2002) *Extremities: Trauma, Testimony and Community* (Urbana and Chicago: University of Illinois Press).

Moss, J. (2001) 'The Drama of Survival: Staging Post-traumatic Memory in Plays by Lebanese-Québécois Dramatists', *Theatre Research in Canada*, 22, 2, 173–89.

Munk, E. (2001) 'Before the Fall: Yugoslav Theaters of Opposition', *Theater*, 31, 1, 5–25.

Murdoch, I. (1991) *The Sovereignty of Good* (London: Routledge).

Murphy, S. (2007) 'Traumatizing Feminism: Prevention Discourse and the Subject of Sexual Violence', in K. Ball (ed.) *Traumatizing Theory: The Cultural Politics of Affect in and beyond Psychoanalysis* (New York: Other Press).

Neelands, J. (2007) 'Taming the Political: The Struggle over Recognition in the Politics of Applied Theatre', *Research in Drama Education*, 12, 3, 305–17.

Nicholson, H. (2004) *Applied Drama: The Gift of Theatre* (London: Palgrave Macmillan).

NURC (2007) *National Unity and Reconciliation Commission, Government of Rwanda*, http://www.nurc.gov.rw/index.php?Comm (accessed 31 October 2007).

Obeyesekere, G. (1990) *The Work of Culture: Symbolic Transformation in Psychoanalysis and Anthropology* (Chicago: The University of Chicago Press).

Patraka, V.M. (1999) *Spectacular Suffering: Theatre, Fascism, and the Holocaust* (Bloomington: Indiana University Press).

Perera, S. (2001) 'Spirit Possessions and Avenging Ghosts: Stories of Supernatural Activity as Narratives of Terror and Mechanisms of Coping and Remembering', in V. Das, A. Kleinman, M. Lock, M. Ramphele and P. Reynolds (eds) *Remaking a World: Violence, Social Suffering and Recovery* (Berkeley: University of California Press).

Perpich, D. (2005) 'Figurative Language and the "Face" in Levinas's Philosophy', *Philosophy and Rhetoric*, 38, 2, 103–21.

Phelan, P. (1997) *Mourning Sex: Performing Public Memories* (London: Routledge).

— (2004) 'Marina Abramović: Witnessing Shadows', *Theatre Journal*, 56, 569–77.

Phelan, P. and Lane, J. (eds) (1997) *The Ends of Performance* (New York: New York University Press).

Philpott, S. (2005) 'A Controversy of Faces: Images from Bali and Abu Ghraib', *Journal For Cultural Research*, 9, 3, 227–44.

Police CID HQ, Bandarawela (2000) From the transcript of an interview with Captain Abeyratne, the officer in charge of the Bindunawewa camp, taken on 6 November 2000 at Police CID HQ, Bandarawela.

Pottier, J. (2002) *Re-imagining Rwanda: Conflict, Survival and Disinformation in the Late Twentieth Century* (Cambridge: Cambridge University Press).

Prunier, G. (1995) *The Rwanda Crisis: History of a Genocide* (New York: Columbia University Press).

Pugliese, J. (2002) 'Penal Asylum: Refugees, Ethics, Hospitality', *Borderlands*, 1, 1, e-journal http://www.borderlands.net.au/issues/vol1no1.html (accessed 30 January 2009).

Rancière, J. (2004) *The Politics of Aesthetics*, trans. G. Rockhill (London: Continuum).

Ranck, J. (2000) 'Beyond Reconciliation: Memory and Alterity in Post-Genocide Rwanda', in R.I. Simon, S. Rosenberg, C. Eppert (eds) *Between Hope and Despair: Pedagogy and the Remembrance of Historical Trauma* (Oxford: Rowman and Littlefield Publishers).

Reynolds, J. (2001) 'The Other of Derridean Deconstruction: Levinas, Phenomenology and the Question of Responsibility', *Minerva – an Internet Journal of Philosophy*, 5, 31–62.

Richmond, S. (2004) 'Remembering Beauty: Reflections on Kant and Cartier-Bresson for Aspiring Photographers', *Journal of Aesthetic Education*, 38, 1, 78–88.

Rockhill, G. (2004) 'Translators Introduction', in J. Rancière (ed.), *The Politics of Aesthetics* (London: Continuum).

Roth, M.S. and Salas, C.G. (eds) (2001) *Disturbing Remains: Memory, History, and Crisis in the Twentieth Century* (Los Angeles: Getty Research Institute).

Rovit, R. and Goldfarb, A. (eds) (1999) *Theatrical Performance during the Holocaust: Texts, Documents, Memoirs* (London and Baltimore: The Johns Hopkins University Press).

Rowe, N. (2007) *Playing the Other: Dramatizing Personal Narratives in Playback Theatre* (London: Jessica Kingsley).

Salas, J. (1996) *Improvising Real Life: Personal Story in Playback Theatre*, 2nd edn (Dubuque: Kendall Hunt).

Salverson, J. (1996) 'Performing Emergency: Witnessing, Popular Theatre, and The Lie of the Literal', *Theatre Topics* 6, 2, 181–91.

— (1999) 'Transgressive Storytelling or an Aesthetics of Injury: Performance, Pedagogy and Ethics', *Theatre Research in Canada*, 20, 1, 34–51.

— (2001) 'Change on Whose Terms? Testimony and an Erotics of Injury', *Theater*, 31, 3, 119–25.

Sartwell, C. (2004) *Six Names of Beauty* (London: Routledge).

Saunders, R. and Aghaie, K. (2005) 'Introduction: Mourning and Memory', *Comparative Studies of South Asia, Africa and the Middle East*, 25, 1, 16–29.

Scarry, E. (1985) *The Body in Pain: The Making and Unmaking of the World* (Oxford: Oxford University Press).

— (1999) *On Beauty and Being Just* (London; Duckbacks).

Schaffer, K. and Smith, S. (2004) 'Conjunctions: Life Narratives in the Field Of Human Rights', *Biography*, 27, 1, 1–24.

Schauer, M., Neuner, F. and Elbert, T. (2005) *Narrative Exposure Therapy: A Short-Term Intervention for Traumatic Stress Disorders after War, Terror, or Torture* (Toronto: Hogrefe).

Schechner, R. (1988) *Performance Theory*, 2nd edn (London: Routledge).

— (2006) *Performance Studies: An Introduction* (London: Routledge).

Schininà, Guglielmo (2004) 'Here We Are: Social Theatre and Some Open Questions about Its Developments', *TDR: The Journal of Performance Studies* 48, 3, 17–31.

Sedgwick, E.K. (2003) *Touching Feeling: Affect, Pedagogy, Perfomativity* (Durham and London: Duke University Press).

Segall, K.W. (2005) 'Stories and Song in Iraq and South Africa: From Individual Trauma to Collective Mourning Performances', *Comparative Studies of South Asia, Africa and the Middle East*, 25, 1, 138–51.

Shaviro, S. (2002) 'Beauty Lies in the Eye', in B. Massumi (ed.) *A Shock to Thought: Expression after Deleuze and Guattari* (London: Routledge).

Simon, R.I., Rosenberg, S. and Eppert, C. (2000) (eds) *Between Hope and Despair: Pedagogy and the Remembrance of Historical Trauma* (Oxford: Rowman and Littlefield).

Skloot, R. (1996) ' "Where Does It Hurt?": Genocide, the Theatre and the Human Body', *Theatre Research International*, 23, 1, 51–8.

Sontag, S. (2001) *Against Interpretation* (London: Vintage Books).

— (2003) *Regarding the Pain of Others* (London: Penguin).

Spencer, J. (1999) *A Sinhala Village in Time of Trouble: Politics and Change in Rural Sri Lanka* (New Delhi: Oxford University Press).

— (2007) *Anthropology, Politics and the State: Democracy and Violence in South Asia* (Cambridge: Cambridge University Press).

Spivey, N. (2001) *Enduring Creation: Art, Pain and Fortitude* (London: Thames and Hudson).

Sri Lankan Observer (2000a) 'Politics, Media and the Bindunawewa Massacre', 27 October 2000.

— (2000b) 'Pre-Planned or Wilful neglect of Duty', 29 October 2007.

Tambornino, J. (2002) *The Corporeal Turn: Passion, Necessity, Politics* (Lanham: Rowman and Littlefield).

Tamil Students Forum (2000) 'Request to Observe Hartal – 1st November 2000', Leaflet, Colombo District, Tamil Students Forum.

Tankint, M. (2004) 'Not Talking about Traumatic Experiences: Harmful or Healing? Coping with War Memories in Southwest Uganda', *Intervention: International Journal of Mental Health, Psychosocial Work and Counselling in Areas of Armed Conflict*, 2, 1, 3–17.

Taussig, M. (1987) *Shamanism, Colonialism, and the Wild Man; a study in Terror and Healing* (Chicago: The University of Chicago Press).

— (1999) *Defacement: Public Secrecy and the Labor of the Negative* (Stanford: Stanford University Press).

Taylor, C. (2002) 'The Cultural Face of Terror in the Rwandan Genocide of 1994', in A.L. Hinton (ed.) *Annihilating Difference: An Anthropology of Genocide* (Berkeley: University of California Press).

Taylor, D. (2002) 'DNA of performance', *TDR: The Journal of Performance Studies*, 46, 1 (T173), 149–69.

Taylor, P. (2003) *Applied Theatre: Creating Transformative Encounters in the Community* (London: Greenwood Press).

The Island (2000a) 'The President Expressed Shock', 27 October 2000.

— (2000b) 'Bindunuwewa', 31 October 2000.

The Law and Society Trust Review (2000) 'The Bindunuwewa Massacre: Interim Report of the Human Rights Commission', 11, 158.

Thompson, J. (2003) *Applied Theatre: Bewilderment and Beyond* (Bern: Peter Lang).

— (2005) *Digging Up Stories: Applied Theatre, Performance and War* (Manchester: Manchester University Press).

— (2006) 'Performance of Pain, Performance of Beauty', *Research in Drama Education*, 11, 1, 47–57.

Thompson, J. and Schechner, R. (2004) 'Why Social Theatre?', *TDR: The Journal of Performance Studies*, 48, 3 (T183), 11–16.

Thrift, N. (2007) *Non-Representational Theory: Space, Politics, Affect* (London: Routledge).

Turner, S. (2005) 'Suspended Spaces – Contesting Sovereignties in a Refugee Camp', in T.B. Blom Hansen and F. Stepputat (eds) *Sovereign Bodies: Citizens, Migrants, and States in the Postcolonial World* (Princeton and Oxford: Princeton University Press).

UNICEF (2004) 'Children Being Caught Up in Recruitment Drive in North East', http://www.unicef.org/media/media_21990.html, newsnote 26 June 2004 (accessed 4 October 2006).

UTHR (J) (2005) 'Special Report No. 19: The Curse of Impunity Part I – Bindunuwewa, the Thin End of the Wedge of Impunity', University Teachers for Human Rights (Jaffna), UTHR, http://www.uthr.org (accessed 30 January 2009).

Uttamanathan, J. (No date) Court Transcript: A Statement to One of the Court Hearings Dealing with the Bindunawewa Massacre from Survivor, Jaganathan Uttamanathan.

Verdery, K. (1999) *The Political Lives of Dead Bodies: Reburial and Postsocialist Change* (New York: Columbia University Press).

Wainaina, B. (2006) 'How to Write about Africa', in *The View From Africa, Granta*, 92, 91–6.

Wehle, P. (2005) 'THÉÂTRE DU SOLEIL: Dramatic Response to the Global Refugee Crisis', *Performing Arts Journal*, 80, 80–6.

Whitlock, G. (2005) 'The Skin of the Burqa: Recent Life Narratives from Afghanistan', *Biography*, 28, 1, 54–76.

Wikipedia (2008) 'September 11 2001 Attacks', http://en.wikipedia.org/wiki/September_11,_2001_attacks (accessed 6 March 2008).

Winston, J. (2006a) 'Beauty, Goodness and Education: The Arts Beyond Utility', *Journal of Moral Education*, 35, 3, 285–300.

— (2006b) 'By Way of an Introduction, Some Initial Reflections on Beauty', *Research in Drama Education*, 11, 1, 43–5.

Wittgenstein, L. (2007) *Tractatus Logico-Philosophicus*, originally published 1918 (London: Standard Publications).

Wolff, J. (1988) *Aesthetics and the Sociology of Art* (London: George Allen and Unwin).

— (2003) 'The Iconic and the Allusive: The Case for Beauty in Post-Holocaust Art', in S. Hornstein and F. Jacobowitz (eds) *Image and Remembrance: Representation and the Holocaust* (Indiana: Indiana University Press).

— (2006) 'Groundless Beauty: Feminism and the Aesthetics of Uncertainty', *Feminist Theory*, 7, 2, 143–58.

Young, S. (2004) 'Narrative and Healing in the Hearings of the South African Truth and Reconciliation Commission', *Biography*, 27, 1, 145–62.

Žižek, S. (2002) *Welcome to the Desert of the Real* (London: Verso).

— (2007) 'Resistance Is Surrender', *London Review of Books*, 15 November 2007.

— (2008) *Violence* (London: Profile Books).

Index